SOUNDS FROM THE STREET

GRAHAM WILLMOTT

Reynolds & Hearn Ltd
London

This book is for Ellie and Jack.

These songs are more important to you than you realise. Each one, in some way, helped to shape my view of the world as I grew up and that must mean they are also helping to shape yours as you do.

> *To the memory of Stuart MacKinnon, my old best friend at school and fellow Jam fan who died before I had a chance to give him his copy.*
>
> *None of us will forget you Stu*
>
> ---
>
> Stuart MacKinnon 03/04/1964 – 26/11/2003
> (our very own David Watts)
> www.mackinnontrust.org

PHOTOGRAPHY CREDITS
Back cover   Sheila Rock (© Rex Features)
Front cover   Adrian Boot (© Retna)

PICTURE SECTION
Page 1   Elaine Bryant (© London Features International)
Page 2   top, Ian Dickson (© www.late20thcenturyboy.com)
bottom Brad Elterman (© London Features International)
Page 3   top, Paul Cox (both © London Features International)
Page 4   top, Paul Cox (both © London Features International)
Page 5   top, © Graham Willmott, courtesy Bruce Foxton
bottom, Erik Auerbach (© Retna)
Page 8   © London Features International

First published in 2003 by
Reynolds & Hearn Ltd
61a Priory Road
Kew Gardens
Richmond
Surrey TW9 3DH

© Graham Willmott 2003
Reprinted 2004 and 2007

A CIP catalogue record for this book is available from the British Library.

ISBN 978-1-905287-62-8

Designed by James King. Typeset by James King and Peri Godbold.

Printed and bound in Great Britain by Biddles Ltd, King's Lynn, Norfolk

SOUNDS FROM THE STREET

ACKNOWLEDGEMENTS

MY thanks go to Peter Gordon for his continuous support throughout the book, including sacrificing a Sunday to go through all the pre-Polydor material and part of a holiday to read through the first draft. Above and beyond the call my friend! Thanks also to Enzo Esposito and Ross Dilanda (Squire) for their early memories (and my haircut) and to Steve Brookes for his patience. I am indebted to the bosses Richard Reynolds and Marcus Hearn.

Thanks also to Nikki Potter for the extra research and picture editing and to Rachel Ridley for that nugget of information. Respect to Martin Gainsford for the memorabilia and additional information, to Bob Gray in Canada and to Jimmy Edwards in New Haw. Gratitude in no small measure to Paul Ryan and Peter Patsalides (for the encouragement) Joe Hobbs and The Bean Monkeys, Simon Goddard and to Jo Dickie for all her help at the launch party.

The three books I would also like to acknowledge are *Keeping The Flame* by Steve Brookes (ISBN 0 9528062 07 and available in the shop at www.thejam.org), *My Ever Changing Moods* by John Read (ISBN 0 7719 5495 X) and *Paul Weller: The Unauthorised Biography* by Steve Malins (ISBN 0 7535 0087 6) – all well worth having.

And of course respect in equal measures to Paul, Bruce and Rick for the music we grew up to.

CONTENTS

FOREWORD

PLENTY has been written about The Jam over the years. Some of it
has been true, and some of it I didn't recognise at all. When Graham
told me he was going to write a history of the band I was surprised,
as I didn't think there was much more to add to what has already
been written. But he seems to have found plenty more, some of
which I had even forgotten myself.

When I have been interviewed in the past I have always partly
regretted it as much of what I say gets edited or used in a context
other than I would have liked. In this case, however, Graham has
stuck to the facts as I remember them and told the story of The Jam
as it actually happened. This shouldn't be too surprising as Graham
is a Woking Jam fan. He saw the band play live on countless
occasions and was at many of those small gigs we played in the
1980s in venues such as the YMCA and The Cricketers. Much of
what he has written is from first-hand experience.

Over the years the attention for many has often focused on The
Jam's so-called acrimonious split, or the supposed bitterness between
myself, Paul and Rick. In fact The Jam didn't break up badly at all.
And as for the bitterness – we were young when we started,
schoolkids in fact. We grew up together, made some pretty decent
music, saw the world and had the time of our lives. That's nothing to
be bitter about at all, and none of us are.

The Jam were mainly known as a singles band, and as a result all
the 'best of' compilations have focused on the very well known
songs. After you have read this book I hope you might pick up a
couple of the albums and discover some of the lesser known tracks,
or perhaps some of those hidden away on B-sides. I think you could
be in for a few surprises.

The level of interest there still is in The Jam always pleasantly
surprises me. It is, after all, over 20 years ago now. It must mean the

three of us did something right together, and that is something to be very proud of.

I hope you enjoy reading the story of The Jam and taking a look behind the scenes, so to speak.

Thanks for continuing to make it all so worthwhile.

Bruce Foxton
Guildford
September 2003

PREFACE

I was one of those rare Jam fans who discovered the band via their apparently unpopular second album *This Is The Modern World*. In January 1978 I was 13 years old and a friend of mine pulled the album out and played it to me. He told me they came from the same place as us, Woking, so we sat and listened to it one afternoon. He reckoned his elder sister had seen them play down at Michael's Club some years earlier. A few hours later I was out washing cars to raise the money for my own copy, and a copy of the band's debut album *In The City*.

That's possibly the reason why I still regard *Modern World* as such an important set of songs – and why the constant criticism that album has come in for frustrates and irritates me. So, in these pages I will try to make it clear why that release was, and still is, so important.

With the demise of the band in 1982 it became hip in some Jam circles to diminish drummer Rick Buckler and bassist Bruce Foxton, and even to forget about original bandmember Steve Brookes, while collectively agreeing that the whole thing had been The Paul Weller Show. That, too, has irritated me. As far as some writers are concerned, Buckler and Foxton feel hard-done-by and are bitter and bemused at Paul's decision to move on. But both Rick and Bruce are friends of mine and at no point in the last 20 years have I heard either of them say an unpleasant word about anything. They know the value of the part they played in the band and so do I. Steve Brookes, in his honest and accurate account of the early Jam, *Keeping The Flame* (an essential read for Jam fans), clearly indicates that he too knows the value of the part he played. But, characteristically, Steve understates the case. I hope I can give him the credit he deserves here.

When I wrote and published The Jam website, www.thejam.org, I made a point of ensuring it was even-handed, reflective and honest.

The millions of visitors it has attracted, and the tens of thousands of e-mails I have received, seem to confirm that very few fans bought in to the rewriting of Jam history, just as I didn't. There is no doubt that The Jam would never have made it without their charismatic front man, and to suggest otherwise is ludicrous. There is, however, a reasonable case to be made for the idea that the band would never have made it without the others, either.

As I wrote this story I had four imaginary readers sitting on my shoulder and I owe them my thanks for their imaginary criticism. The first reader is the Jam fan, who will be the most critical of all. All of them know The Jam better than the next one (and that is part of the mystique of the band) and I already realise I could be picked up at every turn by fans who say 'This isn't right and that isn't right'. So I have taken great care to be as accurate as possible. The second reader is the non-Jam fan who wasn't present on the 70s/80s scene, and who therefore needs some of the details explained – details which the big Jam fans will consider a case of 'stating the bleeding obvious', for which I apologise in advance.

The third group of readers are Messrs Brookes, Buckler, Foxton and Weller, who need no introduction and who I hope will read this story. I want to emphasise that criticism is not the intention, the intention is to create an honest picture and to tell the story as it actually happened. My research suggests that it was Foxton and Brookes who were crucial to The Jam's emergence and subsequent stability. But I make no apologies to those who cry 'sycophant', as I am an obvious Weller and Buckler fan too. The fourth reader is my publisher, Reynolds and Hearn. I know that sensationalism would sell them a warehouse-full of books but they didn't want that and nor did I. They simply asked me to 'tell it as it happened'. And that, quite simply, is the reason I agreed to write it.

There are two further motives for writing this book. The first is Ian MacDonald's *Revolution In The Head*, which tells the story of The Beatles. When I read it in 1999 it fascinated me and I still refer to it when I hear Beatles tunes. I thought that weaving the story around the important thing, the songs, was a wonderful idea and my immediate reaction was to look around for such a balanced account of The Jam, but there wasn't one. Like Ian I wanted to create a chronology of the music. But, instead of labouring too hard over the technical details of each song, I saw the opportunity to tell the inside story of a group of schoolmates, who grew up to dominate the music scene of a generation.

The second reason came earlier this year when I was sitting in a pub in Guildford with Bruce Foxton. A young fan came over for an autograph and a chat. Bruce duly obliged and after a short while the lad made to leave and said, 'It's great to meet you, I have always loved your music and I don't believe any of the shit that's been written about you.' Bruce just laughed and replied, 'Thanks very much. Nor do I.'

I decided that I too had heard enough of that sort of thing and that it was time the true story of The Jam was told, without slant or spin, name-calling, side-taking or rancour. What's the point in all that? It's the music that matters.

Graham Willmott
Guildford
August 2003

ONE

AS IT WAS IN THE BEGINNING. . . .

'How would I like The Jam to be remembered? I like to think that we've done it more honestly than anyone else before. I'd like to see young groups on the way up – and this is probably going to sound pompous – [being] able to use The Jam as a guideline. To look at us and think, well that's the way to do it...'

Paul Weller, 1982

PAUL WELLER has always been a Beatles fan. Like many teenagers of his generation, he wanted to emulate his hero Paul McCartney, and it was obvious that the musically minded Weller was looking around at an early age for a John Lennon to complement his McCartney. At the age of 13 he found his Lennon in the playground of Sheerwater County Secondary School in Woking.

Steve Brookes, in his own account of the part he played in the formation of The Jam (*Keeping The Flame*), remembers their meeting: 'It was my first day there and I was dragged across the playground by one of the other boys to meet Paul who then looked me up and down, grunted and wandered off for a fag.' But Weller soon discovered that the stranger shared his love of playing guitar and took a new interest in Brookes, inviting him over to his home in Stanley Road to try out his new electric model. The two soon became inseparable and were learning Beatles tunes, teaching each other new riffs and writing their own songs.

In the late 1970s Paul Weller described his hometown of Woking as a 'small green hick little place', but it's hard to see why. With a vibrant and long-time multicultural community, Woking has produced some of the world's finest creative talent. The building of the Shah Jehan Mosque in 1889, the first mosque in Britain, resulted in the town becoming the spiritual focus of Victorian Britain's Muslim community. Also in the late 19th century, Woking was home to H G Wells (his fictional Martian invasion, in *The War Of The Worlds*, took place at the sandpits just outside the town), and a little later George Bernard Shaw and Sir Arthur Conan Doyle also took up residence. Later in the century, the novelist Hilary Mantel and composer Dame Ethel Smyth both hailed from the town.

The areas of Woking and nearby Guildford have produced musicians such as Eric Clapton, Peter Gabriel, Phil Collins and Rick Parfitt of Status Quo. From the late seventies' New Wave movement, Squire, The Stranglers, The Vapors and The Jam's very own Bruce Foxton, Rick Buckler, Steve Brookes and Paul Weller are all from the area. Far from being 'hick', Woking is as creative, cosmopolitan and cultured as you can get. Even though, admittedly, you wouldn't want to take your friends there.

In the early 1970s Steve Brookes' and Paul Weller's out-of-school activities soon revolved exclusively around music. Evening practice sessions became lunchtime get-togethers and soon schoolmates were taking their sandwiches down to the music room to watch the 'Lunchtime Jam', who had been joined by the slightly older pupil Rick Buckler, replacing original drummer Neil Harris while he was away on holiday. Within a year, Brookes (lead guitar), Weller playing rhythm and Buckler on a self-made drum kit were playing sixties R and B at various social clubs around town and people were talking about 'The Sheerwater Jam'.

Weller's father John had also taken an interest and took on the role of hustler/manager, coercing friends, acquaintances and social club managers to give them gigs and then persuading as many people as he could to be there on the night to see the boys play. John Weller remembers the time well: 'I didn't have a thousand pounds to give them, but I did have a thousand hours so I gave them that instead.'

Keen to complete their Beatles-type line-up, Weller and Brookes sought a fourth member. Guitarists were auditioned but only one stood out, another Sheerwater pupil, Bruce Foxton. Bruce, however, initially wasn't keen and it took another three months before he was finally persuaded to join as rhythm guitarist to Steve Brookes' lead. And so the four-piece Jam was established.

But Paul was struggling to play bass and sing simultaneously, a surprisingly difficult skill as melodies and bass lines often move in different directions, and The Jam were faltering. Paul had passed the rhythm guitar duties over to Bruce when he joined and the sound and balance of the band had been severely affected. It was suggested that Paul and Bruce switch instruments. Foxton wasn't keen on the idea, especially as the 17-year-old had never really played a bass guitar before.

But his commitment prevailed, not for the last time, and after a series of 'up all nighters' and repeated rehearsal sessions, Bruce finally began to get to grips with the new instrument. This appears to be the reason why there were so few gigs in 1976, but by the end of that year Foxton was an accomplished bass player and Weller was free to play guitar and sing. In later years, an affable Steve Brookes recalled Bruce's reluctance and added: 'But I bet he's glad he did, look at him now.' Another Woking musician, Squire's Enzo Esposito, agreed. 'Listen to Bruce's bass playing,' he points out. 'He's become one of the best there is.'

And in that sentence Enzo sums up how exceptional The Jam were. Most bands settle on their line-ups after the best musicians available come together through a varied range of circumstances. For a group of boys, not just from the same town but from the same school, to grow up together and develop their ability, and for each to become as accomplished and inventive on their respective instruments as anyone else in the country, is extremely rare.

But the four-piece wasn't to last long. Despite having an established set of more than 35 songs, of which over half were Weller/Brookes originals, and having played an unbelievable 151 local gigs in just 18 months, the 16-year-old Weller and Brookes drifted away from each other. Competitiveness, questions about commitment, girlfriends, creative differences and a host of other reasons forced them apart and by the autumn of 1975 Brookes had left, leaving the Jam as a three-piece. The remaining members

auditioned again for another guitarist without any success and then looked around instead for a keyboard player, but no other suitable musician from Woking could be found to fill Brookes' creative shoes. Attempts were made to persuade him back into the fold, but Steve steadfastly refused as he had set his sights on a solo career.

He was missed but, as Rick Buckler later recalled, 'Maybe him leaving made the difference. No disrespect to Steve, who is a fine guitarist, but maybe that switch in instruments created the sound we had. For a start Bruce is a far better bass player than Paul was ever going to be and as a three-piece we all had to play a bit more to fill out the sound. Sometimes it's those things that make a difference and maybe we would never have got anywhere if we had stayed as we were.' Paul Weller added: 'Once Bruce and I swapped instruments, and Steve had left, we developed as a three-piece, more out of necessity though than by choice.'

So the world came to know 'the lunchtime jam' from Sheerwater School as a three-piece instead of a four. Weller was rhythm and lead guitarist, Foxton was bass player and backing vocalist and Buckler sat impassively as ever behind his drum kit. Collectively the Sheerwater School Lunchtime Jam created music that would remain popular around the world for decades and provided a legacy for hundreds of other groups who followed.

EARLY STUDIO RECORDINGS

BLUEBERRY ROCK / TAKIN' MY LOVE
(August 1973 – Eden Studios, Kingston)

SOME KINDA LOVIN' / MAKING MY WAY BACK HOME
(November 1973 – Fanfare Studios, London)

LOVING BY LETTERS / MORE AND MORE
(1974 – Potter's Studios, Mytchett, Surrey)

WALKING THE DOG / I WILL BE THERE / ONE HUNDRED WAYS / FOREVER AND ALWAYS
(1 March 1975 – TW Studios, Fulham)

AGAIN / TAKIN' MY LOVE / WHEN I NEEDED YOU / PLEASE DON'T TREAT ME BAD

(10 December 1975 – Potter's Studios, Mytchett, Surrey)

LEFT RIGHT AND CENTRE / NON STOP DANCING

(28 May 1976 – Potter's Studios, Mytchett)

These songs were played live on countless occasions over a period of three or four years and became firm favourites in The Jam's set. Although two of these demos would eventually make it onto the band's debut album, *In The City*, the rest would lie in the archives unheard by anybody apart from those close to the group. Steve Brookes' part in the formation of The Jam has often been understated and unrecognised by many, but the fact that he left the band only after some four years of writing and performing with Paul Weller, Rick Buckler and Bruce Foxton is testament to his significant influence.

Rick Buckler points out that Steve's leaving may have been the catalyst for the band's change of direction and subsequent worldwide success, but it can equally be maintained that without Brookes the band might not have got anywhere in the first place. It is important to remember that Paul Weller left The Jam in 1982 when he was still only 24 years old, about the age when most musicians are still finding their sound and attracting the attention of the record industry. Therefore it is entirely possible that, without Steve Brookes, The Jam might never have made it past the school dinner room and Paul Weller might still have been playing the Woking working men's clubs well into the 1980s.

Steve Brookes started The Jam with Paul Weller, wrote with him, played live and recorded with the band, so essentially the recordings listed above are all Jam songs.

The similarities between the 13-year-old Paul Weller and Steve Brookes were plain to see almost from the moment they first met. Their birthdays are a single day apart – 25 and 26 May 1958 respectively – and they shared a love of sixties music in the shape of Tamla Motown and Merseybeat. Both were also given guitars for

Christmas – Paul in 1969 (the instrument then lay under his bed for
a year until being rediscovered and dusted off) and Steve in 1971.
A series of family disasters had led Steve's mum and younger brother
to a flat above a shop in Byfleet in November of that year and, come
Christmas, he had been compensated with a gift of a six-string
acoustic, a pitch-pipe tuner and a Bert Weedon songbook.

By the time the two met early in 1972, Paul had been learning
Beatles songs for a year, Steve for just a few months. He had already
mastered the basic chords, however, together with several melodies
popularised by artists such as James Taylor, Carol King, Leonard
Cohen and The Faces.

The two were soon spending much of their out-of-school time
together, practising, swapping ideas and techniques and, virtually
from day one, experimenting with their own tunes to complement a
growing list of Beatles and Chuck Berry covers. In Paul's mind,
Woking's version of the Lennon/McCartney songwriting team was
well and truly establishing itself.

By Christmas 1972, Weller and Brookes were appearing live as
often as they could get gigs. Local agent Wally Dent then offered
them a New Year's Eve slot at a pub called the Ball and Wicket in
Upper Hale, near Farnham. As 31 December is the one date in the
year when every artist should be performing, Wally had clearly
booked up all his regular acts and was looking around for anyone
local who could fulfil this commitment in Farnham. Jumping at the
chance of a proper professional gig booked by a real agent, the
schoolboys loaded up Paul's father's car and made their way across
the Hog's Back to perform. On arriving, however, they realised that
Dent had forgotten to tell them they were expected to play between
9.00 pm and 1.00 am. But they only had about 20 songs – around
one hour's worth – in their repertoire.

With no option other than to run, they decided to play four sets,
mixing up the songs and hoping that no one would notice they were
being repeated. But The Jam were only halfway through their second
set when it became obvious, to the landlord at least, that they were
blagging it. He came over and explained, as politely as possible, that
if the band carried on like that they might empty his bar before

11.00pm, regardless of the 1.00am extension he had obtained. They were given their marching orders and had to pack up all their gear in front of a full pub, leaving with the words 'Don't give up your day jobs, lads' ringing in their ears.

As a footnote to this story, Steve Brookes played a solo gig at the Ball and Wicket many years later and was surprised to see the same landlord still in charge. Afterwards, Steve couldn't help asking the old man if he remembered the schoolboys he threw out all those years previously and was amazed that he did. As they parted company the landlord thanked Brookes and commented that he had come a long way since he last played there. 'Yeah,' replied Steve. 'But you should see what my mate [Weller] is doing now' – and couldn't resist backing out of the door, leaving him guessing.

Before long another twist of fate led the Brookes family back to their home suburb of Colindale in north London, a move that subsequently saw Steve packed off to boarding school near Brighton in west Sussex. On his own and with nothing else to do, he picked up his Jedson Telecaster and repeatedly practised blues scales and Chuck Berry rock 'n' roll licks. His only relief came at weekends, which were mostly spent living with the Wellers back in Stanley Road.

During this time the two recruited other musicians from school to make up their first band, namely school band drummer Neil Harris, who was then replaced by the slightly older Paul Buckler (later known as Rick). Secondly, a close friend of Weller's, Dave Waller, was encouraged to learn guitar and play rhythm to Steve's lead. In a further attempt to emulate his hero, Paul had switched from guitar to a Hofner bass, and it was this four-piece line-up that booked into Kingston's Eden Recording Studios to record their first-ever demo.

BLUEBERRY ROCK (Brookes/Weller)
recorded August 1973 at Eden Studios, Kingston
unreleased

'Blueberry Rock' wasn't one of The Jam's earliest original songs, but as their writing improved it was considered to be one of their better efforts by the time they were due at Eden Studios in August 1973. In the weeks running up to the day, it was that tune, and 'Takin' My Love', another Weller/Brookes original, which the 15-year-olds repeatedly rehearsed. The song is heavily influenced by the sound of Chuck Berry, a likeness confirmed by Steve Brookes: 'Both Paul and myself were listening to a lot of Chuck Berry records at the time. People always recognise The Beatles' influence in The Jam's early music, which is true enough, but we were definitely both Chuck Berry fans as well.'

Eden Studios was built and managed by 24-year-old Philip Love, who set the facility up mainly to record his own songs on a neat Amplex 1100 four-track tape machine. In an attempt to make the new studio pay for itself, Philip and business partner Mike Gardner advertised in *Melody Maker* and that was how The Jam secured an evening rate of £7 per hour, including engineer.

On a midweek evening the schoolboys dragged their equipment upstairs, set up and tried to familiarise themselves with this new environment. Nerves were frayed and Dave Waller, who was in the group as a mate rather than for his rhythm guitar skills, managed to produce only a basic effort which was eventually left well down in the mix. As frustration mounted, Weller and Brookes almost came to blows.

Despite this, the end result is strong and accomplished and the listener needs to keep reminding himself that 'Blueberry Rock' is an original song being performed by schoolboys. Weller's voice is mature and soulful, with little indication of his coarser vocal style during The Jam's Polydor years and none at all of his Style Council experiment. Instead, this is an early version of the sound the singer would return to a full 20 years later, as he gathered a hatful of awards for his mid-nineties albums.

Shortly after the recording sessions, Steve was taken off to Spain for a holiday with his father and spent a fortnight there, imagining the scene as he arrived home and the demo had been heard by the music industry's movers and shakers. Brookes sat on the beach fully confident that a contract would be awaiting his signature back in Woking, and that fame and fortune were now but a formality. He was wrong, but not disappointed.

During that summer the group utilised the remainder of their school holidays working out how to emulate the Beatles' final rooftop concert, which they had seen in the film *Let It Be*. Paul's house in Stanley Road was the location of choice as it was so close to the town centre and the boys imagined their sound resonating across the high street, attracting film crews, reporters and an audience of thousands. Unfortunately, the pitched roof on the Victorian terrace made that a little awkward so they set up their equipment on a sunny afternoon in the back garden with Paul, Steve and Dave facing Buckler's drum kit. Curtains twitched in curiosity and, as they opened their set with 'Blueberry Rock', the boys smiled at each other and imagined the scene from *Let It Be* repeating itself round the front of the house. Unfortunately, the only aspect of The Beatles' legendary rooftop performance to be replicated was the arrival of the police, who pulled the plug on the garden matinée only a few songs in.

Woking was, however, a hot bed of talent among the teenage generation. Within earshot, and above a hippie shop called Squire, a young band of the same name regularly rehearsed. Lead singer and songwriter Enzo Esposito formed a close friendship with both Weller and Brookes, which they all retain to this day. He is now a successful hair salon owner and restaurateur in Godalming; it was Enzo who was responsible for Weller's distinctive haircut in the late 1990s.

It has been recorded that, in a genuine act of kindness, Weller actually gave Squire 'Blueberry Rock' as the fast-moving Jam rapidly grew out it, but Enzo denies this. 'We played it once at a gig,' he recalled, 'but only once, and we never recorded it. It's a good song though.' Squire's drummer, Ross Dilanda, also remembers playing 'Blueberry Rock'. 'I think Steve Brookes was mainly responsible for it and it definitely had his sort of Chuck Berry feel to it, but all those early Jam songs had a joint credit in the same way Lennon and McCartney had worked together.' Steve Brookes confirms that he and Paul always shared the songwriting credits: 'But you know what it's like when you're writing in partnership', says Brookes. 'One person comes up with the initial idea and then the two of you work the rest of the song out together. So it's true, we wrote it jointly but I seem to remember 'Blueberry Rock' was Paul's initial idea.'

This supposed act of generosity towards Squire sits curiously with Weller's public image, and is certainly in stark contrast to drummer Buckler, who, on gatecrashing Squire's rehearsals one day, actually smashed up what he thought was Esposito's guitar by throwing it down the stairs. 'The funny thing is, it wasn't mine,' Enzo remembers. 'It belonged to Perry Clapton, the cousin of another local guitarist who was slightly better known than us, Eric. Once, it might have even been the great man's himself.' But Weller and Brookes didn't see the funny side and could imagine how they would have felt if the roles had been reversed. Dilanda: 'That was quite out of character for Buckler. Usually he was fairly reserved and shy, he didn't really associate with the rest of us that much. I don't know what was going on there.'

TAKIN' MY LOVE (Brookes/Weller)
recorded August 1973 at Eden Studios, Kingston
unreleased

'Takin' My Love' is another joint effort recorded at Eden Studios and produced by Philip Love on the same evening as 'Blueberry Rock'; it was also played during the garden gig in Stanley Road. Steve conceived it as The Jam's version of the Beatles song 'The One After 909', which had a country and western feel to it. He maintains that as young songwriters they never deliberately set out to steal other people's ideas but, in using them as an influence, they could 'borrow' chord progressions and structures and produce something similar. By adding their own feel to it they found that almost no similarity could be detected by anybody.

Whether by accident or design, Weller and Brookes had hit upon the very formula used by almost every songwriter at one time or another during their careers. Steve points out that, when he started listening to The Everly Brothers and Roy Orbison, he could see how Lennon and McCartney themselves had been similarly influenced in their early days. Paul Weller later admitted: 'I was always emulating my heroes, some of my songs have been out-and-out copies but I wasn't expecting anyone not to notice.'

'Takin' My Love' has been recorded by varying line-ups of The Jam on four separate occasions. On this version Paul plays bass and sings, with Dave Waller once again on rudimentary guitar, Buckler drums and Steve carrying the guitar parts almost alone. It became clear during this recording that, with the best will in the world, Dave wasn't up to the role of guitarist. Paul and Steve both realised this but, being fond of Waller and unwilling to offend him, they turned on each other instead. By the time the backing track was finished and the vocals were due, a row had erupted as neither Weller nor Brookes could agree on where they should come in with their respective vocal parts.

Both refused to back down and studio engineer Philip Love finally came out of the sound booth to inform them that, as he was being paid by the hour, he was happy for them to shout at each other all night if they could afford it. The schoolboys calmed down and were then horrified by Love's suggestion they should hold hands while singing. After a brief stand-off, Brookes and Weller agreed and Steve maintains that the mutual aggression, and subsequent hand-holding, actually worked and resulted in a professional vocal performance from both of them. The song ended up with a very strong R and B feel to it, and with a mature blues vocal from Paul which is markedly different from the speeded-up version which appeared on the 1977 debut album *In The City*.

Brookes has never previously been credited in any way for creating 'Takin' My Love' and insists he never wanted to be. 'It's shit,' he says, a curious judgment on a song good enough to be chosen ahead of dozens of others for the band's debut album, and then to actually appear on the flip side to their first single, long after Steve had left.

At the time, crooners and glam rockers were still dominating the UK charts but early salvation arrived in 1975 in the shape of a movement known as Pub Rock. The Dr Feelgood album *Down By The Jetty* was released in January 1975 and finally Brookes and Weller could see others who shared their love of 60s R and B back in the charts again. The Feelgood's dogmatic stage presence, and in particular Wilko Johnson's high-powered technique of rhythm and lead guitar playing, made perfect sense to Paul and a vision of his own style and sound began to form. In late 1974 Enzo Esposito had been to see Dr Feelgood play live while they were touring with Cocomo and Chilly Willy and the Red Hot Peppers, and returned to Woking raving about the band. Within months Weller and Esposito had also been to see them play live at Guildford Civic Hall, a gig Paul remembers well: 'I used to love Wilko, he was like an English Chuck Berry. For me, when I saw him at Guildford Civic, it was like that old John Lennon quote "Now that's a good job, I'd like to do that."'

If Paul Weller had any single influence on his style of rhythm and lead guitar playing, especially during the days of The Jam, then that influence must be Wilko Johnson. One of the first things Paul did after that gig was to change 'Takin' My Love' from a soulful, bluesy sound into the fuel-injected, harsher and more energetic track it became. Its final version was recorded when The Jam entered Polydor's Stratford Place studios in Oxford Street, London in March 1977 and cut the album *In The City* in just 11 days. 'It was easy,' says drummer Rick Buckler. 'It was basically our live set and as such we had been rehearsing it for three or four years already. We were able to go into the studio and virtually record the whole thing in only a few takes.'

It explains much about the development of a song when it is regularly being played live; in the period between writing 'Takin' My Love' and recording the final version for *In The City*, The Jam played no fewer than 181 gigs. It also says much about the ability of the young musicians who made up the various line-ups of The Jam that what started life as a copy of a Beatles country and western pastiche could end up on the B-side of a 1977 punk classic. And, as Brookes says, 'You would never notice.'

Squire's Ross Dilanda remembers 'Takin' My Love' being an early favourite in The Jam's live set. 'They used to play regularly at a local disco in The Delta, which was a community centre opposite our old school. The Jam, which included Dave Waller at that time, used to wear stage outfits of bomber jackets and flares and started their set off-stage, then walked on playing the opening bars of Status Quo's 'Caroline'. We were all only about 14 or 15 at the time.'

In an ironic twist, Eden Studios has since grown into one of the longest established independent recording studios in the UK, working with such artists as Tom Jones, Stereophonics and U2. A few years after The Jam's visit they were recording Madness, Elvis Costello and Blondie. Still owned and managed by the same partnership, they were surprised to hear of their part in Jam history. It is a shame no one at Eden remembers the early Jam demos as many of them were, and remain to this day, big Jam fans.

SOME KINDA LOVIN' (Weller)
recorded November 1973 at Fanfare Studios, Swiss Cottage, London
unreleased

The teenagers were now gigging nearly every week and the Brookes/Weller songwriting partnership was growing stronger and stronger, but, even as they were improving, various weaknesses, real and perceived, were causing friction. Buckler, already dozens of gigs and a studio session into his Jam career, still didn't possess a full drum kit and was disorganised to the point where Paul's dad John had to borrow drum sticks for him when he turned up without any. Dave Waller, meanwhile, simply wasn't learning fast enough and Weller and Brookes were leaving him way behind.

Shortly after the Eden Studios session they had a gig arranged for them at the Sheerwater Youth Club by its then manager, Dave Stryke. The teenage foursome, flushed by the thought of imminent stardom, took to the stage but were brought quickly down to earth when an early electrical failure led to the apparent cancellation of the show. The entire band retired to the pub next door in order to drown their sorrows, but within the hour a friend of Rick's rushed in to say the fault had been repaired and they could play after all. So the group returned to perform their new set of songs in front of all their friends and relatives. Unfortunately, by then they were all drunk and the result was a shambles.

For Squire's Ross Dilanda the evening held another memory. Halfway through the set Dave Waller's guitar lead broke, so Paul handed him the lead from his bass guitar and dragged an old piano over from the corner of the room, the set continuing with Weller playing the bass lines on that instead. 'We were only 15,' said Ross. 'I didn't even know he could play piano. It was incredible really but you somehow expected that sort of thing from Paul. You wouldn't expect it of any other 15-year-old though, would you? I suppose that's why he always stood out.'

Dave Waller's last gig was a few weeks later at Chobham Youth Club, after which Paul and Steve bit the bullet and told him he was out. 'He wasn't really bothered though,' remembers Brookes. 'And I think that was part of the problem in the first place really.' Drummer Rick Buckler, meanwhile, was on a learning curve. 'I remember that night,' he says. 'I had this idea of setting the drum kit up on a large mat, to help improve the acoustics. The problem was I didn't realise I should have stuck it down and, as we played, the whole kit, including me and my stool, kept moving towards the front of the stage. I would be up with the guitarists before I had to pull it back again between songs. That was when I discovered gaffer tape.'

At those gigs the band debuted two new Weller/Brookes songs, the first of which was 'Some Kinda Lovin'', which was a mid-tempo song with a country feel to it and, in its recorded version, includes Paul singing a sometimes wayward lead vocal. Steve provides strong backing vocals in the shape of 'ooh's and 'aah's and, with Rick's gentle drumming complementing Paul's subtle bass lines, the song to some resembles an early Gerry Marsden composition.

The track was recorded without Dave Waller in November 1973 at Fanfare Studios in Swiss Cottage, London. Swiss Cottage was a good two hours (pre-M25) from Woking but Paul insisted on recording at a studio close to Abbey Road, the home of The Beatles. The band had been told by telephone not to bother bringing their amps and on the journey up they fantasised about a room full of equipment and effects. However, when they arrived they realised the real reason for not bringing their own amplifiers was that the studio was so small there was barely enough room for the guitarists, let alone their equipment.

Still learning, Steve and Paul couldn't understand what the engineer meant by plugging the guitars directly into the mixing desk and, once again, tempers flared. But the thought of losing their deposit meant the boys had to give it a go. By the time Rick had set up his drum kit there was barely enough room for Weller and Brookes. But they worked around it and, all things considered, the results are smooth and professional – although Brookes would later remember that his Jedson was slightly out of tune... 'which is what sometimes happens when you tune up through headphones. Still, it wasn't a bad session for 17 quid.'

MAKING MY WAY BACK HOME (Brookes/Weller)
recorded November 1973 at Fanfare Studios, Swiss Cottage, London
unreleased

The second track laid down that day was a rock 'n' roll song called 'Making My Way Back Home', another Weller/Brookes concoction and a much stronger 12-bar R and B melody than the others they had recorded. The song races along with Paul once again on lead vocal, although he seems to have adopted the American accent he would use to great effect three years later when recording The Jam's debut album *In The City*. Also, Steve Brookes' guitar is apparently Merseybeat-influenced, which is a general theme running through many of the pre-Polydor Jam tracks. Steve Brookes: 'We used to use that thin Fender guitar sound all the time, with loads of treble on it. It was definitely similar to those early 1960s British bands attempting American R and B, so I wouldn't say we were necessarily copying Merseybeat. Although it does sound like it, but I think perhaps we were all trying to emulate 1950s American R and B.'

The four recorded songs were now being used to secure new gigs all over town, including a residency The Jam had been given at Michael's Club in the Goldsworth Road, running from January 1974 through to their last appearance there in September 1975. For some it mirrored The Beatles' stint at the Star Club in Hamburg and it certainly gave The Jam the chance to play live on a regular basis. This provided the youngsters with a whole new set of opportunities, including a place to practice in the afternoons and to be seen by other venue owners. They also got the chance to play to an audience closer to their own age group, something they didn't get in the social clubs unless the members brought their kids along. Regular bookings soon started flooding in and The Jam embarked on a run of over 146 live performances in the next 18 months.

Although still two years away from being old enough to legally buy a drink, Michael's Club became a way of life for The Jam. It was a real demi-monde full of comedians and strippers and, on the fire escape steps behind the stage, the youngsters could take a cigarette break and simultaneously watch the strippers changing between acts. 'They couldn't see us,' remembers Rick Buckler, 'but we could see them all right.'

'Making My Way Back Home' became a firm live favourite with the after-hours drinkers and dancers in town and the band began to develop a positive reputation, although many of the regulars still saw them as kids. Rick Buckler had by now got himself a job and invested in his first proper drum kit, but Weller and Brookes still had school to go to on Monday. Although attendances by the pair were becoming increasingly rare it would be another five months before they officially left Sheerwater and could embark on their professional career in music.

Until then they would have to make do with weekly gigs amongst the dancers at Michael's Club. The audiences were enthusiastic enough but many a time, in the tightly packed venue, their waving arms would connect with the microphone stands and deliver the singer a whack in the mouth. A volatile Paul Weller often had to be restrained from retaliating with the neck of his guitar but he loved the overall atmosphere of being able to play live in that hot and frenzied environment. By the time they had made it to the pubs, clubs and other venues of London's punk movement three years later, The Jam could handle anything.

LOVING BY LETTERS (Brookes/Weller)
recorded April 1974 at Potter's Studios, Mytchett, Surrey
unreleased

With the Michael's Club residency under their belt, and the new three-piece line-up of Weller, Buckler and Brookes happy with the Fanfare Studio recordings, The Jam were keen to get back into a studio and record more of their original songs. Paul was convinced his vocal was now sounding like Otis Redding and he was probably right. So, fuelled with a new enthusiasm, the band booked into Potter's Studio in Mytchett, Surrey, just a few miles across the ranges from Woking.

Bob Potter was a local businessman involved in running nightclubs and country clubs and had a small recording studio built to the rear of his offices with a small but professional drum booth and an eight-track tape-recording facility, which was close to the cutting edge of technology in 1974. Still several months away from turning 16, The Jam were earning around £15 per week each and had been able to improve their equipment and instruments. Paul had acquired a maple-coloured Jedson Les Paul copy (which he later sold to Enzo Esposito for £50) and Steve opted for a three-pick-up Welson semi-acoustic guitar similar to the Epiphone George Harrison used, and also resembling the Gibson 335 his guitar hero Chuck Berry played.

The atmosphere in the studio that day was light-hearted and positive, contrasting strongly with the band's two previous studio sessions, and the result was polished and professional, although Steve Brookes recalls that he and Paul were dominating affairs at the time and Rick Buckler seemed isolated. 'He just went along with what we were doing and from time to time he would get pissed off,' recalls Steve. 'It must have been difficult for him as he was on his own and we didn't really involve him much, apart from playing.'

Status Quo's Rick Parfitt saw the band play a set, including 'Loving By Letters', at one of their early Michael's Club gigs and came away moderately impressed. He found the young band refreshing and different but didn't feel they would get anywhere. 'I seem to recall John Weller asking if I would help out on the management side, but by then Status Quo were really flying and I didn't have time for anything else.'

Steve Brookes: "'Loving By Letters' uses the same chord progression as 'More And More' which in turn emulates many Beatles tracks.

C Am F G – a medium-tempo middle-of-the-road dance-along. Perfect for the social clubs we were playing the time.' Brookes had written the song only a short time prior to the booking and the band had to spend the previous Sunday afternoon rehearsing it at the Woking Working Man's Club just behind Stanley Road. That was back in the days when licensing laws meant the hall was empty between the lunchtime bell at 2.00 pm and re-opening at seven in the evening.

Despite the sessions going well, Weller and Brookes were still looking around for a replacement guitarist for Dave Waller. Throughout the recordings Paul had played both bass and rhythm guitar and on stage he was playing only rhythm. Steve Brookes: 'He obviously couldn't play both and although he wanted to be the band's bass guitarist, like McCartney, we didn't really need a bass player for the sort of songs we were playing at the time. Paul had such a naturally strong rhythm style, which drives a song along, we found that between us we could pretty much cover the bottom end of anything we were playing live with two guitars.'

Despite this, The Jam set up a series of auditions in the summer of 1974, at which only one guitarist stood out. Bruce Foxton had grown up listening to his older brother's Motown records and, like Weller and Brookes, was heavily under the spell of that label, even though he was playing in a heavy rock band at the time. Initially, Bruce declined an invitation to join but changed his mind in a matter of months, attracted by the thought of playing live. 'The Jam were the only band in town actually getting gigs,' he recalls, and in the summer of 1974 he became a full-time member.

Once again a four-piece, The Jam's line-up now consisted of Paul Weller (bass and vocals), Steve Brookes (lead guitar and vocals), Bruce Foxton (rhythm guitar) and Rick Buckler (drums). But they soon found that, stripped of Paul's guitar style, the live balance of the band had altered considerably.And that, coupled with his difficulty in simultaneously singing lead vocal and playing bass lines, led to a rethink in which Paul and Bruce switched instruments as an experiment. After lengthy rehearsals and solo practice sessions, Foxton began to master the bass guitar and the sound of The Jam began to fully develop.

'Loving By Letters' was one of the songs listed for a gig at Bunters Club in Guildford on 5 October 1974. That night, with the band sound-checked and ready to play, Bruce wandered off into the High Street intending to meet friends who were going to the gig at the Horse and Groom pub but found his way blocked by the police as ambulances raced around town. That was the night the IRA had chosen to devastate the town with two massive pub bombs, one at the Seven Stars and one in the Horse and Groom that Bruce was heading for. Foxton had missed being caught up in the carnage by a matter of minutes. In the mayhem that followed the group had to leave their equipment where it was and return to Woking. It wasn't until the following day that Bruce discovered his friends had all miraculously avoided injury and managed to climb to safety through a shattered window.

Foxton's good fortune didn't end there, for 27 years later, in September 2001, he was in America with his band Stiff Little Fingers and fate once again went his way. The hotel they were staying at after a New York gig was located only a few blocks from where the World Trade Center stood and was badly damaged in the terrorist attack of 11 September. Luckily, the band members and their entourage had checked out the evening before and flown to Los Angeles.

However, on departure storms delayed the flight and the plane waited on the runway for a full five hours before clearance could be given for take-off. Knowing the delay meant arriving in LA at the dead of night, the band discussed disembarking and spending an evening on the town in New York. But, realising that would mean the aircraft returning to the terminal and disrupting the other passengers' plans, they decided to stay put and wait. The following day, as they watched the horrific events unfold on television, they found out that the alternative flight they would have caught in the morning, had they stayed in New York, was the one that crashed into the Pentagon. Bruce appears to be blessed with good luck and, as Rick Buckler noted, 'The next time we go out, I'm standing next to Foxton.'

MORE AND MORE (Brookes/Weller)

recorded April 1974 at Potter's Studios, Mytchett, Surrey
unreleased

The second song to be recorded at Potter's Studios in April 1974 was 'More And More', yet another Brookes/Weller collaboration. The duo were becoming prolific and by now over half of their set of 42 songs were self-composed, an impressive feat for a pair of 15-year-olds.

Steve Brookes clearly remembers the day he and his songwriting partner wrote the track: 'We didn't have any recording facilities so we had adopted a method of singing a song repeatedly to each other and that way try to commit it to memory. We decided if we couldn't do that then the hook probably wasn't good enough and not worth remembering anyway. Although we had some strange looks walking around Woking singing these tunes to each to other, it seemed to work for us.'

The recording sessions at Potter's Studios had been a complete success and for the first time Weller and Brookes didn't have a cross word between them. The result was their best-recorded work to date and The Jam were clearly taking shape. A copy of the demo followed their previous efforts around London's record labels but Brookes remembers the painful experience only too well. Paul and Steve, still only 15, would sit waiting while various record company executives listened emotionlessly to their best efforts and then hand the tape back to them. Steve summed up his feelings in his book *Keeping The Flame*, and they're worth repeating. 'There are ways to tell someone their baby is ugly, but in the music business they tend to lean over your offspring and retch.'

'More And More' was one of Weller and Brookes' better songs to date and unsurprisingly they found its rejection a little hard to handle. Despite having now left school, and the band regularly playing live, it may well have been these dispiriting experiences which kept the boys away from a studio for the best part of the following 12 months.

'More And More' was also one of the numbers played by The Jam at The Greyhound in Croydon when they secured an unlikely supporting role to heavy rockers Thin Lizzy on 27 October 1974. By that time Phil Lynott's band were four years into their recording career, had just released their sixth album, *Night Life*, and were achieving some international recognition.

Rick Buckler remembers the night well, and the nerves they all felt: 'This was our first experience of playing in a proper venue,' he said. 'There was a sound engineer and lighting system, the works, but no one was particularly interested in us, they were all there to see Lizzy.' Bruce Foxton also has fond memories of the gig. 'I had only recently switched from guitar to bass and didn't know the whole set list, so the three-piece played all the songs I didn't know and then I joined them for the second half of the set. I got a huge cheer as the crowd thought I'd turned up late and the others had started without me.'

WALKING THE DOG (Rufus Thomas)
recorded March 1975 at TW Studios, Fulham, London
unreleased

With the new four-piece now establishing its sound, the band made their way up to TW Studios in Fulham on 21 March 1975 to record a set of songs featuring Bruce Foxton for the first time on bass guitar.

The novelty song 'Walking The Dog' had been a big hit for Rufus Thomas (of 'Funky Chicken' fame) in 1963 and had also turned up on the Rolling Stones' eponymous debut album in April 1964. It was also a regular feature in Dr Feelgood's live set during 1976, although Steve Brookes maintains it was the original version which attracted his attention and The Jam's attempt to cover it was inspired by that. Sung by Paul, the track has a distinct Beatles feel to it with Bruce reworking the Paul McCartney bass line from 'Taxman', which he would later use to great effect on their 1980 number one 'Start!'.

'Walking The Dog' is an interesting inclusion as it clearly indicates the influences on Weller and Brookes at the time. The song was a regular in The Jam's social club set, along with songs from the likes of Martha and The Vandellas, Chuck Berry and James Brown. Not only had Paul by then discovered The Who's 'My Generation' on a tatty 1960s compilation album (which led to the discovery of other edgy tracks such as 'I Can't Explain' and 'Substitute'), but he had also learned that the mod gods formed their own sound after listening to the same American R and B and Tamla Motown as himself. Discovering the 1960s mod movement proved to be a pivotal moment for the 15-year-old songwriter. From then onwards Paul would immerse himself it its music and culture, almost to the exclusion of anything else.

In fact, The Jam's set list at the time even resembled that of the early Who and included classic Chuck Berry songs like 'Roll Over Beethoven', 'Little Queenie' and 'Johnny B Goode', some early Motown in the shape of 'Mickey's Monkey' and 'Hitchhike' and some of the classic R and B tracks The Beatles had also covered in the shape of 'Twist And Shout', 'Kansas City' and Larry Williams' 'Slow Down'.

Brookes, however, sat himself firmly on the blues side of R and B and was never truly taken by the mod culture or its music. His tastes remained with the likes of Smokey Robinson, while the high-octane vibe Paul liked so much in the Feelgoods, coupled with Paul's increasing emulation of the windmilling guitar-playing and jumping-around bands epitomised by The Who, left Brookes feeling uneasy about his band. 'Walking The Dog' and the other songs recorded at the session in TW Studios were far more Brookes' style, but Weller himself was changing direction and Steve didn't like what he was seeing. Ross Dilanda:

'That was definitely when they started drifting apart. Prior to then it was always Weller and Brookes and you never really saw them apart. They used to come up to our rehearsal sessions and we all got on well. Often we would end up back at Stanley Road sitting around drinking tea and always talking about music. Everybody around Paul and Steve in those days was associated in some way with music, there were no other interests.'

I WILL BE THERE (Brookes/Weller)

recorded March 1975 at TW Studios, Fulham, London
unreleased

Despite Paul Weller's new influence in the shape of Dr Feelgood, The Jam were still writing songs with a distinct 1960s feel to them and 'I Will Be There' is a clear example of this. The song is supplemented by Steve's obviously Merseybeat derived guitar riff, as popularised by The Shadows. Bruce's bass playing is subtle and inventive, which is surprising given that he had only been on the instrument a matter of months.

"I Will Be There' is a big song for a big vocal, 'Riders On The Storm' style,' says Steve Brookes. 'We had a guy called Vic Black come down and sing it with us in rehearsals one day. He was a singer in the Tom Jones mould and it sounded fantastic with his voice on it. But he had the idea of us being his backing group, and that wasn't what we had in mind at all so we parted company after just one rehearsal'.

'I Will Be There' was on the set list when The Jam played a New Year's Eve gig at the Woking Liberal Club just yards from the Weller household in Stanley Road. With Bruce now firmly established in the band, Weller and Brookes had become more confident and had noticed that the more animated they were on stage the better the audience reacted. Before long Brookes would be jumping off stage to play guitar solos amongst the dancers, which started to annoy Weller, who felt his partner was being more visual than anyone else in the band.

However, on this particular night Brookes went too far and leapt aboard a baby grand piano to play a final solo, which resulted in a couple of committee members racing up to try to drag him off mid-performance. Weller aimed a kick at one of them and as the evening descended into farce Foxton found himself searching his equipment case for a weapon as the music abruptly ended. It was the first time a Jam gig had ended in violence, but it wouldn't be the last and, although they all stood together on this occasion, friction between Weller and Brookes was growing as the pair competed to be the biggest influence on their band. For the time being however, they were all agreed that it was time to move on from the social clubs and find a younger, more like-minded audience.

All was not well within The Jam camp, as Rick Buckler recalls: 'I remember on several occasions John [Weller] being given a hard time by his wife Anne about spending so much time with us instead of at home with the rest of the family.' Steve Brookes also remembers discontent in the Weller household but plays it down: 'John did everything for us,' remembers Brookes. 'He was always out getting us gigs, blagging vans to take us along and it all took up time. But in the same way as any dad who is manager of the boys' football team, he's going to find it takes up a lot of spare time. I think Anne did get fed up with it, but you know what it's like. Married couples are always going to argue, it's only a question of what it's about. In John's case it was us.'

Enzo Esposito recalls trouble at the Buckler household too: 'There were some occasions when we would all go round in the van to pick him up for gig, and he wasn't allowed out until he had finished his tea. We all had to sit outside and wait for him.'

ONE HUNDRED WAYS (Brookes/Weller)
recorded March 1975 at TW Studios, Fulham, London
unreleased

In this recording, written with a clear Beatles influence once again, Bruce Foxton's extra vocal makes a big difference and the harmonies improve the sound of the band compared to their previous efforts.

'One Hundred Ways' was one of the songs The Jam played at their first record company showcase on a Sunday morning at Michael's Club on 2 March 1975. Just ten days earlier they had performed a gig at the Hindhead British Legion which, as luck would have it, was attended by Sheila Slater, the wife of EMI A&R man Terry Slater. Terry was always on the lookout for new young talent and agreed on a trip to Woking to hear The Jam play for himself. He was impressed enough to recommend that EMI take a closer look at the youngsters.

This was the main reason why the TW Studio sessions were hastily arranged for later that same month, and why time was taken to record four of the band's latest tracks instead of the usual two. But, unsurprisingly, EMI, who were on the lookout for new Glam Rock bands in the style of Gary Glitter and T Rex, simply didn't think the 60s-sounding Jam fitted the bill. Despite Slater's enthusiasm, The Jam were not considered worth investing in.

'One Hundred Ways' had also been played live since the autumn of 1974 and was included on the set list for the group's second high-profile London gig on 21 April 1975, this time at Chelsea Football Club during a testimonial dinner for their legendary coach Harry Medhurst. Being a Chelsea fan, Paul was particularly pleased about the chance to play in front of his favourite team, although that didn't stop him repeatedly mentioning the name of the side who had recently beaten Chelsea in response to some good-natured heckling by a few of the players. The Jam's mixed set of rock 'n' roll, ballads and beat songs went down a storm, despite Glam Rock being the chosen fashion of the legendary seventies Chelsea side, and they all returned to Woking well pleased with their performance.

Soon afterwards the band secured their first public London gig at the Greyhound, 175 Fulham Palace Road, London W14. These days it's a restaurant called The Puzzle, but in the 1970s The Greyhound was a big music venue. Squire's Ross Dilanda remembers climbing into the back of The Jam's transit for the journey to London: 'We all piled in to go and watch them play. Myself and Enzo with Paul, Rick, Bruce and Steve Brookes all crammed in the back.'

Enzo Esposito also remembers the importance of the London gigs: 'Those London venues were always packed at the time, there was a real scene going on. It was a bit like clubbing is these days, people would cram into places like The Greyhound, The Red Cow and The Nashville regardless of who was playing that night. You had to get there early and if it was full you simply went to another one down the road. And for the bands it was a big deal to get a gig in any of them because you were guaranteed a ready-made audience.

'We all took in demos and made phone calls trying to get on the band lists but none of us ever did, except The Jam. That was down to

Paul's dad, who knew someone up there. He hustled and persuaded and finally started getting them gigs and once they were on he would get as many people along from Woking, who would all be in there geeing everybody up and creating a big vibe for the band. Once the venue promoters saw all these people digging The Jam, followed by phone calls the next week asking when they would be back again, they started getting regular bookings. It was easy to see what John was doing. It was down to him that The Jam started breaking into the big London venues, no doubt about it.'

FOREVER AND ALWAYS (Brookes/Weller)
recorded March 1975 at TW Studios, Fulham, London
unreleased

'Forever And Always' was the last of the slow-tempo, 60s-influenced songs The Jam would record and is more Everly Brothers than Dr Feelgood, indicating that Paul's new influences had not yet filtered through to his recorded work. The song has an obvious Gerry Marsden feel to it which is clearly Brookes' style, although the main vocal is from Paul and complemented with Beatle-style harmonies from Bruce and Steve.

Now on the verge of leaving school, Weller was convinced it was time to move away from this type of song, especially as he wanted to find a younger audience, preferring to recreate the sort of music Dr Feelgood and the early Who had done by injecting energy into his music in the style of Motown and Northern Soul. It is important to note that The Who in 1975 stood for everything in the music industry the young Weller hated, but he was mature and eclectic enough to look past his own current prejudices and to regard their earlier work with such respect. Weller and his peers had nothing in common with the hairy Who of the 1970s but Paul once again disregarded perceived fashion by still citing them as one of his favourite bands.

Despite it being 10 years out of date, Weller had completely embraced the look of the 1960s, to the point of spending nearly all his earnings on records, clothes and a scooter costing £70. Paul riding around Woking wearing loafers with his parka flapping in the wind behind him, at a time when all the hip young things were wearing platform shoes, flares and having their hair permed (even the men), made for a bizarre picture. The young Weller was an image of a decade gone by. Ross Dilanda remembers Paul's scooter: 'He did look strange, but that was Paul – he didn't care. The main thing for him was his music; even at that early age it was in his soul. He has often been criticised for trying to copy [Steve] Marriott or [Pete] Townshend but Paul has always been the same Paul. His feel for music made him stand out, not because he was trying to be someone else.'

But Steve Brookes was unconvinced and was increasingly restless about Weller's backward-looking stance. Throughout the summer of 1975 The Jam geared up the tempo of their songs and, following the New Year's Eve debacle at the Woking Liberal Club, were now determined to avoid playing social clubs, preferring to break into the pub and club scene, attracting a younger and much livelier audience. Steve Brookes enjoyed the performances but wasn't into the mod culture in the way Weller was; he also began to feel outnumbered as Buckler and Foxton increasingly went along with Paul's ideas.

The atmosphere became even more strained when Paul began showing Steve pictures of The Who and The Small Faces dressed in slick black suits. He insisted he wanted the band to adopt the same image and Brookes was appalled at the thought of dressing like pop stars from a previous decade. 'But it wasn't only the suits,' remembers Ross Dilanda. 'Steve has a much calmer nature and style to Paul and when he started hammering it Pete Townshend or Wilko-style, I don't think Steve liked it. It probably embarrassed him a bit.'

Steve also had a new girlfriend and had to choose between spending time with her or continuing the drive to London three or four times a week, playing music he wasn't totally struck on while dressed in a ten-year-old stage uniform. The decision seemed easy enough to him and in September 1975 the 17-year-old guitarist announced that he was leaving The Jam. Whether or not that was the right decision for him, there remains no doubt that, a few years

later, the same black suit/red Rickenbacker image The Jam had would become one of the lasting visual images of the decade. Paul had been right, but his single-minded determination had cost him his best friend.

Rick Buckler remembers the split well: 'Paul always cuts people off totally once they are not involved with him and it was like that with Steve,' he recalled. 'One minute they were closer than close and the next there was nothing between them at all.' Ross Dilanda doesn't entirely agree: 'I don't think any of the Wellers were like that. His mum and dad seemed to be fond of all of us and we were always welcome at Stanley Road, whether Paul was in or not, especially Steve. They continued to keep in touch with him for years and probably still do. I don't remember Steve being cut out or ostracised. I think Paul was just pissed off he had left the band and didn't want him to.'

Once again the balance of The Jam had been disrupted and other tensions surfaced when both Buckler and Foxton left the band after a row about the way the gig money was being shared out. With Weller adrift and on his own, his dad even went to the lengths of recruiting professional musicians to back him, but no one could be found to reproduce the sound Foxton and Buckler were developing.

With the regular Friday night commitment at Michael's Club due at the end of the week, Paul asked Squire's drummer Ross Dilanda to join him in a one-off performance. Ross: 'Paul called up one day and said he needed a drummer for a gig at Michael's the following Friday night. He told me Buckler had left the band and would I step in.' Dilanda was reluctant as he didn't know any of The Jam's songs and there was no time for rehearsals: 'Paul told me not to worry about that. He told me just to tap along in the background and we would get away with it. What he didn't tell me was that Bruce wouldn't be there either, it was just the two of us. It was a nightmare and I couldn't believe it, but we got away with it.' There was a suggestion afterwards that Dilanda would join The Jam, but he wasn't keen. 'They were just the same as us at the time, another band around town without a record deal,' says Ross. 'I wouldn't have left Squire, we were all mates. Nearly 30 years later I still haven't left Squire.'

Ultimately Paul needed The Jam's established rhythm section and a meeting was called, the dispute sorted out and, within a week, Foxton and Buckler returned. Weller took the problem in his stride but he never quite forgot what he regarded at the time as gross disloyalty from his band mates.

Paul also became increasingly frustrated by Foxton's refusal to give up his apprenticeship at a Woking print firm until he had qualified. Paul was so convinced the band would turn professional, sign to a major label and achieve worldwide success that he had never bothered looking for other work – and as such has never had a 'proper job' in his life. Buckler and Foxton were less convinced and perhaps a little more realistic, neither giving up their jobs until The Jam signed to Polydor in 1977. This, coupled with Brookes' absence, left Weller feeling agitated about the band.

TAKIN' MY LOVE (Brookes/Weller)

recorded 10 December 1975 at Potter's Studios, Mytchett, Surrey
unreleased

On stage, however, where it mattered most, things had never sounded better. Buckler, in an attempt to fill out the band's sound, was developing his heavy, rhythmic drum patterns and Paul was playing more and more like Wilko Johnson by mixing lead and rhythm guitar parts in Steve's absence. Bruce, meanwhile, had all but mastered the bass guitar. And by the time the band booked into their first studio recording session without the pivotal Brookes, the distinctive musical style the public came to recognise later as 'The Jam sound' was starting to become recognisable. The first thing they did that day in Potter's studio was to record a second version of Brookes' 'Takin' My Love'', despite it being two years old and, by then, was being credited to Weller alone. Unsurprisingly, the end result is harsher than the original.

AGAIN (Weller)

recorded 10 December 1975 at Potter's Studios, Mytchett, Surrey
unreleased

The second song recorded in Potter's Studios that day was 'Again', the first of Weller's efforts without Brookes' involvement. Competent and solid, its lyrics hint at the social observation of day-to-day living and the desperate need to escape it, which Weller would constantly return to throughout his career.

The track also features a guitar solo which is instantly recognisable as a Paul Weller riff and could have appeared on any of the tracks that would later appear on *In The City*. It also has a much livelier drum track than on any previous recordings, full of fills and off-beat snares, that would become Buckler's trademark style in later years.

With Brookes now gone, Bruce Foxton grew into the role of second band member and his own influences were starting to show in the recordings. But the group were still actively looking for another guitarist. Advertisements were placed and auditions held in a room above the Red Lion pub in Woking, but the only suitable applicant, Pete Jessop, failed to appear for any of the upcoming gigs. Paul once again turned to Squire and invited Enzo Esposito to consider joining The Jam.

Enzo: 'I remember being told by John Weller that one of the record companies interested in signing The Jam were insisting on the band being a four-piece, so he asked me to come down to rehearsals to see how we got on. They were held at Sheerwater Youth Club and they had a keyboard player there as well. They were going to chose between that or another guitarist but after a few weeks Rick Buckler told me they were going to remain as a three-piece.'

This was the last time The Jam considered any other full-time band members and the line-up was now settled.

WHEN I NEEDED YOU (Weller)

recorded 10 December 1975 at Potter's Studios, Mytchett, Surrey
unreleased

PLEASE DON'T TREAT ME BAD (Weller)

recorded 10 December 1975 at Potter's Studios, Mytchett, Surrey
unreleased

Records indicate that the above two songs were also recorded at Potter's Studios that day, but it has proved impossible to establish any further details about them.

Paul was still unsettled by Brookes' absence and was becoming even more temperamental and volatile than usual. In Potter's studio on 28 May 1976, Foxton bore the signs of that temper: a peach of a black eye. Two weeks previously, while packing up after a gig at the Hope and Anchor, Bruce had accidentally sat on Paul's guitar in the back of the van and the singer lashed out at him before being pulled off by friends.

Foxton quickly shrugged off the incident but Weller began to isolate himself from his band mates and started spending more time with other friends who had discovered the Northern Soul movement spreading south out of clubs like The Wigan Casino, north of Manchester. Bisley Pavilion, just outside Woking, was one of the southern venues for the Northern Soul All-Nighters and Weller was a frequent visitor to the Thersday [sic] Club at the Pavilion, promoted by the Inter City Soul Show, which was playing the soul and Tamla Motown favoured by the 60s mods. Weller was hooked and immediately started writing songs that reflected this new experience.

LEFT RIGHT AND CENTRE (Weller)

recorded 28 May 1976 at Potter's Studios, Mytchett, Surrey
unreleased

The melody of 'Left Right And Centre' has The Supremes' hit 'Back In My Arms Again' written all over it, and Paul is developing what he thought at the time to be an Otis Redding-style vocal.

'Left Right And Centre' mirrors many of the early Motown songs and studio engineer John Franklin remembers that, as most bands around that time preferred to use the modern multi-track method of recording, he fully expected The Jam to do likewise. But the engineer hadn't reckoned on Paul's single-minded determination to sound like his 60s heroes. The singer was adamant that he wanted the songs to be recorded in the same way the Motown bands had worked – and that was virtually live, with all the musicians playing together. In the end Franklin wasn't entirely happy with the raw result but the band were well pleased. The session was a clear indication that Paul Weller, only three days past his 18th birthday, knew exactly what he wanted and wasn't prepared to compromise with anyone, regardless of their experience.

The gentle melodies of the earlier Jam songs are still evident but have been enhanced by the tension and nervous energy displayed by the 60s mod bands. Paul was also listening at the time to the music of bands like Martha and The Vandellas; their hit 'Dancing In The Street' had also found its way into The Jam's live set. But the edginess of the recordings are still a long way from the 100 mph energy The Jam would apply only a few months later when Paul's next big influence emerged: The Sex Pistols.

NON STOP DANCING (Weller)
recorded 28 May 1976 at Potter's Studios, Mytchett, Surrey
unreleased version

'Non Stop Dancing' was the second track recorded during the session at Potter's on 28 May 1976 and is Paul's offering to the Northern Soul scene of that year, about which Weller would comment: 'That for me is what music is all about, all night dancing.' Clearly Paul has never tried dancing to some of his later classics such as 'Going Underground' and 'Strange Town', but in 1976 many of his songs had a real Motown thread running through them. Already on the live set list at the time were tracks like 'Time For Truth', 'Sounds From The Street' and 'I Got By In Time', which would all make it onto *In The City* a year later and all have a dance feel to them. Lifting the rhythm directly from 'Dancing In The Street', this demo of 'Non Stop Dancing' once again combines the melodies of Motown with some slightly harsher mod sounds, and this time includes a jumping piano played by Bob Gray.

Five weeks after the Potter's session there were two major events in the space of just a few days, which altered Paul Weller's thinking completely. During the early part of the long hot summer of 1976 he had read a review of young bands in the *New Musical Express* and decided to go and see for himself what was creating such an impact in the music press. 'Anarchy In The UK' was still five months away from release and the Sex Pistols were yet to make their infamous appearance on TV with Bill Grundy, but they were already making a huge name for themselves on London's live music scene.

Having read about the emerging punk movement, which was dominated by people around his own age, Paul was keen to experience it for himself and travelled from Woking to a gig at the 100 Club in Oxford Street, where The Clash and The Sex Pistols were playing on 6 July. Weller: 'When I heard The Clash I starting thinking I should sing as naturally as I spoke, and that The Jam should be an English sounding band.' Paul immediately gave up his Otis Redding affectation. The fact the Pistols also played a cover of The Small Faces' 'What'cha Gonna Do About It?' didn't go unnoticed and Paul was excited about this emerging scene.

Next up, a few days later, was an all-nighter at London's Lyceum Ballroom This proved to be his epiphany. The impact on Weller was immediate; everything he loved about music was right in front of him in the hall. He looked around and found the Lyceum full of people like himself – young, aggressive, dancing, high on energy and a far cry from the social club members in Woking that made up his own audience, and much younger even than his crowd down at Michael's Club. Weller saw it all in one evening. 'There was a scene there and I wanted to be part of it,' he recalled. Paul also realised that he could indulge his love of R and B, speed it up and emulate his new heroes Wilko Johnson and Pete Townshend, and find an energetic young audience in that punk movement.

It was all falling into place for Paul now but The Jam had spent most of 1976 struggling for gigs, since they were refusing to play the working men's clubs. London bookings were few and far between so, desperate for publicity, on 16 October the group set up their PA system in Newport Court, in the heart of London's Soho, and once again emulated The Beatles by playing a live and spontaneous set for the public. 'It was great,' recalls Rick Buckler. 'All the firemen from Shaftesbury Avenue station went up on the roof to watch from there.' The Jam, in true punk fashion, had literally taken to the streets. And the stunt was a major success: they received their first reviews in both *Sounds* and *Melody Maker* the following month.

By coincidence, the band of the moment, The Clash, were having breakfast in a café opposite but showed little enthusiasm; in fact, Joe Strummer dismissed the group as revivalists. But it may well have been as a result of that pavement appearance that The Jam were found supporting none other than The Sex Pistols in Dunstable only a few days later. It was the first time Foxton and Buckler had seen the Pistols and although they weren't taken in the same way as Paul, at least the band were now all pulling in the same direction.

In a tribute to the new punk movement, at the end of 1976 Paul Weller wrote 'In The City There's a Thousand Things I Want To Say To You'. Shortened to 'In The City', this would become The Jam's debut single in early 1977. Things had changed, and in a matter of months The Jam had changed their sound to suit.

SOUL DANCE (Weller)

BACK IN MY ARMS AGAIN (Holland/Dozier/Holland)

I GOT BY IN TIME (Weller)

all recorded September 1976 at Potter's Studios, Mytchett, Surrey
all unreleased

The final three songs The Jam laid down in Potter's Studios in 1976 were the last ever Jam recordings prior to them signing with Polydor six months later. They are notable for a number of reasons, the first being that it was the final time The Jam recorded live (Motown style) apart from when they added 'Heatwave' (another Motown classic) to their album *Setting Sons* in 1979.

The first track recorded that day was 'Soul Dance', which is a slow-tempo soul song written by Paul before he had discovered punk rock in July of that year. The recording clearly indicates that Weller was still following his 1960s influence and illustrates the almost instant change in his writing style following his experience of seeing The Sex Pistols and The Clash play live. The differences between 'Soul Dance' and 'In The City' (written only four months later) could not be greater and, if the two tracks were played consecutively, The Jam could be mistaken for two entirely different bands, were it not for Weller's distinctive vocal performance on each.

The songwriting progress The Jam made during those six months is stunning, and partly due to the fact that Bruce Foxton and Rick Buckler's own styles of playing was far more suited to the energetic music The Jam were progressing towards. No longer restricted within the set structures of soul, the rhythm section, during this period, seems to become far more inventive than before. No longer trying to emulate other musicians and create the music Paul felt was right for the band, Bruce and Rick were developing the distinctive sound that would become the cornerstone of the bass- and drum-driven Jam for the next six years, fundamental to every song the band recorded in that time. The contrast between 'Soul Dance' and 'I Got By In Time' at this recording session demonstrates that quite clearly.

The session was also notable for the open-mindedness of the band, who were still looking for a fourth musician to replace Steve Brookes, experimenting with both trumpet and keyboard players in the studio. The attempt to bring brass into the band's overall sound failed and the results were finally left out of the mix, but the inclusion of a keyboard player worked, especially on 'I Got By In Time'. Weller was particularly keen to incorporate keyboards into the band as he felt that, if they couldn't find a replacement guitarist for Brookes to complete their Beatles line-up, then they would try a keyboard player in order to emulate The Small Faces.

Bob Gray grew up with Bruce Foxton on Sheerwater Estate in Woking and, like all the musicians ever to be in a Jam line-up, attended the secondary school near where they lived. In 1974 Gray emigrated to Canada with his family but, on a return visit during August 1976, he ran into Bruce. Bob, himself an accomplished keyboard player, was immediately invited to audition to join the band. Rehearsal sessions were arranged at Sheerwater Youth Club a few weeks later, where he met Rick and Paul. The sessions were successful enough for Paul to ask Gray to play on a three-track demo due to be recorded a few weeks later at Potter's in Mytchett.

'I remember first meeting Paul at the youth club and being impressed with the amp he was using,' says Gray. 'He told me, with a wink, that it was on loan from Rick Parfitt of Status Quo, who also grew up on the Sheerwater Estate. I don't think Rick ever saw it again. I also remember that when we turned up at the studio Paul had brought along the music teacher from school to play trumpet on one of the tracks we were recording, but it didn't work out. Paul's dad John gave the guy a fiver for his trouble and it always stuck in my mind how respectful both he and his dad were to this guy when it became obvious his trumpet-playing was not suitable for the songs. They felt bad about him going to the trouble of giving up his time only to be told we would not be using the parts he recorded.'

The studio experiments with a keyboard player worked well and, with Bruce and Rick playing heavier parts than they had before, the sound of The Jam, particularly on this version of 'I Got By In Time', belie their teenage years. Since the decision was taken to stop appearing at social clubs around Woking, the band had managed to secure only five gigs all year and were eager to take their new line-up out on the road.

Because of the difficulties of taking a piano to the centre of London, Bob didn't appear during the Soho Market open-air performance in October but he did travel with the band to their famous gig with The Sex Pistols in Dunstable on 21 October. 'The Pistols gig was a total shock to me,' says Gray. 'I remember all of us driving up the motorway in a Bedford van and Paul was doing the *Melody Maker* crossword. Despite the Pistols being on the front cover he seemed perfectly relaxed but I remember thinking it must be a big gig if the band were attracting that sort of publicity. I had never heard their music before and had no idea what I was in for. But when we arrived their road crew were bringing all this expensive gear into the venue, with brand-new stacks of speakers and amplifiers, so it looked pretty impressive. But then I watched Steve Jones, who I initially thought was a roadie, desperately trying to tune his guitar using an expensive scope tuner. But he had no idea how to use it and played the entire gig with an out-of-tune guitar.'

'When The Jam went on stage we were all dressed in smart suits and I was playing a grand piano belonging to the venue. There were about 150 people in the audience and almost as soon as we started a few of the wankers in the front began spitting at us and, having been previously immersed in the music business in Canada, I had no idea what punk was or what was going on. It was a total culture shock to me and I remember getting up from my piano stool to sort out some of these idiots for messing up my suit but Bruce told me to sit back down and carry on playing. Someone later told me it was a sign of respect. When the Pistols hit the stage I thought to myself, "What a fucking noise." Glen Matlock was the only one in tune and I thought Jonny Rotten was no more than an obnoxious wanker. I wasn't interested in that scene at all but I played a couple more gigs with The Jam before calling it a day. Within a few months I was back off to Canada.' The Sex Pistols' Glen Matlock also remembers the gig: 'It was a massive oval room and The Jam had this bloke with a waistcoat on, who looked like a pub pianist with an upright piano.'

Bob Gray played keyboards with The Jam on two other occasions. Once at The 100 Club in Oxford Street on 9 November 1976 and finally upstairs at Ronnie Scott's in Soho on the 23rd. When he next returned to Woking in March the following year, he heard *In The City*'s familiar guitar riff on a pub radio while having his lunch and the following day picked up *Melody Maker* to read about The Jam's new recording deal with Polydor. Two years later, on 10 April 1979, Bob was invited to see The Jam play at The Rex Hall in Toronto and was pleased to meet up with his old mates again, especially Bruce Foxton. By then the band were touring their album *All Mod Cons* and

Bob could see how far they had progressed in the two short years since he had played with them. 'I don't have any illusions about myself at all,' says Gray. 'Although I left the band I know they didn't give a toss and obviously The Jam, without a keyboard player, was the best line-up they had. They really were a fantastic band.'

Bob remains in Canada to this day and works as a professional memory coach, becoming a recognised authority on memory systems in the process. He has a stage show which he regularly takes out on the road under the name 'Backwards Bob the Memory Man', and his special talent for recall has earned him a place in *The Guinness Book Of World Records*.

EARLY LIVE RECORDINGS

All the following were recorded live by either a three-piece or four-piece Jam. Some have already been listed in the pre-Polydor recordings, but are included again here as collectively the tapes make an interesting record of the songs influencing Weller's and Brookes' songwriting in the early to mid-1970s.

TAKIN' MY LOVE (Weller/Brookes)

EIGHT DAYS A WEEK (Lennon/McCartney)

SOME KINDA LOVIN' (Weller/Brookes)

LITTLE GIRL CRYING (Weller/Brookes)

WORLD WITHOUT LOVE (Lennon/McCartney)

[1959; a Number One hit for Peter and Gordon in 1965]

OH CAROL (Neil Sedaka)

REMEMBER (Weller/Brookes)

JAILHOUSE ROCK (Lieber/Stoller) [A hit For Elvis Presley in 1957]

I SAW HER STANDING THERE (Lennon/McCartney)

LOVE HAS DIED (Weller/Brookes)

FEELS SO GOOD (Weller/Brookes)

THAT WAY (Weller/Brookes)

LITTLE QUEENIE (Chuck Berry)

BABY I DON'T CARE (Leiber/Stoller)

TWIST AND SHOUT (Medley/Russell)

LOVE, LOVE, LOVING (Weller/Brookes)

CRAZY OLD WORLD (Weller/Brookes)

LIKE I LOVE YOU (Weller/Brookes)

YOU AND THE SUMMER (Weller/Brookes)

SAY GOODBYE (Weller/Brookes)

SHE DON'T NEED ME (Weller/Brookes)

WHEN I'M NEAR YOU (Weller/Brookes)

LOVE'S SURPRISE (Weller/Brookes)

SHE'S COMING HOME (Weller/Brookes)

ONE HUNDRED WAYS (Weller/Brookes)

FOREVER AND ALWAYS (Weller/Brookes)

I WILL BE THERE (Weller/Brookes)

WALKING THE DOG (Rufus Thomas)

NON STOP DANCING (Weller)

LEFT RIGHT AND CENTRE (Weller)

AGAIN (Weller)

WHEN I NEEDED YOU (Weller)

PLEASE DON'T TREAT ME BAD (Weller)

SOUL DANCE (Weller)

BACK IN MY ARMS AGAIN (Holland/Dozier/Holland)

[A hit for The Supremes in 1965]

TWO

ON THE RECORD

WITHIN a few months of the Dunstable gig with the Pistols, The Jam had signed a one-album/one-single recording deal with Polydor for an advance of £6000 and a subsequent six per cent royalty. Just prior to that the Pistols had received a £40,000 advance and The Clash a £100,000 one from EMI and CBS respectively. The Jam were reported to be embarrassed by the figures, but Polydor's John Pearson put it into perspective. 'Who gives a fuck?' he said. 'It's only a loan anyway. The record company gets it back before any royalties are paid.' Weller himself seemed unconcerned, telling friends: 'To be honest, I was more pleased when I found my old Who badge that day.'

Rick Buckler was equally untroubled. 'The less a record company have to advance the band, which they get back anyway, the more they can spend on marketing and promoting the album,' he explained. 'It probably worked in our favour.'

IN THE CITY

ART SCHOOL (Weller)
Recorded in March 1977 at Stratford Place Studios, Oxford Street, London
Produced by Chris Parry and Vic Coppersmith-Heaven
Album track: In The City (May 1977)

The Jam's debut album *In The City* opened up with the track 'Art School', which is a harsh, spiky mix of Weller's R and B roots and the new punk sounds he was experiencing. As one of the last songs to be written for the album, it reflects the growing assurance of a young band who felt at the time they were onto something special. Confident and strong, it's a two-minute masterpiece.

The 'Art School' reference to young punks had been on Paul's mind for some time; he was beginning to find the whole scene cliquey and elitist, rather than the movement of free expression it was presented as. The old musical establishment had merely been replaced by a new one and Weller's feeling of resentment was reflected in many of his songs. Some people regarded The Jam's image and R and B style as retro, with one journalist, *Melody Maker*'s Caroline Coon, accusing them publicly of exactly that. Weller responded by making a placard reading: 'How can I be a fucking revivalist when I am only 18?' and wearing it down the pub. But Coon didn't speak for many other music journalists. Adrian Thrills, Tony Fletcher, Danny Baker and Gary Crowley instantly connected with The Jam. Author Tony Parsons, then a young staff writer at the *NME*, sympathised with the group's attitude to the punk movement and wrote: 'What does exist is the worth of individual bands. That means something as long as they remain true to themselves.'

In 'Art School', Weller observes young punks attempting to become the 1970s equivalent of the fashionable art school crowd of the 1960s. 'Wear what you want and feel good about it, punk is our Art School,' was the message and Weller makes it clear from this powerful opening track exactly what he was thinking. The song is an early demonstration of just how far removed Weller was from his contemporaries, who were singing at the time about breaking out of borstal and life on the dole. Meanwhile, the music press made people's choices for them, telling them who was in and who was out. As a punter himself, Weller didn't buy into it at all. He wanted to like the music and wear the clothes of his choice and the two didn't necessarily go together. The idea that a mod, dressed in smart suits and button-down shirts, couldn't enjoy punk or any other type of music, in the same way that a Chelsea fan couldn't also support Arsenal, was rubbished by Paul.

'Art School' was one of only two tracks on the album to have a video produced for it, or 'promo' as such films were known at the time. This features the group playing live on stage without their trademark black suits and Red Rickenbackers, and also reveals that it was Bruce who counted the album in: 1, 2, 3, 4... In the background, while the band play, three art students are painting abstract rubbish on giant canvases. Look out for the feedbacking Rickenbacker 'Morse coda' and a scene in which Bruce explodes a TV set by putting his foot through it. The TV, however, was pre-smashed and then lightly glued back together before the actual shot.

'Art School' was performed live during The Jam's first ever BBC radio session on The John Peel Show, transmitted on 2 May 1977. The song was later covered by Silversun for the 1999 Jam tribute album *Fire And Skill*.

I'VE CHANGED MY ADDRESS (Weller)
Recorded in March 1977 at Stratford Place Studios, Oxford Street, London.
Produced by Chris Parry and Vic Coppersmith-Heaven
Album track: In The City (May 1977)

The second song on *In The City* has its roots deep in R and B and, at a fluid 3.31, is one of the longest on the album. Written in mid-1976, it was one of the original songs designed to replace the cover versions in the band's live set and, bursting out of London's pubs and clubs, it quickly became a firm favourite of the growing Jam army.

Lyrically, Weller seems to feel that the best way to deal with an unwanted girlfriend is to simply disappear from view, or even move house altogether, maintaining he is too young to settle down and that having a girlfriend represents just that. Throughout his career Weller has been criticised for his songs being too political, but to believe that all of them are is to misunderstand the songwriter. 'I've Changed My Address' is a good example. At a time when Weller's new heroes of mainstream punk were advocating violence in the shape of The Clash ('White Riot') and The Sex Pistols ('Anarchy In The UK'), Paul was actually enjoying a more lighthearted view of the world around him. 'A lot of our songs have humour in them that probably doesn't come out because people don't go into them, [they] just take them at face value,' he observed in 1977.

Paul's Roger Daltrey-like vocal and a Townshend-esque sliding key change indicate the kind of songs The Jam were listening to at the time, but there were other influences too. 'Some of those early Jam songs were my attempt at being socially aware,' says Weller. 'I was aping The Clash after reading interviews with Joe Strummer and Mick Jones, who were saying people should be writing about what's happening today. I'd never even thought of it before, I was busy rewriting 'My Generation'.' In fact, many of Weller's songs displayed vulnerability and self-doubt, their subjects including love and dancing, areas few contemporary artists dared to explore until after The Jam had shown it was possible to combine them with a blistering tempo.

'I've Changed My Address' was chosen by Weller for the John Peel session transmitted on 2 May 1977, along with 'In The City', 'Art School' and 'The Modern World'.

SLOW DOWN (Larry Williams)
Recorded in March 1977 at Stratford Place Studios, Oxford Street, London
Produced by Chris Parry and Vic Coppersmith-Heaven
Album track: In The City (May 1977)

It had become a policy of Weller's not to cover songs written by his own favourite bands, but instead, as a more discreet mark of respect, to cover the songs they themselves had covered. The inclusion of 'Slow Down' on the debut album, a Larry Williams song, was as much due to its huge popularity as part of their live set (dating back to 1975) as it was to the fact that The Beatles had also covered it. It is easy to imagine the band coming up with a completely original debut album had they been given more time, but Polydor, having missed out on several other acts in the preceding months, wanted to launch them as quickly as possible.

In another anti-anarchy move, The Jam displayed their indifference to punk by having Union Jacks decorating the stage as they embarked on their first major UK tour to promote the album. They even went as far as having Union Jack jackets made for a photo shoot outside one of Britain's best-loved establishment landmarks, Big Ben. The message was clear: we love Britain and we're proud of it, faults and all. Weller even told journalists he would be voting Tory in the next election, but the remark, which was only meant as a humorous poke at punk's trendy left-wingers, backfired when the band were accused of associating themselves with the far right movement, The National Front. As that was never the intention, the jackets were returned to their hangers and the Union Jacks removed from the stage.

I GOT BY IN TIME (Weller)
Recorded in March 1977 at Stratford Place Studios, Oxford Street, London
Produced by Chris Parry and Vic Coppersmith-Heaven
Album track: In The City (May 1977)

Following the 100 mph 'Slow Down', 'I Got By In Time' is a neat return to the R and B vibe running through so many early Jam tracks. This song, written about Weller's former band mate and best friend Steve Brookes, is mature and balanced and gives fans an early glimpse into the real attitude of the young songwriter. The lyrics are far from arrogant yet have gone largely misunderstood; Weller didn't feel he had broken any bonds or codes at all, but seemingly still felt that Brookes had.

Another two-minute song, it sails through the chords, Weller experimenting vocally and the band developing their own unique sound, far too proficient to be punk. It also reveals a sensitivity in Weller that few people understood, even Buckler, who insisted that Paul had cut Brookes out of his life and moved on, almost without noticing. In 'I Got By In Time' Weller lets on that he noticed all right, and that he was still bemused and hurt by Brookes' decision to walk out of the band – and also by his refusal to return when he phoned him personally a few months later to ask him back (usually a job Weller left for his father). Even the song's title reveals that it had taken Paul a long to time to recover from the split.

AWAY FROM THE NUMBERS (Weller)
Recorded in March 1977 at Stratford Place Studios, Oxford Street, London
Produced by Chris Parry and Vic Coppersmith-Heaven
Album track: In The City (May 1977)

By the time *In The City* was being recorded The Jam were only six
months beyond the last Potter's Studios sessions, in which they had
experimented with a trumpet player and had Bob Grey contributing
keyboards. At that time they recorded what was regarded as their
best original work to date, 'Soul Dance' and 'I Got By In Time', and
had time to slip in a cover of The Supremes' 'Back In My Arms
Again'. 'Away From The Numbers' was written in late 1976 and
suggests that, although the Pistols had transformed his attitude, Paul
wasn't about to start thinking like them and neither would he turn
his music into a two-chord rant.

If further proof were needed, 'Away From The Numbers' illustrated
the band's mix of R and B and mod influences, even using the 1960s
mod term for a crowd of people (numbers) in the title. Lyrically
Weller takes a step outside and looks back in at the life around him,
drawing attention to the behaviour patterns to be found in any
English town or city. In doing so, he quickly drew comparisons from
the music press to Steve Marriott, John Lennon, Ray Davies and
above all Pete Townshend. No doubt the 17-year-old Weller was
delighted by such comparisons. Some remarked that the young
Weller lad would one day be regarded as just as important, but others
laughed such comparisons off.

Musically, and sometimes through big Who-type chords, The Jam
were pulling it off and by now even the cynics were listening to this
album and noticing real quality emerging. For Paul the songwriting
was more about honest observation than political posturing. At the
time of writing 'Away From The Numbers' Paul had yet to leave his
parents' house in Woking, although the rebellious nature of the
lyrics had little to do with that. The image is more to do with the
old men and women frequenting the drab little social clubs around
Woking, with little else to do with their afternoons but sitting at
the same tables drinking the same beer year after year. That image

frightened Weller, but he does offer a nod of respect and a sign of maturity.

'Away From The Numbers', more than any other song included on The Jam's debut album, set Weller aside from his angry contemporaries and provided an early indication of his depth and grasp of reality. But once again the general thread is of breaking out and running free from whatever the writer feels trapped by.

'Away From The Numbers' remained on The Jam's live set list for many years and made a one-and-only radio appearance on 4 December 1979, when the BBC broadcast *The Jam at The Rainbow*. In this live performance, 'Away From The Numbers' is tucked between 'Burning Sky' and Bruce Foxton's 'Smithers-Jones', two of the big songs recorded for the album *Setting Sons* earlier that year. Impressively, the three-year-old 'Away From The Numbers' doesn't sound at all out of place.

BATMAN THEME (Neal Hefti)
Recorded in March 1977 at Stratford Place Studios, Oxford Street, London
Produced by Chris Parry and Vic Coppersmith-Heaven
Album track: In The City (May 1977)

'Batman' is The Jam's answer to The Who's fantastic cover of the popular TV theme included on their 1966 EP *Ready Steady Who*, which was a major influence on The Jam in their early days. Fast and punchy, this track's inclusion was also due to its popularity at gigs, and it would keep on making live appearances throughout The Jam's career all over the world.

It's another in a sequence of cover versions cribbed from popular mid-1960s artists, providing more evidence, if any were needed, of the band's roots. Each of their first four albums includes cover versions lifted from the sixties songwriters whom Paul admired and was trying to emulate. It's no surprise comparisons were made, as their recorded work included 'Slow Down' (The Beatles), 'Batman' (The Who), 'In The Midnight Hour' (Wilson Pickett), 'David Watts' (The Kinks) and 'Heatwave' (Martha and The Vandellas). And live the band were playing 'Move On Up' (Curtis Mayfield), 'Big Bird' (Booker T Jones), 'Back In My Arms Again' (The Supremes) and 'Sweet Soul Music' (Arthur Conley). Others popped up here and there: 'So Sad About Us' (The Who), 'And Your Bird Can Sing' (The Beatles) and 'I Got You (I Feel Good)' (James Brown). All of them from the same era, just as every cover The Jam played live in their early social club days was from the same genre.

At the time *In The City* was released the album attracted remarks such as 'highly charged', 'chaotic' and 'intense.' 'Batman', on the other hand, only drew such comments as 'why?' and 'pointless'. But that in itself is to miss the point. It was another small joke made by music's Mr Serious, and predictably was missed by many.

In June 1980, The Jam recorded another version of 'Batman' at Stratford Place. At the time Martin Gainsford was the editor of mod fanzine *On Target*, and had gone to the studio to interview Weller. 'I knew The Jam were very open to kids coming along to soundchecks, and they would often dedicate songs to particular fans that evening,' he says. 'They were all really friendly, but even so I was surprised when, after we finished the interview, Weller asked me if I wanted to stay on while the band recorded some demos for their new album, *Sound Affects*.'

Along with around a dozen other fans who had been invited to the studio, Gainsford contributed to a football chant-style intro on a demo of 'Dream Time' that was ultimately never used. He also saw demos of 'Start!', 'That's Entertainment' and 'Boy About Town' being recorded. In addition to these, the band recorded a demo for a song called 'Jazzy Sleazy' that has yet to see the light of day.

'At about 4 or 5 o'clock they were ready to wind it up when Paul reminded Rick and Bruce that they had something else to record,' says Gainsford. 'He had been contacted by the mother of a fan, who explained that she had bought a stereo as a birthday present for her son, and wanted the first thing he heard on it to be a real surprise. So she sent him a blank cassette and asked him if the band would record something specially. I remember they talked about it for a short while, and all agreed that singing 'Happy Birthday' would be a bit naff. I think it was either Bruce or Rick who suggested doing 'Batman', but changing the words to use it as a way to say happy birthday to this kid. Five minutes later they had finished, and had each left personal birthday greetings at the end. I don't know if that bloke's still got the tape, but it must be one of the greatest Jam rarities ever recorded!'

IN THE CITY (Weller)

Recorded in March 1977 at Stratford Place Studios, Oxford Street, London
A-side released 29 April 1977; Polydor 2058 866; reached number 40
[B-side: 'Takin' My Love']
Album track: In The City (May 1977)

Curiously, the album's blistering title track was left to open the second side. Written towards the end of 1976 after Weller had turned 18, this was his tribute to the emerging punk scene, acknowledging it but at the same time placing himself firmly outside it. Such was the song's popularity The Jam would open their live set with it *and* encore with it during the UK tour promoting the album. It was this song that Polydor signed the band to release as their debut single, and for that reason they were disappointed to see it only scraping into the Top 40 of the UK chart. By contrast the band themselves were delighted, particularly with the chance to perform on *Top Of The Pops* – although they were obliged to mime.

The idea for the lyric came from Paul's experience of travelling into London from Woking for the early punk gigs in the summer of 1976; at the time he actually made up a lapel badge, pretty fashionable in those days, with the words 'In The City There's A Thousand Things I Want To Say To You' printed on it. That homemade slogan was a reference to the thousands of kids who formed part of the punk/New Wave movement, each of them with something to say but not being listened to or taken seriously. Weller was one, but managed to articulate those feelings in a way no other 18-year-old had been able to up until then.

'In The City' was the band's debut single, released on 29 April 1977 and earning them the immediate respect and recognition of their contemporaries. Suddenly everybody knew who The Jam were, and their credibility was assured when Sex Pistol Steve Jones borrowed 'In The City''s descending guitar riff for the Pistols' hit 'Holidays In The Sun', which reached number eight in the UK chart in October of that year. This sparked a confrontation between Weller and punk legend Sid Vicious at the Speakeasy drinking club in Soho. Vicious certainly had a reputation but he was unwise to confront a naturally volatile and aggressive Weller over who stole whose guitar riff. In fact, the wiry punk was left bleeding after Weller allegedly settled the row by smashing a glass over his head. 'I was there but I don't remember it like that,' says Bruce Foxton. 'It was only a punch up, in fact more of a scuffle really – nothing serious.'

To promote the record, Polydor arranged The Jam's first real UK tour playing venues outside London, a rare event for them at the time. The first major date the band played was Leicester (at the Polytechnic on 5 March). Other out of London trips included Leighton Buzzard, Canterbury and Ipswich, but as the single wasn't due for release until 29 April very few people outside London had heard of The Jam. Even the local paper in their home town of Woking made no reference to their new recording contract or growing reputation. Consequently the early shows were poorly attended, but the four-month tour gathered pace and after 'In The City' started receiving radio play in April the group found themselves playing to steadily growing audiences.

'In The City' has long been a favourite among Jam fans. Such is its popularity that when Polydor reissued it on seven-inch vinyl in 2002 to celebrate the song's 25th anniversary, it once again broke into the UK Top 40. A staggering achievement considering it was released on an outmoded format (vinyl) and in limited numbers, with hardly any promotion at all. 'Yeah, I was surprised about that,' admitted Weller at the time. 'But then again I think that's a testimony to the music. The mark of a great band, if I may say so.'

That same week, a new compilation, *The Sound Of The Jam*, reached number three in the UK album chart and turned gold. 'In The City' was the album's opening track, as it has been on every other Jam compilation album to be released since 1982. It is also the first song they ever played live on radio, during their first John Peel sessions on 26 April 1977 (transmitted on 2 May). The song also opens the track list on *The Jam At The BBC,* a collection of all their live radio appearances throughout their career.

The original picture sleeve was designed by Polydor art director Bill Smith, who took its DIY style from Jamie Reid, the youth responsible for the cut-and-paste lettering technique The Sex Pistols had used on *Never Mind The Bollocks*; the spray can graffiti image for The Jam's first logo was a very similar homemade idea. A 10 x 6 sheet of plywood was set up and tiled over to give the impression the band were leaning against a subway wall, and then 'The Jam' was simply sprayed onto it. For the back sleeve Smith literally took a hammer to some of the tiles, re-photographed the board and then pasted Paul, Bruce and Rick's photographs onto it as an effective way of using the same cheap prop twice.

SOUNDS FROM THE STREET (Weller)
Recorded in March 1977 at Stratford Place Studios, Oxford Street, London
Produced by Chris Parry and Vic Coppersmith-Heaven
Album track: In The City (May 1977)

Despite punk being the main image in 1977, The Who were still the major influence on Weller's songwriting. Although the album *In The City* had plenty of aggression and fury stitched into it, many of the melodies remained very close to the style of the previous decade. Via The Who, and in particular drummer Keith Moon, Paul had discovered surf sounds (in the shape of Brian Phillips and The Beach Boys) and was particularly keen to develop the harmonic interplay between his vocal and Bruce Foxton's. 'Sounds From The Street' is their first successful attempt at this and Weller has always regarded it as a surf-style song, though cleverly mixing the Californian beach atmosphere with the gritty London streets of the lyric.

Once again Weller was creating painfully honest images supported by a simple chord progression and, in this case, a cheerful melody. Once again he depicts himself as the lonely kid watching all the others having fun and hoping he might be allowed to join in – almost

in the way a new boy at school might feel when he arrives on his first day, desperate to get involved but weighing up the others first.

Prior to the release of *In The City* Paul often complained about what he call the cliquey art school set making up London's music scene, although he was complaining as a fan, not as an artist. At the time of writing 'Sounds From The Street' in late 1976 very few people even knew who The Jam were, let alone were accusing Weller of being a fraud. So he is virtually apologising in advance, on the one hand displaying confidence bordering on arrogance for a 17-year-old (that his songs would get him a record deal and therefore be heard by anyone at all) but on the other displaying his insecurities by feeling the need to explain himself.

But by the time he was accepted in the new London scene Weller wasn't interested anyway. 'One of the biggest disappointments I ever had was in early 1978 when I saw [Clash guitarist] Mick Jones outside The Music Machine in Camden Town with a bottle of whiskey in his hand, staggering about. There was someone I really believed in, hanging around with [former Bowie guitarist] Mick Ronson and some other old rockers.'

Overall it's an accomplished song and a favourite part of the Jam's live set, both with the band and their audience. It had one general radio airing on 1 June 1977, when the BBC broadcast a gig live from their Paris Theatre in Regent Street as part of a ten-track session which also included 'Billy Hunt', 'In The Street Today', 'The Combine', 'Don't Tell Them Your Sane', 'Modern World', "A' Bomb In Wardour Street', 'News Of The World', 'Here Comes The Weekend' and 'All Around The World'. These days the tune is covered regularly by ex-Haircut 100 frontman Nick Heyward as part of his live set.

NON STOP DANCING (Weller)
Recorded in March 1977 at Stratford Place Studios, Oxford Street, London
Produced by Chris Parry and Vic Coppersmith-Heaven
Album track: In The City (May 1977)

A lively R and B song, further removing The Jam from the emerging punk scene by proving they could actually play a bit. Inspired by Northern Soul all nighters at the Bisley Pavilion just outside Woking, the song was written in 1975 (when Weller was still only 16) and a demo recorded in Potter's Studios in May 1976. For the song to appear on an album largely aimed at the punk rock audience reveals much about the attitude of the band and of Weller in particular. Many of his contemporaries were attracting a violent element in their audience and the nature of their songs encouraged this. The Jam, however, had songs like 'Non Stop Dancing', a lively copy of Martha and The Vandellas' 'Dancing In The Street''. It was familiar territory for Weller and Foxton, and suited their styles and tastes perfectly, but the adolescent punks didn't understand it at all.

One school of thought suggests that as nothing was left off the album, the band were actually short of material, despite having been together for over three years. Weller had already decided The Jam would not record any songs he co-wrote with Steve Brookes, but in the two years since Brookes had left the band Paul had only managed to come up with a handful of new songs (nine to be exact) good enough to be recorded. This explains why the album has two cover versions on it and why 'Takin' My Love' was reworked, with Weller dropping Brookes from the credits.

It is reasonable to suggest that if the band had produced enough original material in early 1977 then 'Non Stop Dancing' would probably not have appeared on the debut album, although it would have been perfect for the second album released later in the same year, *This Is The Modern World*. But appear it did and it is a lively dance number that proved popular in their live set, though too stylish for the pogoing punks and therefore needing to be speeded up considerably, and rendered virtually unrecognisable, when it was played throughout 1977.

During that year, and since the release of *In The City*, The Jam were often invited to play at the punk festivals appearing all over Europe and on 6 August they were on the bill of the second Mont-de-Marsan festival in Bordeaux, France. By then they had been on the road around Britain in an old Ford Cortina (referred to in the sleeve notes on the band's final album *Dig The New Breed*) and had played over 80 gigs in five months, spending almost all that time away from home. August of 1977 had been planned as a break from touring during which the group could record their follow-up album, written largely on the road by Weller and Foxton and knocked into shape during soundchecks. But the appeal of a second trip abroad, the first also being to France in order to play the Paris Punk Festival on 28 March, proved hard to resist.

The festival had been put together by a slightly shady group of Frenchmen but the fact that other major bands like The Stranglers, The Damned and The Clash were also appearing alleviated any fears. Also, the organisers had chartered an aircraft which would fly all the acts to and from Biarritz, and the scene was pretty bizarre as all the young punks descended upon Heathrow.

No sooner had the flight taken off than a food fight had broken out and rolls were being bounced all around the cabin. By the time the groups arrived in France most had taken full advantage of the drinks trolley. Then, as the coach provided reached the small town holding the festival, Bruce and Paul decided to cool off in the town square's fountain. Approximately two minutes later the local gendarmes arrived in an old black van and the two guitarists were bundled into the back of it without a word. In a scene directly out of an Inspector Clouseau movie the van was then driven away at speed with John Weller, Paul's dad, running after it shouting for them to stop. Weller and Foxton were finally released without charge later that day and returned, looking sheepish and soaked to the skin. And the trip didn't improve much from then onwards.

The festival was being held in an old bullring and on the day of The Jam's scheduled appearance a row broke out over the billing order, with John Weller insisting the band take top billing over established acts such as The Clash and The Stranglers, who were supposed to be headlining. In the bizarre stand-off that followed, John Weller actually refused to let the group play unless they were given the top slot, causing a great deal of friction and souring the event. Neither side would concede and the end result was that the group didn't play. The whole trip had been wasted and a chance to impress a European audience for only the second time was lost.

The Mont-de-Marsan debacle was unfortunate as the differences between The Jam, with their set including such songs as 'Non Stop Dancing', and the hardcore punk bands who were also playing would have seen the group stand out from the others; they then could have achieved much-needed overseas publicity, which was far more important than the billing order.

TIME FOR TRUTH (Weller)

Recorded in March 1977 at Stratford Place Studios, Oxford Street, London
Produced by Chris Parry and Vic Coppersmith-Heaven
Album track: In The City (May 1977)

Still 18 when he wrote most of the debut album, many of Weller's songs centred around his own experiences. But the political nature, albeit sloganeering, of many of his contemporaries impressed Weller and gave him something new to think about.

His previous influences, sixties bands such as The Small Faces, The Who and The Beatles, rarely dealt with controversial matters or political themes, so Weller had found a new muse for his songwriting. But to label him political and lump him in with artists like Billy Bragg is to misunderstand Weller completely. As he put it in 1977, 'We are against things such as fascism and communism but I don't want to get too involved in politics. The important thing is the music.'

'Time For Truth' is The Jam's first song in which the lyric has a clear political theme, containing a thinly veiled attack on the then Labour government, which was to be the last in the UK for some two decades. Mixing rhythm and soul, the song carries a powerful anti-government message directed at the Prime Minister, James Callaghan. Another target was the British police, widely suspected of having killed amateur boxer and nightclub doorman Liddle Towers while he was in custody. The inquest ruled that the six policemen involved were defending themselves and called it 'justifiable homicide', provoking a wave of protest. The incident became the subject of several songs in 1978, notably The Angelic Upstarts' track

'The Murder Of Liddle Towers', but as was often the case The Jam were original in their reference.

The song was always on the band's live set list during 1977 but, not surprisingly, was never broadcast on either radio or television.

TAKIN' MY LOVE (Brookes/Weller)
Recorded in March 1977 at Stratford Place Studios, Oxford Street, London
Produced by Chris Parry and Vic Coppersmith-Heaven
Album track: In The City (May 1977)
also B-side to In The City single April 1977

The speeded-up version of 'Takin' My Love', the one appearing both as the B-side to the debut single and on the album, was one of the more popular live tracks with American audiences when The Jam first travelled to the States on 6 October 1977. Starting a few days later at the legendary Whiskey A Go Go on Sunset Boulevard, Los Angeles, the band played an exhausting 16 shows in just 12 days, including appearances at New York's favourite punk venue, CBGBs.

The way The Jam was being run by Paul's father John was a little unorthodox at times. When the band went out on tour, their office, which was located in the Weller household, literally closed down as everyone went off with the boys. This caused friction with record label promoters and TV and radio producers, as no one could get hold of anyone connected with the group other than by leaving messages at venues they were due to arrive at. In America many were left bemused by this – John could often only be found down at the local laundromat, drying out the boys' black suits between afternoon and evening performances – which meant that many important opportunities were lost. Several times professional managerial representation was suggested but the band always resisted, preferring to leave their set-up as it was.

This first trip to America was a disaster for several reasons. It also marked the beginning of Paul Weller's indifferent attitude towards the country, although this wasn't an attitude shared by band mates

Bruce Foxton and Rick Buckler, who have always enjoyed their American adventures and still do.

For a start Weller was scared of flying, and his first long-haul flight from England descended into an alcoholic haze as he tried to settle his nerves with vodka, arriving in Los Angeles drunk, bad-tempered and resentful. This atmosphere continued as The Jam made their way through their schedule, often playing two shows a day at the same 'shitty club.' 'It was always the same when we went to America,' says Buckler. 'The bigger we became in Britain and some other parts of Europe, the better we were treated and the larger the venues we played in were. Then someone would come up with the bright idea of going to the States to promote this or that and we would be back in the small clubs playing to a few hundred people again. We couldn't see the point and more often than not we just wanted to get home again.'

There were other problems too, less obvious but just as disappointing for Weller. One was that the legal drinking age in the States was 21, preventing the teenagers whom Paul regarded as The Jam's natural audience from getting into the venues. Another was that the 19-year-old singer couldn't have a beer himself, which only added to his irritation. The result being that most of the people who saw The Jam on their debut US tour had media or record company invitations and Paul's readiness to tell the press at later conferences to 'Fuck off' unsurprisingly angered both the promoters and their record label.

Because the American division of Polydor was using the tour as valuable promotion for the stateside launch of the album *In The City*, they were trying to cram in as much publicity as they could and make the most of the opportunities the tour provided. Needless to say, tension between the band and the label continued to increase, the Wellers becoming belligerent and difficult to deal with, to the point of actually cancelling a show at San Francisco's Old Waldorf because the sound engineer couldn't get the PA loud enough for them. Polydor's Chris Parry was furious. 'It killed me,' he later said. 'I just couldn't take that attitude.'

Also, America's mistrust of the violence associated with UK punk bands such as The Clash had led the record label to promote The

Jam as the English band kids could take home to meet their moms and share her apple pie with. They used phrases like 'pro-monarchy' and associated them with the Queen (always a winner in America), and even promised presenters that the band wouldn't give them a kicking if they had them on their show. They also went as far as promoting the idea that The Jam voted Conservative, but then Paul Weller would come out with a remark like: 'We don't lean to the left or to the right in politics, I actually don't give a fuck either way about any of it.' And comments like 'Nowhere is as creative as Britain' didn't help matters either.

And if it seemed things couldn't get any worse, Weller was missing his new girlfriend of three months, Gill Price, and wanted go home from the moment he arrived. The Clash's Joe Strummer taunted Paul, claiming he didn't like leaving Woking and took a postcard of the town with him whenever he went on tour. Weller didn't even bother to disagree. 'Well, that's almost right,' was his only response.

It's surprising Weller took such an instant dislike to a country that had provided him with so many influences in the shape of Tamla Motown and modernist culture. 'The only thing I like about America is the clothes,' he would say, 'otherwise I'm really disappointed.' It's difficult to understand why a 19-year-old whose musical tastes, and to some extent personal style, could be traced directly to the USA wouldn't want to grab the opportunity to experience it all for himself. But Weller just wasn't interested, and by the time the mini-tour reached New York's CBGBs, only five days in, he was announcing onstage that the band were splitting up. It wasn't the first time morale within the group had reached such a low, and it wouldn't be the last.

BRICKS AND MORTAR (Weller)
Recorded in March 1977 at Stratford Place Studios, Oxford Street, London
Produced by Chris Parry and Vic Coppersmith-Heaven
Album track: In The City (May 1977)

The arrival of Weller's new girlfriend had a negative effect on the band, but for the man himself it seemed to be entirely positive. As soon as the group returned from America the first thing Weller did was move out of Woking and into a Baker Street flat with Gill, isolating himself from the band and other friends in his home town. 'I never went out with other people,' he explained. 'I never mixed or spoke to other people, even within the band.' Rick Buckler remembers the change in Paul's domestic life: 'For long periods, when Paul first met Gill, Bruce and I would work through the evenings on arrangements and Paul would sod off home at five o'clock for his tea and to watch *Coronation Street* or something,' he complained.

On the positive side, Weller developed a lifelong love of literature, particularly the work of novelist George Orwell. As his political enthusiasms sharpened they could be seen reflected in his songs, and *In The City's* closing track 'Bricks And Mortar' illustrates this. Written in Woking, the song deals with the local planning authority knocking much of the character out of the town. Town centre residents were being relocated to out-of-town council estates, including the Wellers themselves, and rows and rows of Victorian town houses were being replaced by soulless office blocks, shopping centres and car parks.

Opening with a big Who-style chord progression and Bruce Foxton's distinctively heavy and intricate bass lines, the song is classic mod rock, simple of lyric but effective. The lyrics took on a personal prescience when, in the 1980s, Weller's own family house at 7 Stanley Road was flattened by Woking Borough Council, making room for a car park and subsequently luxury flats.

'Bricks And Mortar' was included in The Jam's second live broadcast from the BBC, transmitted on 25 July 1977. A live version also appeared on the B-side of the single 'The Modern World' released in October 1977.

In The City is a class debut album and arguably the best of any teenage band in British rock, an argument reinforced by the fact the album can still be seen on the racks of most major record stores 26 years after its original release. In May 1977 the album sold a

staggering 60,000 copies in its first week, eventually reaching number 20 in the UK charts. Incredible for a largely unknown band with audiences averaging only a few hundred and whose only single had been released just 21 days earlier.

Polydor had timed *In The City*'s release to coincide with The Clash's White Riot Tour, which kicked off at The Playhouse Theatre in Edinburgh on 7 May. The tour had been billed as punk rock's first major national offering since The Sex Pistols' aborted Anarchy Tour in late 1976, and The Jam's record label bought the band a place on the coach as the main support act for £1000. The importance of such exposure for The Jam couldn't be overstated, but by the time the road show had reached London's Rainbow Theatre only three days later, mayhem was already prevailing.

Out front, fans ripped up seats and threw them onto the stage in scenes described by the music press as resembling a riot. Back stage, animosity between the acts was developing, with The Jam claiming their soundchecks were poor, some even suggesting a deliberate attempt by The Clash to undermine the band's performance. At the same time Bernie Rhodes, manager of the headline act, was insisting that Polydor should finance the tour, claiming that this was the original agreement.

The Jam, in typical non-negotiable fashion, simply pulled out of the tour and went home, with Rhodes claiming he had sacked them. Either way the agreed tour 'buy on' fee was never paid and The Jam's £100-a-night appearance fee withheld. It was a disagreement that left the band with no live appearances for nearly a month; at such a vital time it would have been best avoided.

The final word about The Jam's debut offering should go to Paul Weller, who in the summer of 1977 said: 'I thought *In The City* was a great debut album. It was rough but that's how we were at the time, it was how it should be. Hopefully in years to come it will be a well-respected album. I'm sure when the second album comes out people are going to say it's not as good.'

ALL AROUND THE WORLD (Weller)

Recorded in May 1977 at Stratford Place Studios, Oxford Street, London
Produced by Chris Parry and Vic Coppersmith-Heaven
A-side released 8 July 1977; Polydor 2058 903; reached number 13
[B-side: 'Carnaby Street']

Without a major tour to help promote their records The Jam quickly signed to the Cowbell Agency, who were instructed to organise some dates in a hurry. As a result, the band were back on the road in early June. A month later, right in the middle of both the Jubilee celebrations and Sex Pistols mania, The Jam distanced themselves yet further from the punk scene with a calculated broadside aimed at its empty values and sloganeering. The group's second single, 'All Around The World', was distinguished by the fact that neither side had appeared on their debut album. The track opens up with a distinctive drum pattern before it explodes into guitar-driven life with nerve-shredding energy. It simply has one of the best openings of any of the 1977 recordings and if the song didn't quite signal the end of punk rock, it certainly called for it.

Its anti-punk theme was clear enough in Paul Weller's best piece of social observation to date, and carried with it a positive message. Tired of bored teenagers moaning about having to sit around with nothing to do, Weller's response is simple: 'Get out and do something about it then.' He might have added, 'or shut the fuck up.' The penultimate line a clear rejection of the famous punk maxim. Paul Weller: 'I didn't buy into the whole scene lock stock and barrel and could see all the bollocks that went with it. I preferred to try and stay positive about things.'

The song also earned the band a vital TV appearance after taking them into the UK Top 20 for the first time. The Marc Bolan TV show *Marc* was broadcast at around teatime, its format attracting the vast record-buying market represented by schoolboys. Nervous to the point of paralysis, Paul, Bruce and Rick were only comforted by the fact that the show was pre-recorded and a retake was possible if everything went horribly wrong. Which it did, in what Rick Buckler describes as his own TV nightmare.

With their stunning black suit/red Rickenbacker stage image, the band put in a faultless display until, during an elaborate drum roll, Rick let go of his drumstick, which then flew between Paul and Bruce and brought about an unplanned end to the song. Rick maintains that the producers reassured him they would do another take later in the day, but in the end they ran out of time and decided to broadcast the only version they had. Available now as part of *The Complete Jam* DVD, Weller is seen catching sight of the stick spinning past his feet and stops playing, knowing there'll be no point without the drum finale. Bruce hears the drumming disappear from his monitor and instinctively does likewise. It almost looks planned.

However, the TV appearance was a huge success and, with the band out on the road for virtually the rest of the year, it had been a massive six months for them. Unsigned at the beginning of March, an album, two singles and numerous TV appearances by July and a second album in the pipeline is just about as good a start a band can have. 'All Around The World' also made two live BBC radio appearances on the John Peel Show, one to round off The Jam's *In Concert* appearance at the Paris Theatre on 1 June and one on 25 July.

The sleeve was once again designed by Polydor art director Bill Smith, using the same spray can logo as *In The City*, this time on a yellow plastic sheet. The band was photographed by Martin Goddard in their black suits standing in front of it. Unusually for groups at the time, especially those involved in the punk movement, The Jam employed professional hairstylists Shumi, who also receive a credit on the sleeve.

In Thailand 'All Around The World' was released on a four track EP with 'Pretty Vacant' (The Sex Pistols), 'This Perfect Day' (The Saints) and 'I Knew The Bride' (Dave Edmunds).

CARNABY STREET (Foxton)

Recorded in March 1977 at Stratford Place Studios, Oxford Street, London
Produced by Chris Parry and Vic Coppersmith-Heaven
B-side to 'All Around The World' (July 1977)

After an exhausting six months Paul Weller began to run out of steam. Never a prolific songwriter, he had struggled to come up with enough original material for the first album. So bass player Bruce Foxton, who had been contributing enormously to the arrangement of Weller's songs, had been penning his own lyrics. The dynamic between Weller and Foxton was clear and, musically at least, they were very much on the same wavelength, with Bruce laying down the solid underpinning to Paul's chopping Rickenbacker. With the band struggling to find the time to come up with new ideas and Paul's domestic arrangements more settled, the baton passed to Bruce to keep up the momentum.

Polydor's Chris Parry recognised Weller as the main driving force behind The Jam's songwriting but also recognised that Foxton was keen to contribute his own efforts, either in part or in full. By the time 'All Around The World' was recorded, The Jam only had three other original songs, two of Weller's ('The Modern World' and 'London Girl') and Bruce's 'Carnaby Street'. Parry: 'There was an increasing awareness that Paul was the main songwriter and if the other two were to benefit from any of the writers' royalties they would have to come up with some songs for themselves. Now Rick wasn't going to, but Bruce felt he could contribute and wanted to get his songs out.'

The centre of the London mod scene in the 1960s was Soho and Carnaby Street, a pedestrian thoroughfare running parallel to Regent Street and lined with shops and boutiques famous for their mod fashions. Although that culture had never really disappeared from the area, The Jam did more than anyone to reawaken interest in the street, with all the band members regularly visiting and spending their new-found wealth. For Bruce to choose a London street as the setting for his first self-penned Jam song is no real surprise, especially as he was as interested in its culture as Paul himself was in mod fashion.

The scene set out in Bruce's lyrics isn't as subtle as those Weller routinely conjured up, but it could be argued that very few contemporary songwriters could match Paul's creativity at that time.

The recorded version of 'Carnaby Street' somehow fails to capture The Jam's unique qualities, but, produced by any other band at the

time, it would almost certainly have been an A-side. However, played live it came across entirely differently and sounded (musically at any rate) as good as any other Jam offering of that year, as the version they played on the television show *So It Goes* (featured on *The Complete Jam* DVD) proves.

Rick Buckler, who usually prefers the live versions of Jam songs, has an explanation for why the recorded 'Carnaby Street' isn't as rounded as the one played on stage: 'Once we had a song out on road for a while the tunes would develop properly and often differed from the already recorded version. One of my few regrets about my time in The Jam was that we didn't take the songs out on tour and *then* record them, but there was never any time for that. As soon as we had a song knocked into some sort of shape Polydor wanted to release it.'

THREE
TOO MUCH TOO SOON

IN retrospect, it seems a mistake for The Jam to have considered a follow-up album within six months of their debut release, especially as the band had also undertaken such a busy live schedule. In 1977 The Jam went from relative obscurity to international success in the space of a few months and it's a miracle they found the time to come up with anything new at all. But having been together as a band in one form or another since 1973, they felt it had been a long apprenticeship and were now keen to capitalise on their success.

It's fair to say that, had the group taken a few months off and had the time to develop a new collection of songs, they could have produced an album that picked up where *In The City* left off. One of the reasons for rushing out the second album was the impending Christmas market; another was that the group had a handful of new songs proving popular at their live shows but which were as yet unreleased. But the deciding factor was that Paul's father John had agreed a new percentage deal with Polydor, which was sweetened by a £20,000 advance.

THIS IS THE MODERN WORLD

THE MODERN WORLD (Weller)
Recorded on 21 September 1977 at Basing Street Studios, Notting Hill, London
A-side released: 21 October 1977; Polydor 2058 945; reached no 36 in UK chart
Produced by Chris Parry and Vic Coppersmith-Heaven
Album track: 'This Is The Modern World' (November 1977)
B-side: 'Sweet Soul Music' (live); 'Back In My Arms Again' (live); 'Bricks And Mortar' (live)

'The Modern World' (the single) was written in April 1977, just after the recording sessions for *In The City* had finished but prior to its release. Other songs were written during the course of those few months: 'London Girl', 'Carnaby Street' and 'All Around The World'. It seemed as if, even before their debut album came out, the band were halfway towards a follow-up already. But with his father already having committed to a second album Weller's creative process ran aground. And his lack of songs was made worse by the release of 'All Around The World' as a mid-year single, which caused Weller to block its inclusion, along with 'Carnaby Street', on the new album. Weller was appalled at the thought of releasing an album 'in instalments' and insisted on giving fans value for money. It was an attitude that remained with the band throughout their career, ensuring that only one or two tracks from each album ever sneaked out as singles or B-sides. The same attitude extended to their live shows, where entrance fees were kept to a minimum and merchandising was intended as a non-profit making exercise, with items sold virtually at cost price.

For a while, during the summer of 1977, Polydor had considered releasing a live album in an attempt to capitalise on the quality of The Jam's concert appearances, and a gig at the 100 club on 11 September had been recorded for that purpose. The idea was scrapped, however, when Weller and Foxton put together enough original songs considered good enough for a second studio album.

When 'The Modern World' was released as a single in October, the fact it had a supporting flip side of three live tracks lifted from the 100 Club recording suggested to many that the band were drying up creatively. As a result the upcoming album was viewed with suspicion, but the A-side itself was pure Jam in its structure and intensity and was well reviewed. 'The Modern World' was recorded at a much faster tempo than the live version they were performing and shows Weller, apparently unaffected by the criticism he had received over the band's mod image, rounding on his detractors and literally sticking two fingers up.

At school Weller had been derided for his ambition and told he would amount to nothing; now his band had been criticised for not being punk (they never tried or claimed to be) and Weller himself had been told they were a one-album act. The lyrics made it clear

TOO MUCH TOO SOON

that Weller was highly driven and that criticism, especially from those with influence and perceived authority, was never going to affect him. Paul could not have made it clearer than that, although to his dismay he was obliged to replace the 'two fucks' he threw at his reviewers with 'a damn' for the radio-friendly version. Musically the song once again looks back to the previous decade and is full of swinging power-chords reminiscent of The Who's 'Pictures Of Lily'. But it also includes a snapping drum pattern and bass line that drive the tune forward.

'The Modern World' was first heard on the John Peel show on 2 May, three weeks before *In The City* was released, so it came as a surprise to many when it wasn't included on the album. The track remained popular with fans across the world right through to the very end of the band's career; it was played both on the Beat Surrender tour and on The Jam's last ever live television appearance (on *The Tube* in 1982). Though criticism at the time of its release seemed to be supported by its eventual chart position (much lower than that of the previous single), the song's longevity speaks for itself.

But the track's poor chart performance affected Weller's confidence more than at first appeared. It would be a full year before he could produce another A-side, when 'Down In The Tube Station At Midnight' was released in October 1978. In the meantime, the singer effectively passed the reins to Bruce Foxton.

In 1999 'The Modern World' was covered by Ben Harper for The Jam tribute album *Fire And Skill*.

LONDON TRAFFIC (Foxton)

Recorded on 25 August 1977 at Basing Street Studios, Notting Hill, London
Produced by Chris Parry and Vic Coppersmith-Heaven
Album track: This Is The Modern World (November 1977)

In the summer of 1977 it appeared, to the outside world at least, that The Jam were on the ascendant. They had bagged a Top 20 debut album, released two successful singles and were building a following

all across the UK and some parts of Europe. But behind the scenes, those close to the group knew that Paul Weller was losing interest. It had taken Weller two years to come up with enough original songs to fill an album and one of those ('Takin' My Love') can be traced back four years to the Eden Studios session in Kingston.

Bruce Foxton had always worked closely with Weller, and made a number of valuable contributions to The Jam's songs. Critically slaughtered at the time, 'London Traffic' must have shaken Foxton's confidence in his lyric-writing, but musically the track is as strong as any of the early Jam songs. Fast and energetic (and very popular live), the arrangement and structure are as good as any. The listener cannot fail to be impressed by the backing track and, although the vocal melody is not as inventive as many of Weller's, it is still very much a Jam song.

The main criticism lay with the song's storyline, in which Foxton attempted to create an image of the London of the time in the style of Ray Davies. Although it's fair to say the lyric doesn't quite deliver the word-picture Jam fans had become accustomed to, its message did precede the pro-public transport lobby by about ten years, proving that Foxton did have a point to make about the capital city grinding to a fume-filled halt. (Weller himself later said that 'Not every song has to be a lyrical masterpiece, although it sometimes helps.') As it is, the Who-style harmonies and questioning lyric are very much in the style of The Jam at that time.

The fact remains that Bruce was more than able to fill the gap left by Weller's creative drought, coming up with enough decent tunes to meet their album commitment, contributing to both sides of the band's next single 'News Of The World' and providing the vocal for the single after that (a cover of The Kinks' album track 'David Watts'). He also found time to musically complement Paul's next a-side; where would 'Down In The Tube Station' be without that bass line?

It is possible that without these contributions from Bruce Foxton The Jam's momentum would have ground to a halt and, conceivably, would never have reached their defining moment a year later when *All Mod Cons* was released.

STANDARDS (Weller)

Recorded on 26 August 1977 at Basing Street Studios, Notting Hill, London
Produced by Chris Parry and Vic Coppersmith-Heaven
Album track: This Is The Modern World (November 1977)

This Is The Modern World springs into life at track three, with Paul once again lifting the guitar riff from an old Who song, this time 'I Can't Explain', which was the older band's second single, released in 1965.

In the summer of 1977 Paul and Bruce had become absorbed in literature, possibly as a result of being on the road for so long and having little else to do other than read or listen to music. Two of the authors they were reading at the time were George Orwell, whose books would influence Weller in many ways, and Ken Kesey. Two of their stories, *1984* and *One Flew Over The Cuckoo's Nest* respectively, would provide the inspiration for three of the songs on *This Is The Modern World*, marking it as Weller's first half-hearted attempt at a concept album. (The second being *Setting Sons* in 1979). The theme of *This Is The Modern World* was to be totalitarianism, an unshakeable authority controlling the lives and minds of the people, and 'Standards' was the first of the tracks fitting that theme.

With scenes lifted straight from Orwell's *1984*, Weller creates his first real character song by assuming the role of a faceless government bureaucrat and condemning The Sex Pistols' 1976 Anarchy Tour. The Pistols had found themselves banned from television, radio and even from making live appearances after venues were persuaded to cancel shows. Their record label, EMI, had also come under pressure to drop the group after the Conservative MP for Christchurch and Lymington, Robert Adley, wrote to EMI's managing director, Sir John Read, saying: 'Surely a company of your size and reputation could forego the doubtful privilege of sponsoring trash like The Sex Pistols.'

The Pistols were fired by EMI soon afterwards and Weller was furious, responding in 'Standards' by creating the image of an Establishment figure reminding us that standards and rules have been made which must be obeyed. Weller had seen such figures

abusing their influence to censor bands on grounds of taste alone.

Weller was drawing directly from *1984*'s Big Brother and makes a chilling reference to the story's tragic central character, Winston Smith, who was found not to be following the rules and sent to the dreaded torture chamber Room 101.

The song is a crisp highlight of the album and was an instant hit on the live circuit. It could easily have been a successful second single if drawn from the album but once again Weller refused, allowing only one, the title track, to be released. 'Standards' never appeared on the BBC live recordings, possibly due its stark anti-establishment message.

LIFE FROM A WINDOW (Weller)
Recorded on 29 August 1977 at Basing Street Studios, Notting Hill, London
Produced by Chris Parry and Vic Coppersmith-Heaven
Album track: This Is The Modern World (November 1977)

Another average track on this much-maligned album is the wistful but lifeless 'Life From A Window', where the writer, once again using the first person, places himself in various elevated positions to observe and record what he sees going on around him, but doesn't actually let us know us what it is. The song has much to offer musically but is crippled by a lifeless lyric that strangely failed to attract the kind of criticism given to 'London Traffic'.

On the sleeve of the album, music journalist Barry Cain, who later formed the popular *Flexipop* music magazine, is credited with inspiring parts of 'Life From A Window', in particular the phrase 'teenage blue', which is arguably the only memorable thing about it. The track did, however, provide the first signs of The Jam beginning to experiment musically by using acoustic guitars high in the mix, a distinct change from the highly charged, one-dimensional guitar sounds used in almost every recording prior to it.

Also, preceding the opening bars, background studio sounds have been added in the shape of a couple of bass notes and a single guitar chord leading into the intro. Weller can be heard addressing Foxton across the studio ('You got your bass line?') before counting the song

in. The idea behind such sound fills, which were to feature regularly
in The Jam's subsequent studio albums, was to give a vague impression
that the songs were being recorded live. Little imperfections like
guitar tuning, practice melodies or the odd word or cough might be
expected to appear on a live recording rather than a studio one. The
effect of a vocal 1,2,3,4 often adds to the atmosphere of a track,
giving the listener the impression that all the musicians are playing
along at the same time.

The track was never played in a live set by The Jam. Paul Weller:
'A song like 'Life From A Window', without getting too technical, has
intricate acoustic and electric guitar parts that would be lost if we
played it live. I wouldn't want to spoil a song by doing that.'

THE COMBINE (Weller)

Recorded on 2 September 1977 at Basing Street Studios, Notting Hill, London
Produced by Chris Parry and Vic Coppersmith-Heaven
Album track: This Is The Modern World (November 1977)

'The Combine' was the first of two songs influenced by Ken Kesey's
classic novel *One Flew Over The Cuckoo's Nest*. The track's title refers
to the name Kesey gave the totalitarian system, or governing force,
in his fiction, and the song deliberately follows 'Life From A
Window' to provide a stark contrasting image. Indeed, its opening
lines relate directly to the preceding track.

Once again the song is written in the first person and the subject
has something to escape from. The phrase 'The smell of fear and
hate', which would reappear in another of Weller's songs that year
(''A' Bomb in Wardour Street'), borrowed from one of Kesey's
effective descriptive techniques ('the smell of machinery' or 'the
smell of motors') and is used in 'The Combine' as a powerful way of
creating an image with a menacing undertone.

But otherwise the song is a jumble of images, another Weller
songwriting technique, in that parts of one song may be about one
thing and others parts about something entirely different. Often
there is no connection at all between the sections other than it

'sounds good'; for example, the middle-eight section here provides real-life images of 1977, referencing Sunday newspapers and Ena Sharples. Page Three girls and the ongoing war in Rhodesia also make an appearance, as does the *News At Ten* television programme. Ena Sharples, as played by Violet Carson, was the hatchet-faced, hairnetted battle-axe of TV's *Coronation Street* and Page Three girls, introduced into the tabloid press eight years earlier, had become a national institution by 1977. On *News at Ten*, meanwhile, every evening the war in Rhodesia (now Zimbabwe) headlined every bulletin. It was a conflict in which Robert Mugabe triumphed and took control of the country he still governs to this day.

But overall the song is distinctive only for its lack of imagination and is regularly pointed to by Jam fans when they say, 'Sure, Bruce Foxton didn't write the best Jam songs. But then again, he didn't write the worst of them either.' The song's only radio appearance was during the band's *In Concert* performance for the BBC at The Paris Theatre in Regent Street on 1 June 1978. Songs like this helped focus criticism of the new album, largely from contemporary bands dominating the 'London clique'. Such scorn from bands Weller had admired and been inspired by began to dent the songwriter's confidence, more than was ever revealed at the time.

DON'T TELL THEM YOU'RE SANE (Foxton)
Recorded on 26 August 1977 at Basing Street Studios, Notting Hill, London
Produced by Chris Parry and Vic Coppersmith-Heaven
Album track: This Is The Modern World (November 1977)

'Don't Tell Them You're Sane' was the second song on the album inspired by Kesey's novel and provided an instant return to form with an immediately likeable guitar riff, once again provided by Foxton's bass line. Also sung by him, the lyric tells the story of a sane young man arbitrarily institutionalised and unable to convince the authorities that he should be leading a normal life. Written in the first person Bruce sings about a boy he knows who has been written off by the medical profession and locked away in his room for hours at a time, whilst staff attempt to convince him he is mad. But the lad rebels and insists they will never persuade him he is actually insane. It is a common enough story and one that is easily related to.

Slaughtered by reviewers, the song at least stands the test of time musically, featuring chord changes and harmonies as good as any other track on the album. Once again Foxton was carrying the can for the creatively spent Paul Weller and, although clumsy drumming leaves the song feeling bumpy and unfinished, it does provide early evidence that the band were maturing and breaking songs down into the kind of separate musical parts used to great effect on their following album.

'Don't Tell Them You're Sane' was popular live and played by The Jam during their *In Concert* performance for the BBC at The Paris Theatre in Regent Street on 1 June 1978, eight months after the studio album it appeared on was released.

The song was also played throughout The Jam's second ill-fated visit to America, which began at the Harvey Hubbles Gymnasium in Connecticut on 16 March 1978, in an attempt to promote both *In The City* (the tour for that album four months earlier had proved a disaster for all concerned) and *This Is The Modern World*. Despite misgivings, the band were persuaded to travel to the States for a six-week period and to perform 35 times. The main difference this time was Polydor's enthusiasm, together with assurances that the tour would be supported by extensive television and radio coverage. And as a measure of how seriously The Jam were now being taken in Britain, the *NME* even sent a reporter to cover the entire first week of the trip. Polydor had secured the band a supporting slot with Blue Öyster Cult, of '(Don't Fear) The Reaper' fame (who shared the same record label as The Jam in America), and it appeared to be a big opportunity for the band to play in front of over 10,000 people.

But the moment The Jam stepped on stage in front of Blue Öyster Cult's audience, another managerial blunder became apparent. Instead of winning over a vast new audience, The Jam found themselves performing to a sea of student faces, gawping back in amazement. Band and audience were equally bemused by the culture shock involved, and the *NME*'s Phil McNeill, in a report for that paper, described Paul Weller as 'positively surly'. Once again the US experience was proving unsatisfactory; The Jam even found themselves third on the bill in one Arizona venue to British Prog Rockers Be Bop Deluxe. Although The Jam had long since dropped the black suit image in the UK, they had been persuaded to return to it for the tour, but American audiences who were largely unaware of mod culture were merely confused by their appearance. To them, in their herbal haze, The Jam resembled a bunch of British bank clerks launching themselves into a 200mph set of two-and-a-half-minute, guitar-led pop songs.

The tour wasn't a complete disaster but neither was it the success that had been hoped for. Foxton later admitted: 'We weren't big enough to be playing in such big venues, the idea backfired.'

IN THE STREET TODAY (Weller/Waller)

Recorded on 25 August 1977 at Basing Street Studios, Notting Hill, London
Produced by Chris Parry and Vic Coppersmith-Heaven
Album track: This Is The Modern World (November 1977)

Another song played live on the US tour, and which failed to impress the bewildered collegiate audience, was 'In The Street Today'. At only 1'29" from start to finish, it doesn't even cover the time taken up by the average American guitar solo, and audiences simply failed to understand the song's (admittedly clumsy) attempt at creating a picture of violent life on English streets.

Desperate for ideas, Weller borrowed the theme from his old friend, and original member of The Jam, Dave Waller. Waller had by now turned his attention to street poetry, achieving some recognition for his work, and Weller, to his credit, was tireless in his promotion of Waller's poetry, once again disproving the notion that he is an emotionless user. For years Weller campaigned on behalf of Waller; for his part, the young poet was in regular attendance backstage at Jam gigs.

Paul saw music as only one of the arts, only one form of expression among many, and he took the opportunity to promote the others as often as possible. He even published six of Waller's poems in the very first Jam songbook, produced in July 1978, and wrote: 'I thought it may be necessary for a few lines explaining the six poems included in the book. As in all cultures, which hopefully the NEW WAVE will evolve into (or maybe it has?), there are a lot of other Art forms not only music, but why not NEW WAVE painters, playwrights, authors and poets. One such person, and I'm sure there are a lot more, is DAVID WALLER, a very talented young poet. So please read the poetry and if you give a Reaction maybe a book will follow, I relate very deeply to his works. I hope you can.'

Weller had just turned 20 when he wrote those words and a book did indeed follow. A year later, in the summer of 1979, Paul formed a publishing company called Riot Stories Ltd, which he would use to publish the works of what he called the New Wave Poets. The first of those collections was *Notes From Hostile Street* by Dave Waller.

Riot Stories Ltd became a publishing outlet for scores of fanzines and the work of dozens of young writers. *Notes From Hostile Street* portrays a city in decay, mirrored by the quality of life of its population. The compilation's anti-capitalist nature was clearly shared by Weller at the time, with Waller presenting himself as a bleak observer of the urban decline that was visible in any major town during recession-hit 1977. But he manages to retain his humour and dignity, avoiding any bitterness in the process. Unfortunately, a bright future eluded the tragic Waller, whose friends and family (Weller included) failed to prevent his troubled decline into drink and drugs. The schoolboy who had been part of The Jam's first line-up later died of a heroin overdose in a shabby upstairs room at Woking's Wheatsheaf Hotel in August 1982, at exactly the same time as The Jam themselves were playing out their final act.

Weller was distraught and lost interest in Riot Stories. He remained affected, however, by Dave Waller's undoubted influence. Shortly after Waller's death, Weller wrote 'Man Of Great Promise', a searching and tender eulogy to his one time closest friend.

A touching tribute to one of Woking's fine teenage talents and Paul continues to play the song on his acoustic travels to this day, but it was recorded after he had left The Jam in 1982 so was never a

Jam song. 'In The Street' was, however, though probably best forgotten. It was featured in The Jam's set for the BBC on 1 June 1978, broadcast live from The Paris Theatre on Regent Street, London.

LONDON GIRL (Weller)

Recorded on 21 September 1977 at Basing Street Studios, Notting Hill, London
Produced by Chris Parry and Vic Coppersmith-Heaven
Album track: This Is The Modern World (November 1977)

'London Girl' was yet another song written in May 1977, just too late to be considered for *In The City*, but was one of those listed instead as a B-side for The Jam's second single 'All Around The World'. Very much in line with the street stories Weller was absorbed in at the time, the song tells the familiar tale of a young homeless girl living out a bleak existence on the streets of London, having run away to the capital in search of her fortune but finding only squalor and isolation instead. Ominously Weller then illustrates how easy it is to learn how to blag cigarettes and pills on the streets of London in the late 1970s. With little else on offer it was duly included on the album, and is only notable these days for the fact that those same 'London Girls' can be found from all parts of Britain shuffling around the streets of the capital to this day. Twenty-five years later and nothing much has changed.

Spanning 25 performances across just 30 days. Despite the criticism *This Is The Modern World* received in the music press, by the time the band reached Leeds on the 19th they were enjoying huge success and playing to packed venues. But it was yet another violent confrontation involving Weller that would earn the band national publicity.

After a successful gig at Leeds University, The Jam tour party found the small hotel they were staying in packed; an Australian rugby team had checked in with their entourage. The hotel bar was closed and frustration developed as guests queued at a small hatch while the night porter dispensed drinks from there instead. After queuing for some time Weller eventually collected his drinks and, as he turned around with his tray, bumped into an elderly man (who later turned out to be the rugby team's accountant). Angry at spilling his drinks, Weller lashed out at the old man, allegedly hitting him with a glass, and before they knew it the rugby players were looking for the young punk who had attacked their friend.

Buckler watched the scene unfold from the safety of the adjoining bar but decided not to get involved, though Foxton was faster to help Paul, who by this time was being chased around the hotel, and jumped to his defence. Unfortunately for Bruce, Weller carried on running, leaving him to take a savage beating in his place, resulting in severely bruised and cracked ribs for the remainder of the tour. Leeds police, who were quickly on the scene, were unable to calm the Australians, still searching the hotel for the chief culprit, and insisted the band were escorted to another hotel for their own safety. Meanwhile, Weller was arrested and spent the night in the relative safety of a police cell before being charged with a breach of the peace.

But the incident created even more publicity for The Jam and further enhanced their status among their peers. Local radio reported the incident and young fans queued outside the courthouse, chalking 'Paul Weller is innocent' on the steps of Leeds Crown Court. It was a gesture Weller never forgot and referred to six years later in the sleeve notes of The Jam's closing album, *Dig The New Breed*. But for many, Foxton especially, Weller hadn't exactly covered himself in glory. And, already, the distance between himself and drummer Buckler was becoming evident. Weller was already starting to describe him as 'fucking awkward'. Rumours of 'unfinished business' circulated in the rugby fraternity and, whether they were true or not, The Jam certainly never visited Australia. In fact, it would be a full year before they even went near Leeds again.

I NEED YOU (FOR SOMEONE) (Weller)
Recorded on 21 September 1977 at Basing Street Studios, Notting Hill, London
Produced by Chris Parry and Vic Coppersmith-Heaven
Album track: This Is The Modern World (November 1977)

Paul's new girlfriend, Gill Price, had not only encouraged him to discover literature and other art forms, moving his songwriting in new directions, but she had also provided the inspiration for an entirely new style of lyric in the shape of love songs. 'I Need You' is a simple, self-explanatory tale reflecting everybody's feelings when caught up in the first flush of new love, and is one of the album's shining highlights.

The lyric not only reveals, for the first time, the softer side of Weller's abrasive character but also a new confidence in attempting the kind of songs avoided by most bands in 1977. At the end, Paul adds a disarming touch of reality and shows he is prepared to reveal his faults to us too by suggesting the problems in the relationship are being caused by himself. If nothing else, Weller had clearly grown both as a person and a songwriter since writing the shallow 'I've Changed My Address' less than a year earlier.

The Jam were touring *This Is The Modern World* throughout the following year, starting with their first major tour of America and Canada and followed by a summer seaside tour of the UK. Though known as The Bucket and Spade Tour, the latter stint kicked off at Guildford Civic Hall on 20 July 1978, over 50 miles from the nearest beach. At the Civic, Paul invited his old schoolfriends Squire to support the band, not only to earn them much-needed publicity (which seemed to work, given that Squire signed their own recording deal with ROK Records six month afterwards) but also because he was just keen to see his old mates again.

The Jam had been on the road almost constantly since January 1977, and the gig at Guildford was the first time they had played in the Woking area since their last appearance at Michael's Club on 26 September 1975, nearly three years earlier. It was very much their homecoming and Squire's Ross Dilanda remembers the gig well. 'It was a hot night' he says, 'and the Civic Hall was crammed. Half of Woking was there that night to see The Jam. It was unbelievable, the last time we saw them play locally it was to 20 or so people like the rest of us did, now it was thousands.

Lead singer Enzo Esposito also remembers it well, though for different reasons. Apparently, Paul was unhappy with his old friends, thinking they had started treating him differently. Esposito: 'I suppose we did treat him differently, but not deliberately. We were just grateful to be playing such a big gig and we didn't want to get in their way. By then they had this huge rig, tour bus and road crew, but we had all still only just turned 20. I remember when we arrived at the Civic Hall in the afternoon, Paul was sitting on the top step of the stage entrance and our guitarist Steve Baker, who was in Paul's class at school, walked straight past him and that pissed him off completely. He sarcastically called out after Steve: "Yeah, nice to see you Paul, cheers for the gig mate."

'He wasn't happy, but I could sympathise with Steve really. It isn't easy when such a close mate becomes so famous so quickly. We hadn't seen Paul, Bruce or Rick for quite some time, apart from on television like everybody else, and didn't really quite know what to expect of them. But people's *perception* of what Paul is going to be like is the only thing that changes. Paul himself hadn't changed at all. He was exactly the same as he always had been and he still is 25 years later.' For the title of 'I Need You (For Someone)', Paul lifted directly from a 1962 George Harrison song of the same name which was penned as a direct plea to a lost lover, though Weller is singing to a current one in the Jam track.

HERE COMES THE WEEKEND (Weller)
Recorded on 26 August 1977 at Basing Street Studios, Notting Hill, London
Produced by Chris Parry and Vic Coppersmith-Heaven
Album track: This Is The Modern World (November 1977)

Once again turning to his mid-sixties heroes for inspiration, Paul came up with another Who-style track and even picked up the *Ready, Steady, Go!* slogan, 'The Weekend Starts Here'. With big Townshend-style Rickenbacker chords, the song carries a positive power-pop message, particularly in its middle eight where the singer suggests he lives only for the weekend and nothing else in life matters once it arrives. Its upbeat positive message is a far cry from the negative punk movement The Jam had been swept up in.

The band themselves were tired of that tag, recognising the movement as virtually dead in the water, and were removing themselves as far as possible from it at every opportunity. Paul, Bruce and Rick never saw themselves as a punk band, though being associated with the movement and thereby attracting a young and vibrant audience was seen by many as a wise move. But, though Weller didn't quite know where next to turn, he did know which direction he would *not* be taking the band in. 'The Clash have just become like any other old rock band,' he said at the time. 'I mean, those pictures of them standing around with biker jackets and with their hands in their pockets like they've got a fucking gun or water pistol or something in there. And the Pistols have just got worse and worse, what's all that multi-layered guitar about? They sound like mainstream rock, don't they? It's only the vocals that make it sound something else.'

A year on from apologising for his Woking roots in 'Sounds From The Street', Weller had begun to sound like the wise old man of pop, winning an army of new young fans who were thinking exactly what he was brave enough to say. But The Jam didn't care about fashion or social cliques, and Weller was equally dismissive of American attempts to break into the British New Wave scene: 'Devo? That is just elitist music dealing with something the average kid knows nothing about anyway. I had to go and look up devolution in the dictionary.' As had thousands of others, who immediately saw Weller as like-minded, speaking for them.

Recording sessions for 'Here Comes The Weekend' overran considerably and producer Vic Coppersmith-Heaven recalled the tension. 'It was those Rickenbackers,' he says. 'They just wouldn't stay in tune, we wasted days in there.' Drummer Buckler agreed: 'Those Rickenbackers never stayed in tune for long. We tried to get Paul to use other guitars but he insisted on staying with the Rickenbacker at the time. After that session he got the message and tried others, but still always used the Rickenbacker on stage because of the way they looked.'

TONIGHT AT NOON (Weller/Henri)
Recorded on 29 August 1977 at Basing Street Studios, Notting Hill, London
Produced by Chris Parry and Vic Coppersmith-Heaven
Album track: This Is The Modern World (November 1977)

Listening to the final tracks included on *This Is The Modern World*, it becomes hard to understand the criticism levelled at the album, for each of them stands the test of time both musically and lyrically. 'Tonight At Noon' carries a strong acoustic melody supported by an inventive bassline, and Paul lifts both the title and much of the theme from two poems written by Liverpool beat poet Adrian Henri in the mid-1960s. Paul had been introduced to Henri's works by old friend and poet Dave Waller, and was fascinated by Henri's descriptive use of language. Short of ideas and lyrics for *This Is The Modern World*, Paul welded together the title 'Tonight At Noon' and ideas from 'In The Midnight Hour' (not to be confused with the Wilson Pickett song), both of which had appeared in *The Mersey Collection*, published by Penguin in 1967. In 1973 Henri recorded a live reading at the Liverpool Academy of Arts Gallery which was released as 'Charivari' in 1974 and included both poems.

Adrian Henri was born in Birkenhead, Cheshire in 1932 and was a renowned poet, musician and artist. His first major London exhibition was held at the Institute of Contemporary Arts in 1968 and he was awarded the John Moores prize for painting in 1972. He died after a long illness in December 2000.

Paul had long been interested in poetry and loved Henri's 'Tonight At Noon', saying: 'I think it is time the band really started getting into ballads and some more acoustic stuff.' Despite Paul's shortage of original contributions to *This Is The Modern World*, *Melody Maker*'s Chris Brazier could see his potential and summed up The Jam in a single sentence: 'Paul Weller will mature into one of our best songwriters, provided he keeps his mind open. This album only hints at what The Jam are capable of.'

IN THE MIDNIGHT HOUR (Wilson Pickett/Steve Cropper)

Recorded on 21 September 1977 at Basing Street Studios, Notting Hill, London
Produced by Chris Parry and Vic Coppersmith-Heaven
Album track: This Is The Modern World (November 1977)

Having run out of original songs, the band once again returned to their live set, which always guaranteed a handful of exhilarating soul classics. Wilson Pickett was one of the most popular soul singers of the 1960s who, working with the excellent studio bands of the Stax Studios in Memphis, Tennessee and the Fame Studio in Muscle Shoals, Alabama, created a series of R and B classics between 1963 and 1972. Those hits included 'Mustang Sally', 'Funky Broadway' and 'In The Midnight Hour' in 1965. Former band mate Steve Brookes remembers in his book *Keeping The Flame* how Weller enthused about the latter track. Brookes: 'We jumped into Paul's dad's car to go round and pick Rick up from his parents' house, where he still lived, to go for a few beers and Paul played the tape of 'Midnight Hour' a couple of times. He was particularly pleased with his harmonica part.'

As *This Is The Modern World* began slipping out of the charts The Jam found themselves with a dwindling audience and a marked lack of direction. It was clear the album should never have been agreed to; that management decision to grab the £20,000 advance and then press the band into delivering was a mistake. The Jam should have been given some time to develop a new batch of songs to match the blistering *In The City*.

The importance of *This Is The Modern World* and its standing among other Jam albums is easily overlooked, however. True, it didn't chart as high as its predecessor but there isn't much wrong with a teenage band having two albums in the Top 30 of the UK charts within six months of each other. Two albums is also one more than either The Sex Pistols or The Clash had managed by then and the content of *This Is The Modern World* proved to be a neat link between the band's debut album and their 1978 masterpiece *All Mod Cons*. Put simply, without *This Is The Modern World* The Jam may never have had the chance to create that third album.

By anybody's standards 1977 had been a year of great progress for The Jam. 1976 had produced only 13 live performances, uncertainty over their line-up, no record deal and only a handful of original songs suitable to attract such a deal. Yet, within a year, everything had changed for them.

NEWS OF THE WORLD (Foxton)

Recorded in January 1978 at Basing Street Studios, Notting Hill, London
Produced by Chris Parry and Vic Coppersmith-Heaven
A-side released 24 February 1978; Polydor 2058 995; reached no 27 in the UK chart
B-side: 'Aunties And Uncles (Impulsive Youths)' / 'Innocent Man'

The criticism *This Is The Modern World* had received late in 1977 had affected Weller's confidence, so he was happy for Bruce Foxton to come up with something suitable for their fourth single first thing the following year. Lyrically 'News Of The World' is a direct attack on the tabloid press, and musically it's often regarded as the inspiration for a new breed of 'power pop' bands in the late 1970s. Indeed, Foxton uses the phrase 'Power – pop' at the start of the song.

Once again, musically at least, Foxton had produced a tune every bit as powerful as any Jam track up to that time. But he immediately found himself in the firing line of a music press critical of what was seen as another Jam effort that lyrically wasn't up to the standards of their earlier work. But the only song Weller had written that charted higher than Foxton's 'News Of The World' was 'All Around The World' in July 1977. Foxton's song outsold all other Weller efforts, including 'In The City', until 'Down In The Tube Station at Midnight' reached number 15 in October 1978. Weller: 'We recorded half a dozen songs around that time, most of which were shit. 'News Of The World' was the best we had until we got into writing *All Mod Cons*.'

'News Of The World' was strangely regarded by Polydor as an 'interim record', an odd judgment given that it rewarded the band with their second highest chart position to date. Things like that further dented the confidence of a young band whom the record label should have been encouraging. They had only signed The Jam one day short of a year prior to the release of 'News Of The World', and in that time they had garnered two Top 30 studio albums, four singles all charting in the Top 40, a seven-month national tour, a US tour and a two-month follow-up tour to come. They also expected two more singles and a third album by the end of that calendar year. It's no wonder The Jam launched a blistering attack on the shallowness of the major record labels in the opening two tracks of their forthcoming album *All Mod Cons*. Despite Polydor's indifference, 'News Of The World' was always popular live and was featured in the BBC *In Concert* performance at the Paris Theatre on 1 June 1978.

As with all previous singles the sleeve was designed by Bill Smith, only this time with some input from Weller, who was taking more of an interest in how Polydor packaged The Jam in order to forestall any continuation of the 'punk' tag. Martyn Goddard's sleeve photograph was deliberately shot in the mod mecca of Carnaby Street. Rick Buckler remembers the shoot: 'We started at one end of the street and simply walked through to the other. It was done in two minutes and we were back in the pub. Two of us had been in the pub beforehand, which is easy to see.

Deliberately continuing to link themselves with London, the band climbed to the top of Battersea Power Station in order to record the video, which simply featured The Jam taking us through the song on a windy rooftop overlooking the city.

AUNTIES AND UNCLES (IMPULSIVE YOUTHS) (Weller)
Recorded in January 1978 at Basing Street Studios, Notting Hill, London
Produced by Chris Parry and Vic Coppersmith-Heaven
B-side to 'News Of The World'

Weller's only contribution to the 'News Of The World' package was easily his best effort for some time. With Weller sounding relaxed and confident, 'Aunties And Uncles' is a melodic mod tune which could easily have come straight from that era, complete with Small Faces-style cockney voiceovers.

The band had never been in more demand as a live act and Paul's father continued to book them into a gruelling schedule of performances, television and radio appearances and press interviews. Running out of creative steam, they were unable to find the time to stop and think, let alone write new songs, and the pressure of being in The Jam started to pull the band members apart. At one point during this time Weller, looking around for new ideas, actually approached former Sex Pistol Glen Matlock and asked if he would be interested in joining The Jam. But Matlock had only just formed his own new group, The Rich Kids, and, despite being tempted by the idea, it came to nothing. When The Jam played The Marquee Club on 24 February 1978, Matlock tried to reverse roles and asked Paul to join his band instead. Weller dismissed the idea immediately, although Matlock insists Paul 'was thinking about the offer.'

INNOCENT MAN (Foxton)

Recorded in January 1978 at Basing Street Studios, Notting Hill, London
Produced by Chris Parry and Vic Coppersmith-Heaven
B-side to 'News Of The World'

Another solid musical contribution from Foxton. Lyrically Bruce tackles miscarriages of justice, a brave enough theme and demonstrating once again the varied topics The Jam were prepared to cover in their songwriting.

For the bands who had surfed into view upon the punk wave, early 1978 was an uncomfortable time. Punk had died off and the boys and girls of the record-buying public had voted with their pocket money by placing Kate Bush ('Wuthering Heights'), ABBA ('Take A Chance On Me') and Brotherhood Of Man ('Figaro') back at the top of the charts. *Saturday Night Fever* was due to land in Britain and The Bee Gees were about to make a major comeback. The *Night Fever* album was recorded in the same studio at the same time as the 'News Of The World' sessions, and Rick Buckler remembers listening to it in the corridor.

A good indication of the general musical mood in 1978: while The Jam were at number 27 with 'News Of The World', Showaddywaddy were at number two with 'I Wonder Why'. Punk had clearly done very little to alter the musical tastes of the paying public. Weller had been right to distance himself from the movement, but for his next move he had to think carefully. Crashing guitars were already no longer the order of the day.

DAVID WATTS (Ray Davies)

Recorded on 29 June 1978 at Polydor Studios, Stratford Place, London
Produced by Vic Coppersmith-Heaven and Chris Parry
A-side released 8 August 1978; Polydor 2059 054; reached no 25 in UK chart
Double A-side with "A' Bomb in Wardour Street'

On Sunday 16 April 1978 The Jam played the last show on their second tour of America and Canada prior to flying home to England. Once again, contracts had been agreed on their behalf and the band were immediately booked into the studio to start recording their third album. Paul hadn't written anything apart from 'Aunties And Uncles (Impulsive Youth)' and, as that had already been released as a B-side, he didn't want it to be considered for the new album. The only other idea he had was lifted from another Adrian Henri poem, 'I Want To Paint', but it simply wasn't good enough; despite trying to shape the song it was soon scrapped. Weller: ''I Want To Paint' was like this great fucking poem that was to be read out against the backing of a strummed A chord. Very weird stuff, and it was during the period when I felt I had to be sort of clever when I wrote, which is the wrong idea to have really.'

All Weller and Foxton had were scraps of ideas that the band hoped they could jam together in the studio. But they knew it wasn't working. The Jam's recording career was still only 13 months old and the pressure they were being put under was starting to show. 'At the time we had simply lost all direction,' said Weller. 'I didn't really know what I was writing and Bruce was off trying to come up with something. One of his songs sounded like The Stranglers and I even played organ on it, but we both knew the stuff we had was shit.'

Polydor also knew and producer Chris Parry, on listening to the playbacks, cancelled the sessions. The only positive thing coming out of the experience was an early version of 'Billy Hunt' and Paul's last raw-edged punk offering "'A' Bomb In Wardour Street'. The other songs that made an appearance at the sessions were 'English Rose', a love ballad Weller had written in his hotel room on the American tour, and Foxton's 'The Night', which later appeared as the B-side to 'Down In The Tube Station At Midnight'. Polydor's Chris Parry explained what happened: 'Paul's dad wanted them to make another album so the session was booked and I went in to see how it was coming together. But they only had bits and pieces, nothing really stood out and the songs just weren't up to it.'

So Rick and Bruce returned home to Woking, and this time Paul joined them. He moved out of the London flat he shared with Gill and back into his parents' house at Balmoral Drive on the town's Maybury Estate, having been freaked out by an apparent stalker in London. 'We lived on the ground floor and people would be peering through the letterbox,' said Weller. 'We ended up crawling around the lounge on all fours so no one could see us, it was ridiculous.' The only thing The Jam had to look forward to now was The BBC *In Concert* performance they would be playing live from The Paris Theatre on 1 June.

Back in Woking a meeting was called with the band's lawyers and accountants, at which Paul was handed his first royalty cheque – for a sizeable amount of money. Just turned 20, the singer now had to consider, for the first time, opening a bank account in order to have somewhere to pay the cheques into; prior to that, all Jam business had been conducted in cash. But Paul showed little interest in the money, being more worried that the band were now adrift, with only a couple of songs up their collective sleeve and no studio bookings in the diary. Foxton was overheard in a bar talking of opening a seaside guest house, and Weller, also becoming restless, talked of starting a secondhand mod clothes store. Instead, he retired for the summer to his parents' back garden in Woking. With an acoustic guitar and a pile of Kinks LPs, he resolved to write and play guitar 'every day'.

Meanwhile, Polydor had switched their attention to Sham 69, whose song 'Angels with Dirty Faces' had given them a Top 20 hit in

May 1978, followed by 'If The Kids Are United', which reached number nine in July. Jimmy Pursey's group were outselling The Jam everywhere and Weller had never felt more alone. He confided in friends that he was thinking about 'leaving music altogether', but also felt he wasn't any good at anything else; music was all he could do. Against this backdrop of rejection, Paul then sat down in his parents' garden and produced the finest set of songs he wrote during that decade. They would go on to make up The Jam's classic album *All Mod Cons*.

'David Watts' is the opening track on The Kinks' fifth studio album *Something Else* (which also included the evergreen 'Waterloo Sunset') and tells the story of a boy who dreams of being the perfect pupil and captain of the school team, sailing through his exams with grade As and getting all the girls.

Paul Weller's own schooldays were mirrored in the song; the Sheerwater Secondary School he attended in Woking even had its own golden boy. 'We had a David Watts at our school,' Weller later admitted. 'In fact he was called Mark Watts and was really infuriating. Whilst I was out smoking in the toilets or bunking off, he would sweep the field both academically and on the sports field. The last I heard he was a copper.' Indeed, Mark Watts remains a Woking policeman to this day.

The Jam began playing a cover version of 'David Watts' when they went out on a mini British tour commencing on 12 June at King George's Hall in Blackburn. But at that time 'Billy Hunt' had been pencilled in as the band's next single and Paul was even introducing it as such on stage. However, when it was recorded during the *All Mod Cons* sessions at Mickie Most's RAK Studios the choice for the single had been narrowed down to 'David Watts' and "A' Bomb In Wardour Street'. Nobody in or around the band could agree on which song should be released as the A-side. And in early July, with an imminent television appearance on *Revolver* during which The Jam intended to debut the new single, a choice had to be made. Paul's father John decided to take both songs to Mickie Most, who was in the studio's office at the time, to ask his advice. After hearing both tracks Most said, 'David Watts, that's the one for me,' and John returned saying:

'If it's good enough for Mickie, then it's good enough for us.'

In the event 'David Watts' and "A' Bomb' were released as a double A-side. But the former, with Paul and Bruce sharing vocal duties throughout the track, was the one that received all the attention, taking the single to number 25 in the UK charts, only a modest improvement on their previous effort. But the version was well received by its originators. 'I think The Kinks went in and re-recorded it after they heard our version,' says Rick Buckler. 'They speeded it up to sound like ours, which was quite ironic.'

Despite only reaching number 25, the song was regarded by many as a turning point in the band's fortunes. Garry Bushell, writing in *Sounds* on 4 November 1978, described The Jam's version of 'David Watts' as 'a sign that the widespread and blasé critical relegation of The Jam to 'spent force' was, to say the least, a trifle premature.' The same edition of *Sounds* demonstrates Polydor's renewed commitment to the band in the shape of a full-page advert featuring *All Mod Cons* and the band's forthcoming Apocalypse Tour.

The Jam played 'David Watts' as their final number at the BBC live Rainbow recording session on 4 December 1979, during which, as violence erupted in the audience, Foxton can be heard swearing at the crowd mid-vocal.

'A' BOMB IN WARDOUR STREET (Weller)

Recorded on 3 July 1978 at Eden Studios, London
Produced by Vic Coppersmith-Heaven and Chris Parry
Double A-side with 'David Watts'

The studio sessions at RAK were notable for friction between the band and Polydor's Chris Parry, who had bluntly brought their previous efforts to a close. John Weller approached Parry in his office and told him, 'You should get down to the studio, they are all saying they don't want you to produce any more.' Parry then spoke to each band member individually, with both Rick and Bruce telling him directly they didn't want him working on the album. Paul was a little subtler and explained to Parry that he liked what he had done for the band but agreed with the others that Vic Coppersmith-Heaven should produce the new album alone. The incident caused even more friction with Polydor, who were not informed of the problem, but ultimately the sessions were going so well that a deal was agreed between all parties and Coppersmith-Heaven completed the album without Parry.

"'A' Bomb in Wardour Street' was created by Weller after a disturbing experience in Soho's Vortex Club. 'It came from a feeling I got in the Vortex one night. It was very heavy and everyone was only there for the violence, kicking each other in. I just thought how that scene had changed so quickly. Everyone used to be there for a purpose – to see new bands play and to talk about new things.'

Despite some criticism to the contrary, Weller wasn't advocating or encouraging such behaviour in the lyric of the song, in fact quite the opposite. 'I'm not preaching,' he said at the time, 'but I am trying to get across a non-violent stance. Street violence isn't necessary.'

"'A' Bomb' is the last of The Jam songs with a punk feel to it and, with its anti-violent message, Weller finally turns his back on the movement that a year earlier he was so desperate to be a part of. In sharing the disc with 'David Watts', Jam fans were given a clear sign of the band's future direction.

Once again, The Jam were criticised for not making any significant progress, but those in and around the band were quietly confident. They knew the quality of what had been going on in the studio – and what was coming next.

DOWN IN THE TUBE STATION AT MIDNIGHT (Weller)
Recorded in August 1978 at RAK Studios, St Johns Wood, London
Produced by Vic Coppersmith-Heaven
A-side released 6 October 1978; Polydor POSP 8; reached no 15 in UK chart
B-side: 'So Sad About Us' (Townshend)/'The Night' (Foxton)

Only two months after 'David Watts'' muted reception The Jam returned to the charts in some style. 'Down In The Tube Station At Midnight' was released on 6 October and signalled a real turning point for the band. Musically the track demonstrates a significant change of style for The Jam. Instead of having Weller's raging Rickenbacker high in the mix, the song is driven along by Foxton's intricate bass line, with Paul contributing single spaced-out chords throughout the verses before raising the tempo in time for a punching chorus – a style Kurt Cobain would use to great effect with Nirvana a decade later.

Weller again tells a story in the first person, this time a witty but at times dark tale of a young man attacked on the London Underground late at night. The scene is set as the song's character fumbles for the right change for his ticket and hears hateful voices whispering behind him. Finally the voices shout out and demand money with menaces. (The phrase in the second verse 'smiling beguiling' was lifted from The Yardbirds' 1965 single 'Evil Hearted You'.)

Weller borrows from Ray Davies' highly evocative style, painting a vivid and disturbing picture of the unfolding horror. First Weller's victim is punched and then kicked by right wing thugs fresh out of prison (Wormwood Scrubs) and then left drifting in and out of consciousness on the platform. Finally, in a sinister twist, Weller reminds us his victim's wife is waiting at home for him – and that the muggers have stolen his flat keys.

Weller himself describes the track as a short television play transposed to a three-minute pop song. 'A geezer is on his way home from work with a take-away and gets beaten up on the platform by some thugs. He assesses his life as it flashes across his eyes and his last thought is his take-away curry getting cold on the floor.' But, in perhaps the greatest image of all, as he slips in and out of consciousness all he can make out is a British Rail poster advertising an Awayday. With that, Weller firmly establishes himself as one of the great three-minute storytellers.

'I remember exactly what happened with 'Tube Station',' says Rick Buckler. 'It was developed around Bruce's bass line, which is pretty obvious, and we had all the musical parts worked out and then Paul came in one day with some lyrics, which are fantastic, and we adapted the song to suit them.' But adapting it wasn't as easy as

Buckler makes it sound. 'Paul wanted to scrap it after a while,' producer Vic Coppersmith-Heaven said. 'He's very impatient in the studio, with The Jam being very much a live band, and he didn't think it was working. He said it was rubbish but when I read the lyrics I was knocked out and told him he must be joking.'

History has proven Coppersmith-Heaven right in encouraging The Jam to persevere with 'Down In The Tube Station At Midnight' and make it work. In 1981 Paul said, 'I still think that 'Tube Station' is the best single we have done and it's not that commercial when you first hear it. I think people are getting more into actually listening to the songs and not just the first hook line.'

'Down In The Tube Station At Midnight' only managed to chart at number 15, failing to beat their previous best position with 'All Around The World', which reached number 13. But, more encouragingly, it was the first song Weller had written since April 1977 (before the release of their debut album) which was good enough to be released as a single. The song illustrated that not only was Weller back, he was far better than he had ever been. In the past his story telling had been at best lumpy, but now Paul was creating identifiable English characters and telling grim real-life English stories.

'Down In The Tube Station At Midnight' was one of the most popular songs The Jam played live at that time, and a haunting version appears on *The Jam at the BBC* during their live concert broadcast from the Golders Green Hippodrome on 19 December 1981. Anybody attending a Jam gig between 1978 and 1980 will remember the thunderous noise of a tube train echoing through the PA system, which would usually attract the largest cheer of the night as the band launched into the song.

But Rick Buckler remembers it all going wrong on one occasion: 'We went off on tour and nobody thought to bring along the taped tube train intro to the song,' he recalled. 'Then someone had the bright idea of going out to a local record shop and buying the single to play the intro off that. The problem was the single was half a beat out from the version we played live and Paul came in at the wrong time. Bruce and I looked at each other and switched to Paul's beat, just as he realised it for himself and switched to ours, which meant we were all out of time again. That time Bruce and I just stayed with it and Paul had to come back to us. We got away with it though, but we didn't bother with the tube recording after that.'

But some recognised pundits missed the point of the song completely, and Radio 1 DJ Tony Blackburn was scathing about the lyric on his show. 'I think it is disgusting the way these punks sing about violence all the time,' he raged. 'Why can't they sing about beautiful things like trees and flowers?'. Weller was furious and phoned the programme to defend his creation on air and explain the anti-violent message he was trying to put across. But 'Tube Station' won The Jam an army of new fans, all eager to find out what was going to be on the upcoming album *All Mod Cons*. The rush to the shops as soon as the LP was released catapulted The Jam to number six in the UK charts.

For students of detail, the tube train intro was recorded by Vic Coppersmith-Heaven just around the corner from the studio at St Johns Wood tube station and the sleeve photographs were taken Polydor art director Bill Smith at Bond Street tube.

SO SAD ABOUT US (Townshend)
Recorded in September 1978 at RAK Studios, St Johns Wood, London
Produced by Vic Coppersmith-Heaven
B-side to 'Down In The Tube Station At Midnight'

On 7 September 1978, The Who's drummer Keith Moon died of an accidental overdose of Heminevrin, which had been prescribed to him in a bid to help overcome his alcoholism. Moon had been addicted to drink and drugs for many years and was, at the time, making a serious attempt to overcome his problem, so his death shocked the music world. At the time The Jam were booked into RAK studios recording their third album *All Mod Cons*, and such was Moon's influence on the band they immediately decided to include a respectful tribute to the wild man of rock on the B-side of their new single 'Down In The Tube Station At Midnight'.

'So Sad About Us' had been a regular cover during The Jam's live sets and as such needed little or no rehearsal; they simply went into the studio, recorded it almost in one take and it was done. When the single appeared, the few who understood The Jam's real influences were not surprised to see a black-and-white photograph of Keith Moon gazing out from the back of the sleeve. Moon had been a massive influence on The Jam (it had been through his love of The Beach Boys that Weller had discovered surf sounds), and coincidentally the song the band had been covering that year included touching lyrics about not being able to turn the clock back and put right what had just gone so horribly wrong. It was the perfect tribute to one of their greatest 1960s influences.

So far was this melodic, mod-sounding song from the hard guitar shape The Jam had perfected in their year at the top that *Record Mirror*'s Philip Hall wrote: 'Forget the crash bang wallop revivalist style of their early days, The Jam have come of age.' The single was pressed in France and due to a mix-up at the factory this version of 'So Sad About Us' also appeared as the B-side to the first pressing of John Travolta's 'Sandy', released in October 1978.

THE NIGHT (Foxton)
Recorded in July 1978 at RAK Studios, St Johns Wood, London
Produced by Vic Coppersmith-Heaven
B-side to 'Down In The Tube Station At Midnight'

Prior to Moon's death the original flip side planned for 'Tube Station' was another Bruce Foxton song, 'The Night'. Once again the song is as solid musically as anything The Jam recorded that year and lyrically it tells a story (*Quadrophenia* style) of a mod night out in any seaside town.

At only 1'47" 'The Night' is short and sweet, but musically accomplished. The song includes a harmonica part played by Paul, and short snappy guitar licks over almost frantic bass and drum parts.

FOUR

A DEFINING MOMENT

WITH the release of *All Mod Cons*, The Jam announced they had at last found their own voice – and people were listening. *NME* reviewer Charles Shaar Murray wrote: '*All Mod Cons* is not only several light years ahead of anything The Jam have done before but it is also one of the handful of truly essential rock albums of the last few years.'

Punk was over for The Jam and *All Mod Cons* proved it, complete with its pop art inner sleeve, featuring a melange of sixties mod images, including scooters, targets, badges and Tamla Motown records. Pop art fascinated Weller and he was easily able to relate to pop artists and their ideas. 'I read somewhere about pop artists and their work is very similar to what we are doing. They take everyday situations and things like washing machines and turn them into art. That's basically what I am doing, taking an everyday experience, like a tube station, and turning it into art.'

The album's packaging presented The Jam as a mod band – Weller, after all, had been a mod since he was 14 years old – and the LP was hailed as the rebirth of the mod movement. The songs, however, were just as hard, crisp and effective as Jam fans had come to expect.

ALL MOD CONS

ALL MOD CONS (Weller)
Recorded on 16 August 1978 at RAK Studios, St Johns Wood, London
Produced by Vic Coppersmith-Heaven
Album track: All Mod Cons

The album is fired into life by a lazy count-in from Paul Weller, followed by a harsh two-chord, Who-style riff and drum pattern.

Lyrically the title track launches a blistering attack on the music industry, and especially Polydor, revealing Weller's deep hurt at the way the band had been treated when their previous attempt at a third album, earlier in the year, had been unceremoniously cancelled. Weller was uncompromising and scathing in his contempt, spitting the lyrics out as if in a rage.

At only 1'18", the track leaves the listener trying to take in all he has just heard, but there is no time as 'All Mod Cons' neatly segues, via morse-coding Rickenbacker feedback, into song two, a characteristic trick the band also used on stage and is still copied by many Jam tribute bands to this day. (The two appear together in this way on *Dig The New Breed*.)

'All Mod Cons' was a staple in the live set as The Jam set off on a February tour of France, Belgium and Germany to play nine shows promoting the album. They were accompanied by Danny Baker, who at the time was a *New Musical Express* journalist. Baker travelled with The Jam as they played the famous Star Club in Hamburg, once the home of The Beatles, and recorded the event in an article published in *NME* on 17 March 1979. Baker: 'A few minutes after they had punched into their set I realised why I wanted to do a piece on The Jam. This trio is just so excellent. It was during this set that I began jotting down [notes] about patriotism, their string of magic muscle music creating a mammoth pride in my chest. 'All Mod Cons', 'To Be Someone', 'Billy Hunt', 'Away From The Numbers' ... I mean, even knowing the catalogue of strength they have to fall back on they were awesome.'

Later, Baker had a chance to talk to Weller about the album. Weller was clearly bristling with anger: 'With the record companies it's OK saying you hate them and that you're not going to have anything to do with them but the only people we meet are the employees anyway, who are just like us and are really OK. You never get to meet the fat cats up top, you only meet the people working for them and you can't have a go at them. The thing you have to guard against is thinking they are all like that and you've got to remember the blokes upstairs, making the decisions, are only interested in what they can get out of you.'

Danny Baker summed up his review with the words: 'Paul Weller is phenomenal and, with Bruce Foxton and Rick Buckler with him, and we must repeat they are not simply backers, The Jam will become tougher, better than the rest.'

TO BE SOMEONE (DIDN'T WE HAVE A NICE TIME) (Weller)
Recorded on 3 July 1978 at Eden Studios, London
Produced by Vic Coppersmith-Heaven and Chris Parry
Album track: All Mod Cons

In more reflective mood, Weller wrote 'To Be Someone' having learnt and understood the limited career span of a pop star. Placing himself on the outside looking in, Weller muses over what it must be like to 'be someone' and, having achieved that ambition, to lose it all again. Revealing a canny disregard for those who once feted his work, Paul uses vivid lyrics as a warning to others with similar ambitions.

From the moment Rick Buckler announces the opening bars of 'To Be Someone' – along with Bruce embarking on a line that was to reappear in 'Start!' a few years later, right through to Paul's soulful guitar at the close – the song simply hooks you in.

'To Be Someone' is both wistful in its longing and direct in its critical message to the shallow, self-obsessed pop world, further establishing its writer as a spokesman (albeit reluctantly) for his generation. Weller portrays his central character once again as a lonely, isolated figure, only this time having been propelled through fame and stardom before finding himself isolated once again. He complains of life without lock-ins at the local pub, after being thrown out with the rest of the 'ordinary' regulars, and of having to stay at home now the bodyguards have gone. Weller can only have been writing about himself in a song that marked an obvious return to the R and B roots of The Jam's earlier days.

But, contrary to the lyric, Weller himself had become someone to be reckoned with via this set of songs and was now a hero to an army of fans, despite being only 20 years old. Weller: 'I liked it at first because that was part of the fantasy as a kid to be whatever The Beatles were.

But it later became frightening when The Jam were at their peak. We kept trying to stay behind at gigs to meet people, as we always had done, but in the end there would be thousands and it became impossible. People would see us differently and even those VIPs who came to meet us in the dressing room would come in shaking.'

'To Be Someone' was the second song on the set The Jam played live at the Rainbow Theatre on 4 December 1979 as part of the BBC's *In Concert* series. The song followed 'All Mod Cons' (as it usually did at gigs) on the live album *Dig The New Breed*, which was recorded during a show at the same venue nine days later.

In 1999 Oasis star Noel Gallagher was asked to contribute to The Jam tribute album *Fire and Skill* and, tellingly, 'To Be Someone' was the song he chose to cover. It was the only time the track ever received radio play, as yet another classic Jam song was never released as a single.

MR CLEAN (Weller)

Recorded on 7 August 1978 at RAK Studios, St Johns Wood, London
Produced by Vic Coppersmith-Heaven
Album track: All Mod Cons

Opening with a haunting three-chord guitar riff, Foxton and Buckler then provide a steady understated rhythm for Weller's menacing attack on the English class system. The central character, described as Mr Clean, could be an establishment civil servant, a town planner, politician, bank manager or a music industry executive. Whatever he may be – and the smart money, given the album's theme, is on the latter – the song delivers a chilling warning that the writer has seen him, understands his motives, has his card marked and, should Mr Clean focus any attention on him again, will destroy him. But the song is anti-violence, the inference being: '...if you just stay away from me, you will be OK.'

The inspiration for 'Mr Clean' clearly emanates from The Kinks and Ray Davies' style of creating easily identifiable characters. As a form of songwriting it also features in many Beatles songs, which

Paul had always been keen to emulate. His only previous attempt had been with 'London Girl', appearing on the previous album *This Is The Modern World*, but the success of The Jam's cover of the Kinks hit 'David Watts' had initially encouraged the 20-year-old songwriter to develop the technique further and introduce some of his own characters, all of whom would pass into legend amongst Jam fans. 'Billy Hunt' was the first of these, but 'Mr Clean' would only be followed by Bruce Foxton's 'Smithers-Jones' and Paul's 'Liza Radley' and 'Alfie', although other unnamed examples did appear in 'Boy About Town' and 'Just Who Is The 5 O'Clock Hero'.

'Mr Clean' was another major success on the live circuit. Jam fans will never forget the sea of arms as thousands pointed back towards the stage when Paul Weller screamed the lyric 'fuck up your life', which was surprisingly left unedited during the BBC *In Concert* performance broadcast from The Rainbow Theatre on 4 December 1979. Although Paul did pull away from the microphone at the crucial moment, slightly diminishing its effect.

ENGLISH ROSE (Weller)

Recorded on 16 August 1978 at RAK Studios, St Johns Wood, London
Produced by Vic Coppersmith-Heaven
Album track: All Mod Cons

During The Jam's second ill-fated tour of America in March and April 1978 (supporting Blue Öyster Cult), one of the few positive things to emerge was 'English Rose', written by Weller in one of the anonymous motel rooms the band were confined to on the tour. Too young to visit bars and clubs, Paul had relied on elder tour members to provide beers from the local supermarkets and shut himself away with his acoustic guitar to produce his first ballad, the type of song he had been talking about experimenting with for some time.

'English Rose' has a beautifully simple melody and a soft, charming lyric which Weller seemed embarrassed about; he refused to sing it in front of anybody, asking for the studio to be cleared when he recorded the vocal part. It has also been said that the lyric was deliberately left off the album sleeve (blamed at the time on the song's last-minute inclusion) as Weller was uneasy about revealing himself in such an obvious way. He himself explained that he felt the lyric meant very little on paper and lost its effect without the music, so it was left off. But the lyrics and music do appear in The Jam songbook published in early 1979, suggesting either Paul had changed his mind, or the real reason it was left off was its late inclusion to the album, after the sleeves had been printed.

The track was recorded on the same day as the powerful 'All Mod Cons' and 'Billy Hunt', providing quite a contrasting day's work for the singer, but the searching feel to the song made it an instant hit with those who bought the album. 'English Rose' opens up with the sound of gentle waves lapping on a beach. In the distance a ship's foghorn can be heard, providing the impression of a cold misty morning in an English port town as the writer steps off a ship, arriving home after a long-distance journey. The lyrics support that image beautifully and tell of travelling the world (via secret mists, the seven seas and the highest peaks) but always longing to return home to the writer's 'English Rose'. It isn't difficult to imagine Weller sitting in a faceless American Motel, missing his girlfriend and conjuring up such images.

The Jam never played the song live, with Paul stating at the time that he couldn't sing it and play the guitar part at the same time, although he did when he embarked on his acoustic tour in 2002 to support his album *Days Of Speed*. 'There was a fantastic atmosphere in there when Paul played 'English Rose',' says Squire guitarist Enzo Esposito. 'He got a standing ovation for that, it was great to hear him play it live for the first time.' The only other Jam songs Paul included in that performance were 'Town Called Malice' and 'That's Entertainment'.

'English Rose' was beautifully sung by Tracy Thorn when Everything But The Girl re-recorded the song for the Jam tribute album *Fire And Skill*.

IN THE CROWD (Weller)

Recorded on 7 August 1978 at RAK Studios, St Johns Wood, London
Produced by Vic Coppersmith-Heaven
Album track: All Mod Cons

On 10 April 1979, The Jam arrived in Canada for their fourth
Stateside tour, this time to promote *All Mod Cons*, and hopes were
high for a better experience than the last. The visit had been
restricted to just two weeks and only nine performances. By now the
band had a large loyal following, especially in the major cities, and
were booked into venues such as The New York Palladium and The
Royce Hall in Los Angeles. In a publicity stunt, New York DJ Mark
Simone offered to give away tickets to the first 50 Jam fans who
recognised him standing at a Manhattan crossroads, but the response
was so great the police had to rescue Simone and take him to safety
at a New York police station. Hundred of fans followed and the stunt
was widely publicised in new bulletins.

Despite this, Weller remained unsettled and his reputation in
America was of being difficult and immature. Weller himself couldn't
see how The Jam would succeed in America at a time when radio-
friendly acts like Foreigner, Rod Stewart and The Village People were
dominating the charts. He didn't help himself much when, at a
packed press conference to promote one of the shows, Weller turned
to the crowd of journalists and announced: 'We are going to do
an interview with a couple of fanzines, and the rest of you can fuck
off.' If that wasn't bad enough he then announced on stage in New
York: 'I have to say, in all honesty, this place just ain't really us.'

During the tour The Jam once again reverted to the black-suited
mod mage and this time insisted on decorating the stage with Union
Jacks, further alienating themselves from their hosts, although not
their audience as fan Mark Cooper remembers. 'I hadn't seen anything
like it for years, nor the feedback that closes 'Bricks and Mortar', the
fifth number of two encores. Weller at the back of the stage thrashing
out the chords and then assaulting the speakers whilst the crowd
seethed.' Paul clearly wasn't in the mood to be in America and it
didn't go unnoticed. In a review for *Rolling Stone* magazine, one writer

noted: 'The Jam's energetic music is enjoyable enough. Too bad their extra-musical behaviour is so embarrassingly immature.'

Despite their behaviour, 'In the Crowd' was a song full of signs of growing maturity. The Jam were now creating music with sophisticated arrangements and clever guitar work, including imaginative backward guitar breaks borrowed from Beatles techniques. Once again drawing from George Orwell and Ken Kesey's influence, Weller came up with the title for In The Crowd and the idea for the song while he was working on 'The Combine', featured on *This Is The Modern World*; indeed, the phrase appears in the latter song's lyric. Once again Weller is creating vivid Orwellian images of a world in which we have no control over ourselves emotionally. Weller: 'It's the feeling that I used to get when I went shopping. In a supermarket as you walk around with a trolley you suddenly start to become dehumanised as we are taken in by advertising slogans and background music.'

Weller's perceptive lyric is supported by an understated bass line (Foxton sending his notes off in directions it would seem impossible to dream up) and Buckler's off-beat drum pattern driving through to the song's coda is pure class. It's hard to believe the drum track was played live and in one take, but Buckler insists all Jam recordings have a 'live' drum track. 'We used to play the song through in the studio, for my benefit, and then I would record the drum part for the others to come in and use when they did the guitars. The drum track went down first and I would always do the whole thing in one take. That's not to say I didn't have several goes at it, but that if any part didn't sound right I would do the whole thing again. We never dropped bits in or borrowed from other takes.'

The image 'In The Crowd' creates is a vast step up from the work of earlier albums and it's easy to forget the creative drought Weller had been through in the year prior to writing the song. It's also worth remembering the pressure he was under, having just had the recording sessions scrapped and been 'invited' to come up with something better. With the bitterness of that rejection written out of him in 'All Mod Cons' and 'To Be Someone' (albeit not entirely forgotten), Weller had been able to create one of the finest songs on the album.

A wonderful live version of 'In The Crowd' was recorded by the BBC at the Golders Green Hippodrome on 19 December 1981, appearing on *The Jam At The BBC*, a collection of live recordings released in 2002. Also, a version recorded at the Edinburgh Playhouse on 6 April 1982 featured on The Jam's final album *Dig The New Breed* in December 1982.

BILLY HUNT (Weller)

Recorded on 16 August 1978 at RAK Studios, St Johns Wood, London
Produced by Vic Coppersmith-Heaven
Album track: All Mod Cons

'Billy Hunt' was, for a while, intended as The Jam's fifth single, although in the event 'David Watts' was chosen ahead of it. It was one of the few songs Paul had written during his creative drought in 1977 and he had introduced it as the band's 'new single' at the BBC *In Concert* performance at The Paris Theatre on 1 June 1978. Weller: "'Billy Hunt' was written just after we got back from the States in 1977. It originally had a longer middle eight and a lot of the words were cut. I wrote it while I was still living in Woking, one day when I was sitting in the garden. I thought at the time it had to be a single, but we held out until we had some other material. Polydor suggested we waited until we had some other numbers.'

'Billy Hunt' is another humorous song, loaded with irony, which many seemed to misinterpret. In its lyric Weller portrays the title character as a cool and popular figure in his own mind, but cynically points out all the personality traits that mark him out as the kind of character that rhymes with the song title.

Some people thought Weller's lyrics were attempting to evoke a hero-type character, exacting his revenge on teachers and work colleagues who bully him, as a sort of call-to-arms for all underdogs. But this is far from the case. Instead, Paul is depicting, with tongue firmly in cheek, young lads around Woking and London's club scene whose only hope of achieving any prestige among their peers is through the use of violence. Billy Hunt was a Billy Liar-type figure (as immortalised in Keith Waterhouse's novel and the subsequent film) who dreamt his days away in aimless fantasy imagining himself as James Bond and living in a world of strippers and 'long legged girls'.

In fact, Paul had created the type of character who wished he was David Watts but couldn't help being Billy Hunt instead. 'There is a bit of Billy Hunt in everybody really,' said Weller. 'He is the sort who is always being put down and can only take so much before he breaks out. He dreams of being Superman and has Clark Kent posters on his wall. There is a bit of me in there as well.' But Weller joked that he had David Soul posters on his bedroom wall instead. Those hearing Weller punch through the lyrics during live appearances were left in no doubt about what he really thought of his new creation, as often he would drop the rhyming slang and sing the song title as intended.

At the time, concept albums, especially Sham 69's That's Life, were achieving chart success. One journalist asked Weller if he had similar thoughts, to which he replied: 'You could just take a character like Billy Hunt and centre an album around him, but in the end I preferred to let it hang loose rather than connect it all.'

IT'S TOO BAD (Weller)
Recorded on 3 July 1978 at Eden Studios, London
Produced by Vic Coppersmith-Heaven and Chris Parry
Album track: All Mod Cons

When The Jam returned from America they went back out on the road to play their spring tour, supported by The Records, starting with two dates at Sheffield University on 4 and 5 May 1979, and covering 15 shows. The tour, initially titled Jam 'Em In, was an unqualified success, with each venue completely sold out in advance; this is what led to the hasty name change. The renamed Jam Pact Tour not only reflected the success of the album *All Mod Cons,* but also saw the birth of The Jam Army, a group of loyal fans who would jump onto scooters or pack into Cortinas and follow the band across the country from town to town.

Their dress code reflected the new image The Jam were creating, with parkas, targets, mohair suits, Ben Sherman shirts and bowling shoes appearing everywhere as the Jam-inspired mod revival gathered pace. Shortly before the tour *Record Mirror* reported that 'The Jam's fans are in the process of reorganising their transport and, in the true spirit of Mod, are planning to have their scooters fitted with all the wing mirrors and accessories. The Jam fans are so keen to keep the Mod style they buy original suits from jumble sales and are as much into the complete fashion as they are into the band themselves.'

But musically The Jam hadn't really adopted a traditional mod sound – the single released in March of that year, 'Strange Town', had a stomping Northern Soul beat running through it. Even so there were touches of mod-inspired genius on the album and 'It's Too Bad' is one such. Again drawn from early R and B stock, the increasingly inventive use of harmonies between the Weller/Foxton vocals were providing the band with a subtle melodic sound. Combined with the free-ranging bass lines Foxton was coming up with and the drum patterns Buckler was perfecting, 'It's Too Bad' has a touch of The Beatles' 'She Loves You' about it and gave the new mods something to dance about.

Lyrically Weller turns to love again, or more specifically lost love (a theme the writer torments himself with regularly), presumably a reflection of his personal situation having moved out of the apartment he shared in London with his girlfriend and back into his parents' house in Woking.

FLY (Weller)

Recorded on 16 August 1978 at RAK Studios, St Johns Wood, London
Produced by Vic Coppersmith-Heaven
Album track: All Mod Cons

The fourth song recorded on a single day at RAK Studios, demonstrating that the band were working through their parts with Beatles-like speed, 'Fly' sounds entirely different to 'Billy Hunt', 'English Rose' and 'All Mod Cons'.

Subtle and tender acoustic sections building up into a harsher bridge and chorus was a style The Jam were developing with a view to creating separate parts to a song, each providing a different emotion. Lyrically Paul takes us through yet another side of love, this time having everything you want, recognising it and determining to keep it.

Although a hugely popular album track, 'Fly' was never broadcast on the radio and never played live. 'It is just impossible to play 'Fly' live,' said Weller. 'I'd have to change my guitar about three times. I wouldn't like to adapt my songs to that extent. Unless it is something you can do really well, it's not worth doing.' The song has also never appeared on any compilation albums, preserving its status as something of a hidden classic.

As *All Mod Cons* was creating national attention, The Jam's appearance at the opening of old band mate Steve Brookes' new guitar shop, in Brookwood on the outskirts of Woking during the spring of 1979, was guaranteed to create a stir. On hearing of Brookes' plans, his old band made it known they would be appearing on the day and were greeted by an army of fans, as well as both the local and music press, outside the new shop, Abacorn Music. Brookes was grateful for the gesture, despite the fact that the number of Jam fans milling around outnumbered potential customers by about ten to one, and for the two old schoolfriends it was a chance to catch up on a few stories. Brookes recalls how it all ended in his book *Keeping The Flame*: 'Paul and I ended up going out for a Chinese and then back to his house in Maybury to drink Harvey Wallbangers and jam together old Everly Brothers songs, me on guitar and Paul on piano. I woke up the following morning lying fully clothed with my head wedged up against the piano.'

As The Jam got bigger they regularly used their influence to help old friends around their home town, turning up at summer fetes to present prizes and playing gigs to packed crowds in youth clubs, pubs and community centres. They continued to see themselves as normal local lads and insisted others treated them the same way. Yet they were increasingly having to come to terms with their newly elevated status. 'One time we played a gig for the benefit of the

Woking YMCA,' remembers Rick Buckler. 'And when I jumped in the car to go home afterwards this face appeared right in front of me, like a rabbit caught in my headlights. The lad had been bent down unscrewing my front number plate at the time.'

THE PLACE I LOVE (Weller)
Recorded on 7 August 1978 at RAK Studios, St Johns Wood, London
Produced by Vic Coppersmith-Heaven
Album track: All Mod Cons

This song's evocation of a beautiful countryside full of colourful moss and goldfish pools is starkly contrasted by the city violence that erupts in "'A' Bomb In Wardour Street', which followed 'The Place I Love' on *All Mod Cons*.

On 1 November 1978 The Jam set out on The Apocalypse Tour to promote *All Mod Cons*. The tour began in Liverpool on 1 November and travelled the length of Britain before closing at The Great British Music Festival in Wembley Arena on 29 November.

Woking had become a mod stronghold and 'The Jam' train, leaving Woking Station for Waterloo of a weekend evening, would carry hundreds of mods into London, making for Soho, Carnaby Street, Leicester Square and other meeting points. On an evening when The Jam had a London show, the train from Woking would be crammed with fans, picking up hundreds more on the way, and Waterloo Station at night would heave with mods catching last trains home. 'It must have been as much fun as the gigs themselves,' said Rick Buckler. 'All part of the night out. I missed all of that though, I was working on those nights.'

But Rick also remembers the growing mod scene, which replaced the dying punk movement in the shape of bands like Secret Affair, The Purple Hearts and The Chords, all of which secured support roles with The Jam at certain London gigs. Other bands like The Jam's old friends from Woking, Squire, emerged on the I-Spy label, while Buckler drummed for The Merton Parkas upstairs at Ronnie Scott's on 19 June 1979, during The Jam's summer lay-off.

During this time Weller became friends with brothers Danny and Mick Talbot of The Merton Parkas and was seen connecting with other bands making up the 'mod' revival, but he was careful to distance himself from the movement in public. Weller was wary of the 'spokesman' tag he had been given and didn't want to be seen as leading any musical movement at all.

By then The Jam had seen for themselves no fewer than four separate audiences at their gigs. First it was the old men and women making up the social club membership at their early Woking performances, then came the groovers at Michael's Club and the contrasting followers of punk. Now, as they faced their audience, The Jam looked out on a sea of khaki parkas making up the vibrant mod movement. Having only just managed to drop The Who and The Small Faces comparisons, the band were careful not to attach themselves to any new movement too closely. 'I just didn't get it,' Paul later said. 'The whole thing to me was about individuality and I could see the irony of someone trying to be an individual but within a great sea of parkas.'

And Weller definitely tried to stay away from becoming a spokesman for anything, preferring instead to let the music speak for him. Despite this, every word he uttered was analysed, edited and reported by a music press determined to place Paul at the front of the mod revival, and the 20-year-old wasn't comfortable with it. Especially as it was his political observations, rather than his natural sense of humour, that made the headlines. 'I am portrayed as humourless because people keep associating me with politics and that's dull,' he complained. 'You should see some of the questions I get asked in interviews and they are so serious and one-dimensional, even though I am prepared to talk about anything in my private life, I just don't get asked.'

As far as the mod movement was concerned, Paul tried in vain to dissociate The Jam from it at every opportunity, telling one magazine: 'I don't consider myself as any leader. I'm not interested in the whole revival thing, it's all a bit pathetic.' Weller had a point, as musically most of the bands involved were sub-standard. In contrast, *All Mod Cons* won The Jam the NME Album Of The Year Award in December 1978.

STRANGE TOWN (Weller)
Recorded in January 1979 at RAK Studios, London
Produced by Vic Coppersmith-Heaven
A-side released 5 March 1979; Polydor POSP34; reached no 15 in UK chart
B-side: 'The Butterfly Collector'

With such a successful album as *All Mod Cons* now in the bag, the temptation was to release another single from it and benefit from a new round of publicity. But The Jam once again insisted on giving value for money and would only consider another brand-new song, a move which significantly increased their reputation as a singles band. In fact, nine of their 17 singles failed to appear on any album and a remarkable 12 album tracks, at one time or another considered as singles, were never released as either an A- or B-side. Even more notable is that 16 B-sides (some singles had two tracks on the flip) also never appeared on an album, some as good as 'Tales From The Riverbank', 'Pity Poor Alfie', 'Carnaby Street' and 'The Butterfly Collector', all of which could easily have charted as a single in its own right, let alone done duty as a popular album track.

In the glow of success from *All Mod Cons* and the Apocalypse Tour at the tail end of 1978, The Jam appeared to take the following January off, but nothing could be further from the truth. In fact Paul, Bruce and Rick were soon back in the studio, writing recording and rehearsing for their upcoming tour. 'We never really had much time off at all,' remembers Buckler. 'The Jam was a business really, like having a job. When we weren't on tour we would be either in the studio every day or writing and rehearsing. We only ever had some time off over Christmas and maybe a few weeks in the year when we could have a holiday, but apart from that it was business as usual.'

During that month in the studio The Jam wrote and recorded 'Strange Town', which was the first of four classic Jam singles to be released over the following 12 months that delivered previously unheard songs on both sides ('The Eton Rifles' came out two weeks prior to the album it appeared on, making both songs on that single brand-new at the time of release). 'Strange Town' offered yet another new sound, this time with Bruce Foxton's bass high in the mix and the bottom end powering through the song supported by an aggressive drum pattern. This driven sound set the tone for each of the following singles, until the softer 'Start!' changed direction for them 18 months later in August 1980.

Lyrically Weller, once again in the first person, draws on his isolation from accepted social circles and illustrates exactly what it's like for a stranger to arrive in a new town (obviously London) and wander up and down with an *A to Z* guide book being largely ignored by the city natives. Millions of visitors to any major British town, especially London, could relate to the theme of the song where the central character feels like an alien, and he might as well be for all the chance he has of being noticed by anybody. Weller later acknowledged new influences and admitted that a vocal part on the song had been borrowed from Buzzcocks' 'What Do I Get'.

In February 1978 Weller had recorded a piano demo of a new track called 'Worlds Apart'. The demo ran to only 1.53 and the idea was scrapped soon afterwards, but the bridge section and lyric were later revived and added to 'Strange Town'. ('Worlds Apart' can be found on disc 5 of the box set *Direction Reaction Creation*.)

'Strange Town' didn't have an easy development and in the end Polydor spent about £5000 on two separate versions, neither of which was deemed satisfactory. Producer Vic Coppersmith-Heaven ended up spending two full days in the studio mixing the track, and Polydor saw this as a chance to find the band a new producer. They were keen to employ Beatles legend George Martin in order to produce an album that might ensure commercial success in America. Many thought Weller would jump at the chance of working with Martin and were surprised when the singer loyally insisted Coppersmith-Heaven stayed. 'Paul was fantastic,' said the producer. 'I couldn't have had a better friend. He totally stood by me and wasn't having any of it. Although Polydor didn't understand it at all they had no choice but to go along with him.'

'Strange Town' was played live at The Rainbow Theatre during the BBC *In Concert* performance on 4 December 1979, sandwiched between two of the other three power pop singles of that year,

'When You're Young' and 'The Eton Rifles'. This was also the first time The Jam ever released a single on which Paul Weller contributed exclusively to both sides of the record, but he would do so again on nine of the following 11 over the next three and a half years.

The poem appearing on the rear sleeve is by Weller himself, in which he attacks pop star revolutionaries for their double standards. In the final verse the so-called angry man of the New Wave revealed once again his inner humour and irony, only for it to be missed, or ignored, by many.

THE BUTTERFLY COLLECTOR (Weller)
Recorded in September 1978 at RAK Studios, St Johns Wood, London
Produced by Vic Coppersmith-Heaven
B-side to 'Strange Town'

The title of the song 'The Butterfly Collector' came from the John Fowles book *The Collector*, published by Jonathan Cape in 1963, in which the central character, a butterfly collector called Frederick (who calls himself Ferdinand) decides to 'collect' himself a girlfriend called Miranda and, having secured the object of his devotion, locks her away in his cellar. But Frederick treats Miranda like a princess and fulfils her every need, creating an image of a sad pathetic character rather than one of a monster.

Musically the song is loosely based on The Kinks' 'Shangri La' and is arranged in separate parts, with the tempo sometimes slowing to almost a standstill before lifting through the bridge, providing a haunting atmosphere. Lyrically Paul writes about a groupie known at the time as Sue Catwoman, or just Catwoman, who used to follow punk and New Wave bands around trying to collect herself a boyfriend. 'I remember Catwoman,' recalls Rick Buckler. 'She used to appear at loads of gigs and followed a number of bands around, mainly the Pistols. Her ambition seemed to be simply to sleep with a pop star and I imagine plenty of them did. She turned up at a few of our gigs but none of us were into that sort of thing, we all had girlfriends.'

The song was a massive hit with fans attending the live shows, where it was a staple in The Jam's set. It was even played live at the Radio One *In Concert* performance on 4 December 1979, which was its only radio appearance. 'The Butterfly Collector' is regarded by many as one of The Jam's finest songs, regularly featuring in fan polls listing their top ten Jam songs of all time. A remarkable feat for a song that was only ever hidden away on a B-side, but it has since appeared on the *Live Jam* compilation, released by Polydor in 1993, and on the compilation *The Sound Of The Jam*, which was released in 2002.

In 1995 Garbage recorded a psychedelic version of 'The Butterfly Collector' as the B-side of their 'Queer' single.

WHEN YOU'RE YOUNG (Weller)

Recorded on 3 July 1979 at Eden Studios, London
Produced by Vic Coppersmith-Heaven
A-side released 17 August 1979; Polydor POSP69; reached no 17 in UK chart
B-side: 'Smithers-Jones'

During the quiet summer of 1979, while The Jam were tucked away at the Townhouse Studios in Shepherd's Bush recording 'The Eton Rifles', Polydor released their eighth single in less than two and a half years, 'When You're Young', which would become their third consecutive Top 20 hit. Musically the song is powered along by the bass line and hinted at what could be expected on the forthcoming album *Setting Sons*, also being recorded at that time. Once again the track is broken down into parts, even including a hint of reggae in the middle eight, before the song explodes back into life with a typical Weller guitar break.

Lyrically, Paul sums up the life of any teenager in just one single illuminating verse, suggesting long timeless days during which they find out about life and love. But Weller, keen to warn of the disappointments ahead, advises that our dreams and ambitions could amount to nothing. 'When You're Young' will forever stand as The Jam's statement on the realities of youth, though Weller cleverly tempers the mood by providing a thick slice of sarcasm throughout the final verse.

The song was released on the crest of the new mod movement as scooter-borne mods convoyed to the English seaside towns in search of bikers, skinheads and anyone else they could pick a fight with. Despite steering clear of any direct associations, the anti-violence Jam couldn't help being caught up in the whole scene, with mod shops concocting 'Jam shoes' and making a small fortune on other, apparently Jam-endorsed, merchandise. The sight of parka-clad mods wading into rockers on English beaches, bearing stitched-on Jam patches and with Jam stickers on their scooters, depressed Weller. On one occasion, as a crowd chanted 'We are the mods' at a later gig, he even spat back: 'This song means more than all those clothes and tribes.

But 'When You're Young' was the song that did more than any to elevate The (reluctant) Jam to status of heroes among Britain's disaffected youth, and it was Weller who was given the spokesman's platform. Author Tony Fletcher recalls: "When You're Young' just summed up life at that time for any teenager. If Weller was elected spokesman for his generation it is only because he deserved it.'

Despite the success The Jam's singles were now having, those around the band were becoming restless. Other bands were achieving far more, commercially speaking, than The Jam, notably The Boomtown Rats, who had a Number One hit in late 1978 with 'Rat Trap' and were the first of the New Wave acts to achieve such success. Ian Dury and the Blockheads were next in the chair with 'Hit Me With Your Rhythm Stick' in January 1979, immediately followed by Blondie ('Heart Of Glass' and 'Sunday Girl'). The Boomtown Rats returned to number one in July with 'I Don't Like Mondays' and were followed by The Police ('Message In A Bottle') and Gary Numan ('Are 'Friends' Electric?' and 'Cars') respectively. Before the year was out The Police once again returned to Number One with 'Walking On The Moon'. The Jam were still nowhere near even breaking into the Top Ten, despite their growing fanbase.

The explanation was that the group was failing to secure any real support from radio and television. The band's media plugger, Clive

Banks, offers reasons for this, claiming that there were always many people who just wouldn't play Jam records or support the band. Banks: 'I worked on the early Boomtown Rats records and Bob Geldof did everything Paul wouldn't do. He would do any television or radio interview that moved and spent 24 hours a day manipulating the media whereas Paul would shy away from that.'

But The Jam, preferring to play their music live rather than giving endless (and frequently misinterpreted) interviews, continued to stay accessible and play their music wherever possible. 'When You're Young' featured on the John Peel live radio sessions on 5 November, together with three brand-new tracks from the forthcoming album – 'Thick As Thieves', 'The Eton Rifles' and 'Saturday's Kids' and was also played in a live television broadcast from Manchester on the cult music show *Something Else* (the performance appears on the *Complete Jam* DVD).

SMITHERS-JONES (Foxton)

Recorded on 1 September 1979 at Townhouse Studios, Shepherd's Bush, London
Produced by Vic Coppersmith-Heaven
B-side to 'When You're Young'
Album track: Setting Sons

On the flip side of 'When You're Young' another of The Jam's great character songs made its debut in the shape of 'Smithers-Jones', an affable character created by Bruce Foxton during the summer of 1979. 'Smithers-Jones' is a lighter and gentler offering than the A-side but it nevertheless takes an equally sarcastic look at an identifiable English character. This time he is a genial London commuter catching the early morning train from Woking in what Foxton neatly presents as production line commuting.

Each morning Smithers-Jones packs into one of the hundreds of trains ferrying corporate types to their day's work. Foxton demonstrates just how meaningless that sort of life-long commitment actually is when his character arrives at the office, only to be made redundant and cast adrift. Smithers-Jones returns home to an uncertain future, and the song leads to a bitter finale as he puts his feet up, presumably for the rest of his life.

Two versions of 'Smithers-Jones' were recorded, the second being a string rendition credited to The Jam Philharmonic Orchestra with string arrangements by Pete Solley (formerly of Whitesnake and Procul Harum).

'Smithers-Jones' was a regular staple in The Jam's live set and was played during in their BBC *In Concert* appearance on 4 December 1979. It also appears on *The Sound Of The Jam*, released in 2002. On extremely rare copies of 'When You're Young' a pressing mix-up resulted in 'Smithers-Jones' appearing on both sides of the disc.

THE ETON RIFLES (Weller)

Recorded on 15 August 1979 at Townhouse Studios, Shepherd's Bush, London
Produced by Vic Coppersmith-Heaven and The Jam
A-side released 22 October 1979; Polydor POSP83; reached no 3 in UK chart
B-side: 'See-Saw'
Album track: Setting Sons

Written in the Weller family's holiday caravan at Selsey Bill (of 'Saturday's Kids' fame), 'The Eton Rifles' is driven by an imaginative, thundering bass line complemented by Buckler's tight machine-gun drumming and Weller's clashing, double-tracked Rickenbacker. Buckler, in fact, regarded it as one of his favourite tracks to play live. The song's live radio debut took place about a fortnight after its release, on the John Peel show on 5 November 1979, and it was played again a month later at The Jam's *In Concert* show from The Rainbow Theatre.

Coming as it did at the end of the year of the mod revival (which The Jam were largely, if unfairly, credited with creating), the power and sentiment of 'The Eton Rifles' surprised many. Traditional mod bands sang loose, poppy songs about love and Friday nights out. Yet here were The Jam thundering out a clever satire on the class system via one of the ultimate Establishment strongholds, Eton College. But rather than uphold the usual all-conquering revolutionary image,

Weller mockingly allowed the gentry to win the conflict by suggesting that 'his side' came out far worse than the boys of Eton during the imaginary battle. But their spirits remained high and they would be back next week for another go.

In fact, the music was pretty much a deliberate message to the band's fans: 'Look, we are not a mod band. You try dancing to this in your mohair suits and loafers.' But once again critics missed the humour in the song, focusing solely on its anti-establishment theme instead.

An acoustic demo of the song appears on the 1992 compilation album *Extras*, which was recorded as Weller played a rough version to the others to demonstrate the new track. Weller: 'I believed then, as I believe now, that if a song still sounds good when you sit down and play it with just a voice and a guitar then you know you've got a good song. With 'Eton Rifles' I certainly did sit down and figure it all out before I played it to anyone. And I can understand how it might have been tough on Rick and Bruce when I presented them with a song like that and virtually told them what to play. It must have been especially frustrating for Bruce because he has such a distinctive style. But 'Eton Rifles' was an exception. Most of the time all I had were rough ideas and fragments and we would hammer them out together, with everybody contributing ideas.'

Unhappy with their lack of airplay, those close to The Jam complained to Polydor that the marketing department just wasn't working hard enough for them. But Polydor saw The Jam as only having limited cult appeal and were not prepared to invest in the band. The Wellers' fractious relationship with the label didn't help matters and it fell to Polydor A&R man Dennis Munday to glue the two sides together. Munday: 'We had problems with Polydor's promotion department, who didn't get on with the Wellers, so Paul's dad phoned me up and said he wanted it changed. When I played 'Eton Rifles' to Polydor they gave me the standard response that they didn't see Radio 1 playing it because of its political content. I then played it to Clive Banks, who was one of the best independent pluggers around, who thought that with some hard work he could get it on a B play list.'

This controversial shot attracted the wrong kind of publicity to Weller, Foxton and Buckler, early in The Jam's career.

ABOVE: Live at the Top Rank, Reading, 13 June 1977.

ABOVE: Rick Buckler shows his support for *Trouser Press* magazine. The seminal publication voted *This Is The Modern World* and *All Mod Cons* two of the greatest albums of 1977 and 1979 respectively.

The band made a number of TV appearances, but disliked having to mime to their records.

Buckler and Weller on stage. The group attracted a loyal live following known as 'The Jam Army'.

The JAM

ABOVE AND BELOW: Appearing on the BBC's *Top Of The Pops*.

ABOVE AND RIGHT: Two of Bruce Foxton's souvenirs from The Jam's live tours.

LEFT: On stage at the Fox Warfield Theatre, San Francisco, on 2 June 1982. This was The Jam's final US concert.

A selection of 7" picture sleeves:

IN THE CITY (April 1977)
NEWS OF THE WORLD (February 1978)
DAVID WATTS/'A' BOMB IN WARDOUR STREET (August 1978)
WHEN YOU'RE YOUNG (August 1979)
GOING UNDERGROUND (March 1980)

THAT'S ENTERTAINMENT (German import, June 1981)
TOWN CALLED MALICE (February 1982)
BEAT SURRENDER (limited edition double-pack, November 1982)
LIVE! EP (free with initial copies of *Snap!*, September 1983)

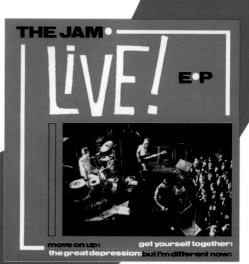

'I want us to finish with dignity,' Paul Weller told Jam fans in 1982. 'Here's to the future…'

That was better than nothing, so The Jam fired Polydor's promotional team and brought in Banks, who managed to promote wide-ranging airplay, taking the single to number three in the UK charts. The band were delighted and from then on the major radio stations just couldn't afford to ignore The Jam.

And the song went by no means unnoticed at Eton itself. The *Eton College Chronicle* of Friday 16 November 1979 (the same day the song's parent album, *Setting Sons*, was released) carried an interview with Weller written by the future music journalist Tim de Lisle. 'Released at the start of Long Leave [ie, half term], the Jam's 'The Eton Rifles' has by now sold an estimated 150-200,000 copies, the most successful single of a pretty successful group,' wrote de Lisle. 'Approved by the critics and picked up by disc-jockeys, 'The Eton Rifles' was top of Capital's Hit Line within five days of release.

'I asked [Weller] exactly what 'Eton Rifles' was about. "Basically, it's, like, taking the mickey out of class. It's meant to be humorous – I think for a start the title's funny. It's an imaginary setting, the two classes clashing, with the trendy revolutionary saying to the man in the pub, 'Come on, sup up your beer, there's a row on up the road,' and it's like, 'The revolution will start after I've finished my pint.' I got the inspiration for the song from watching a programme on the BBC called, I think, *Camera*. They showed an old photo of the Eton Rifles and I thought, what a great name ... It's not a political song in the sense of 10 Downing Street politics, but of everyday politics. Yes, I am against little boys going off to fire blanks at each other ... It's not that I'm bitter about my own education, it was pretty good in fact. But I think that everyone has a right to a good education and they're just not getting it. It's the old story, isn't it. Every man is equal but some are more equal than others. That still exists."

'The song's images are thankfully and surprisingly unhackneyed,' de Lisle concluded, 'and in several cases very appropriate: beer, tea, Slough, rugby, rain stopping play, all are features of Eton life. But Weller has never visited Eton; he happened to know it was near Slough; the song is not intended to be very specific. "I've got nothing against Etonians personally. Eton's just a symbol for the song. They're not annoyed about it, are they?" I said no, they're not,

they're buying it in droves. "Great," said Paul Weller, "that's fantastic. It'll probably go to Number One."'

As it turned out, however, The Jam would have to wait until the following year before attaining that coveted position.

SEE-SAW

Recorded on 15 August 1979 at Townhouse Studios, Shepherd's Bush, London
Produced by Vic Coppersmith-Heaven and The Jam
B-side to 'The Eton Rifles'

The flip side to 'The Eton Rifles' was the lighter 'See-Saw', which was regarded as something of a disappointment by both fans and critics alike. Written shortly after the release of *All Mod Cons* (a year prior to it being issued with 'The Eton Rifles'), lyrically Weller is far from his best here. After flipping over from the thundering 'The Eton Rifles' there was some confusion as to what The Jam were trying to achieve with 'See-Saw', especially as there were some classic album tracks already in the can, having been recorded for the upcoming album *Setting Sons*, any of which would have complemented 'The Eton Rifles' in a more natural way.

Originally Weller had given the song to Polydor label mates The Jolt, who had supported The Jam in Scotland on their previous tour – a gesture that was seen by many as suspiciously generous, given that Weller wasn't known for his warmth towards other bands Polydor were trying to promote. The Jolt had released it on their *Maybe Tonight* EP earlier in the year, but the band had failed to live up to their early promise (and Polydor's high expectations). Possibly The Jam had mopped up 'See-Saw' for B-side purposes in an attempt to keep the new album fresh and as full of as many brand-new songs as possible. Either way, it's largely forgettable and strangely out of kilter with other songs the band were delivering at the time.

FIVE

RISING SONS

ONCE again The Jam had been contractually committed to a new album and, although the quality of their songs was now vastly improving in the shape of 'Tube Station', 'Strange Town' and 'When You're Young', they still had a slight problem. Having spent most of the year touring *All Mod Cons* in the States and Europe (including the UK), by the time the studio dates were booked The Jam had no new songs at all, apart from the impressive demo of 'The Eton Rifles' that Paul had produced in the summer. The band therefore conceived, wrote and recorded the entire fourth album only once they arrived at the studio. This meant working under immense pressure and delivering songs from start to finish at an incredible pace. 'But by then we had the luxury of being able to afford studio time,' says Buckler. 'Although it meant we spent longer in there, and costs naturally increased accordingly, it was far better than rehearsing our ideas at home.'

With deadlines geared to the Christmas market looming, The Jam once again had to deliver and their lack of new material this time was obvious. There would be just ten tracks on the album, and only seven of those were new – but what a fantastic set of songs. They epitomise the powerful Jam sound between 1978 and 1980, which for many was their finest period.

SETTING SONS

GIRL ON THE PHONE (Weller)
Recorded on 8 October 1979 at The Townhouse Studios, Shepherd's Bush, London
Produced by Vic Coppersmith-Heaven
Album track: Setting Sons

Flushed with the success of 'The Eton Rifles', The Jam embarked on a two-month, 29-date national tour to promote their upcoming album, *Setting Sons*. They started in typical fashion with one of the worst kept secrets of the year. As a warm-up to their Setting Sons Tour, The Jam adopted a pseudonym for a small (by their standards) gig at The Marquee Club in Soho's Wardour Street. Under the pseudonym of John's Boys (a slight variation on Marc Bolan's 1960s psychedelic band, John's Children), they were due to appear again the following night at The Nashville billed as the even less imaginative Eton Rifles. Both venues were regular haunts of The Jam during 1977.

Unsurprisingly, word got out and for every fan inside each venue there must have been three more locked outside. At The Marquee Club a near-riot ensued as skinheads charged the doors in an attempt to get at the mods inside; having failed, they then turned on the mods outside instead. Wardour Street ended up resembling a war zone not unlike Weller's descriptive "'A' Bomb in Wardour Street'. When the tour proper got under way, an army of parka-clad fans followed The Jam up and down the land.

'Girl On The Phone', the opening track on *Setting Sons*, was conceived and written in the studio as The Jam struggled to create songs for the new album. It illustrates Weller's increasing discomfort regarding the interest in him, echoing the stalker experience which led to his leaving London and returning home to Woking the previous year. The song tells the story of an imaginary stalker who has taken a disturbing interest in the writer. It also aims a veiled broadside at the press, who increasingly claimed to know all about Paul but who often misinterpreted his sentiments. The voice of the stalker dubbed in by Coppersmith-Heaven at the end of the track is that of a French student who was working on reception at The Townhouse Studio during the summer of 1979.

Paul explained to author John Reed, in his book *My Ever Changing Moods*: 'It's about anyone who tries to sum you up, they think they know what you're about, and they know bits and pieces, but no one knows what I am about because I don't know myself.' Paul was terrified of losing both his perspective and ambition, becoming obsessed with the fear of failure during 1979. He knew that the more successful The Jam became, the further the character he created in 'To Be Someone' had to fall. Paul was determined not to start believing in the hype building up around him.

The Jam opened their set with 'Girl On The Phone' at The Rainbow Theatre on 4 December 1979, a performance recorded and broadcast live by The BBC as part of their *In Concert* series. It was also the first song played at the secret John's Boys gig at the Marquee Club in November. Gary Crowley, writing a John's Boys review in the *NME* on 10 November, commented: 'Paul has developed into an excellent songwriter, laying down statements and views with poetic, cynical and amusing insight.' Clearly the humour of the band hadn't been lost on everyone.

THICK AS THIEVES (Weller)

Recorded on 5 September 1979 at The Townhouse Studios, Shepherd's Bush, London
Produced by Vic Coppersmith-Heaven
Album track: Setting Sons

Originally *Setting Sons* was to be a concept album, focusing on three young men who grew up together as friends and whose lives are then disrupted by war. The tracks on the album were originally meant to provide snapshots of the three at various stages of their lives. As they grew up, embattled and embittered, all three characters would radically change their views of the world they live in. Ideologically they would drift apart, one becoming a right-wing businessman ('Burning Sky'), another a radical left-wing revolutionary ('The Eton Rifles'), while the third, possibly Weller himself, viewed both with an outsider's muse, trying to understand both points of view.

It would be easy to assume that the three characters were loosely based on the three band members, who in fact were growing up themselves, and drifting apart too. By this time they no longer shared the 'all-for-one and one-for-all' mentality and, while they remained friendly (and lived and worked well together), each had developed his own circle of friends and rarely socialised with the others outside of band business, save for Christmas and birthdays.

In fact, the theme of the album, based on a short story by Dave Waller, is more likely to reflect Weller's relationship with Waller himself, a radical left-wing thinker and poet, and Steve Brookes, who by now was a successful businessman with a thriving guitar shop. At Sheerwater School the three had been classmates and best pals, and their changing relationship is portrayed in 'Thick As Thieves'.

The song is a detailed story of close friendships, sharing a sentiment with 'I Got By In Time' on the band's debut album *In The City*. Weller describes a long-standing friendship crumbling around him for reasons he can only attribute to growing up.

'Thick As Thieves' was described in an album review by Tony Stewart, writing in the *NME*, as 'possibly the best song Weller has *ever* written and the key to the album's theme'. It was certainly the first of only five songs on the album to fit the original concept ('Little Boy Soldiers', 'Wasteland', 'Burning Sky' and 'The Eton Rifles' are the others). As time and money ran out, Weller reverted to his Ray Davies-style observation of English street life ('Private Hell' and 'Saturday's Kids') to create enough songs to complete the album.

PRIVATE HELL (Weller)

Recorded on 10 October 1979 at The Townhouse Studios, Shepherd's Bush, London
Produced by Vic Coppersmith-Heaven
Album track: Setting Sons

As Paul looked around for inspiration, he stumbled upon an interview in a 1966 edition of *Record Mirror* with Eddie Phillips, guitarist in the mod band The Creation. Phillips was a highly respected songwriter and innovative guitarist (he was the first to play using a violin bow), and at one time had turned down Pete Townshend's offer to join The Who. During the interview Phillips revealed the titles of two new songs (which were never released by The Creation): 'Private Hell' (which became the Weller song's title) and 'Closer Than Close' (which became the opening line). Weller put down the paper, wrote both titles down and immediately penned a grim tale of middle-aged female depression, impressively perceptive for a 21-year-old man.

'Private Hell' is the easily identifiable tale of an urban housewife whose life is passing by unnoticed by anybody, herself included, and alludes to Siouxsie and The Banshees' 'Suburban Relapse', which appeared on their 1978 album *The Scream* and described a mid-life nervous breakdown. In 'Private Hell' Weller somehow adopts the persona of a middle-aged English lady and describes her daily desperation as she realises that, with her children grown and flown, her own life has become irrelevant and her identity almost erased. Echoing loveless marriages all over the world, Paul describes her fat, balding husband, who takes no interest in her, and how she witnesses her looks fading in the bedroom mirror. Using Ray Davies' style of personalising his characters, Paul gives her children first names, Emma and Edward. Emma has married Terry and now has her own family, while Edward is away at college, leaving a vacuum which she fills with valium as she drifts aimlessly through each day, peering at herself in shop windows and using her fingers to try and smooth out the lines appearing on her face.

It is a stunning portrayal of mundanity, which Weller conceded didn't fit into the overall theme of the album but nevertheless regarded as an important song that 'just needed to be written'. Even so, the songs that fail to fit the concept idea still share a vein of sarcasm and provide a contrasting vision of the class system that Weller was so vocally opposed to and felt was obviously out of date.

Musically 'Private Hell' is driven by a powerful bass line and drum part, which the band decided to open the track with after seeing Joy Division start one of their songs on a television show in a similar way. ('Yeah, we sort of nicked that bit,' Weller later admitted.) The thundering rhythm section underlies Weller's cutting and sometimes wayward Rickenbacker, but Weller and Foxton cleverly combine their instruments, Paul sometimes playing an ascending lead while Bruce plays a descending bass line and vice versa. As musicians, the band were developing very quickly but were becoming frustrated by the drawn-out sessions arising from producer Vic Coppersmith-Heaven's relaxed nature and slow recording pace. He sometimes laboured over details for far longer than the snappy, edgy personalities of the band members could tolerate. The days at The Townhouse Studios that summer were long and uncomfortable.

'Private Hell' is one of those album tracks that could easily have provided the band with a hit single. Punchy, fast and a classic Jam sound, it was always popular in the live set, featuring for the only time on radio in The BBC's *In Concert* recording on 4 December 1979. 'Private Hell' also appears on the 2002 'best of' collection, *The Sound Of The Jam*, providing evidence of its continued popularity.

LITTLE BOY SOLDIERS (Weller)

Recorded on 20 August 1979 at The Townhouse Studios, Shepherd's Bush, London
Produced by Vic Coppersmith-Heaven
Album track: Setting Sons

'Little Boy Soldiers' is the second of the themed tracks on *Setting Sons*, being an anti-war song in the same vein as 'The Eton Rifles'. In its lyric, Weller (once again with tongue firmly in cheek) resigns himself to the futility of protest, adding a chilling sense of empathy with the young Englishmen sent to create the British Empire by killing the inhabitants of faraway lands in the name of Queen and country.

'We are not supplying answers,' Weller later said. 'We are not even asking questions. I'm just stating what I feel at the time and I'm not coming out with my theories on world politics because I don't think it is very important. I am not a spokesperson or anything like that. I just sit in front of the television moaning on about world politics, saying "Look at these bastards."' Weller regarded himself only as an 'armchair radical' who ranted and raved but found that after a few pints he would cheer up anyway. 'It's a lazy attitude' he said at the time, 'but in another sense it's a realistic one. There might be all this stuff going on in the world and nuclear threats but as long as I have enough for a pint I can tolerate it.' That was Weller's basic philosophy.

'Little Boy Soldiers' reflects Weller's Orwellian patriotism, returning to the 'class war' once again by providing images of the establishment using the working class as human fodder for empire building. In many ways the theme mirrors that of 'Smithers-Jones', where Foxton created an image of dispensable corporate fodder rather than military fodder. Musically the song is ambitious, being made up of five separate parts that could easily have been five entirely different songs, until a sweeping drum roll returns the track to part two for the finale. And Foxton displays his musical dexterity by appearing on cello in some sections.

Lyrically, 'Soldiers' attacks naïve patriotism in the shape of Kitchener's famous 'Your country needs you' recruitment drive during the First World War, condemning the use of young men to 'shoot at strangers' under the 'flag of democracy'. But Weller cleverly uses irony to make his point, casting himself as a willing participant, having swallowed the patriotic fervour hook line and sinker as millions of others had.

Like all The Jam's anti-establishment songs (apart from 'The Eton Rifles', but as a number three hit single the corporation had no choice over that), 'Soldiers' never appeared on any of the live sessions for The BBC despite being a firm favourite with the band's live audiences.

WASTELAND (Weller)

Recorded on 15 August 1979 at The Townhouse Studios, Shepherd's Bush, London
Produced by Vic Coppersmith-Heaven
Album track: Setting Sons

'Wasteland' was the third of the album's concept songs and the one in which the third friend (Weller) dreams of a time when the other two, the businessman and the revolutionary (Brookes and Waller), might join him. It is one of the highlights of the album. Written in the first person, the author suggests that the other two destroyed everything they once believed in through either revolution or commercialism, but now invites them back to join him in the rubble of what remains. All three are embittered by their experience and are perhaps longing for the simple days when they all joined hands in adolescent enthusiasm and agreed to 'rule the world' together.

Musically 'Wasteland' is one of the album's shining highs and follows the chopping, harsh 'Little Boy Soldiers' perfectly by slowing the album down and rounding off side one in a melodic, reflective way.

BURNING SKY (Weller)

Recorded on 5 September 1979 at The Townhouse Studios, Shepherd's Bush, London
Produced by Vic Coppersmith-Heaven
Album track: Setting Sons

'Burning Sky' is the third of the themed tracks on *Setting Sons* ('The Eton Rifles' was released as a single but appears after 'Burning Sky' on *Setting Sons*) and in the lyric Weller, writing in the first person again, adopts the persona of the idealist-turned-businessman writing back to his old revolutionary schoolfriend in an unintentionally patronising manner. The letter starts by enquiring how his friend is coping 'in his own little world' and apologising for not staying in touch – but as 'business is thriving' there is little time any more for wishful thinking and romantic visions of a better world. The letter writer remembers their youthful intentions but suggests he has grown up to fit into the real world around him, and that playground revolutionaries, such as the recipient, had better start doing the same, and the sooner the better for everybody.

Apparently the writer and the addressee have by now become polar opposites but are still able to understand each other's principles. The song, despite being written in the first person, is slightly disdainful of both parties, portraying its author as an arrogant businessman who appears to have 'sold out' and joined corporate England, and the revolutionary as a simple dreamer who needs to wake up and see the real world. Is this Weller imagining how Steve Brookes might write to Dave Waller?

Musically 'Burning Sky' is one of the most imaginative Jam songs to date, with a highly complicated bass line demonstrating Foxton's musical dexterity. The track appears in demo form on *Extras* with Weller going through the whole song on acoustic guitar. The contrast with the final recorded version is considerable and it's easy to see how a pretty good Weller song is converted into an exceptional Jam song by Bruce and Rick, who remember writing all their own bass and drum parts on most of the tracks the band recorded.

Songwriter Jimmy Edwards of The Neat Change and Masterswitch, who also worked with Sham 69 during their glory days, is quick to credit The Jam's rhythm section: 'It's very possible Paul would never have emerged at all without Bruce and Rick. There are many fine songwriters who don't get the credit they deserve but with that big sound Bruce and Rick laid down, it was impossible not to notice The Jam. No one else could have done it. There was no better rhythm section around as far as I'm concerned.'

'Burning Sky' was yet another fine Jam song that was only heard by those who bought *Setting Sons* and saw The Jam play live. It made one radio appearance on 4 December 1979 at The BBC's *In Concert* series broadcast from The Rainbow Theatre. A live version also appears on *Live Jam*, a collection of 24 performances released by Polydor during the 1990s.

SATURDAY'S KIDS (Weller)

Recorded on 15 August 1979 at The Townhouse Studios, Shepherd's Bush, London
Produced by Vic Coppersmith-Heaven
Album track: Setting Sons

'Saturday's Kids', described by Tony Stewart in the *NME* as a 'brilliant piece of reportage', could have reflected suburban teenage life in any English town. Paul Weller described it as a documentation of that time and revealed then that it was written about his old school friends in Woking, who 'still all go down my local pub.'

Opening with a harsh three-chord guitar riff complemented by a cow bell, which Buckler had lowered the tone of by wrapping it in gaffer tape, the song thunders into life with yet another powerful

Foxton bass line. Lyrically the track is a template for the soon-to-follow 'That's Entertainment' and utilises clever references to everyday life. The idea for the 'Saturday's Kids' lyric was conceived when Paul was experimenting with Dave Waller-style urban poetry as the two developed their publishing company, Riot Stories. The original lyric (almost unchanged) appears as one of Weller's 11 poems published in the back of the *All Mod Cons* songbook, published in 1978. A vivid account of Saturday afternoons in the local pub, waiting for the football results before doing a bit of shopping and getting ready to go out for the big night of the week, it's a classic observation of working-class life.

Paul's continued interest in poetry eventually led him to appear at the 'Poetry Olympics', held at London's Young Vic Theatre on 30 November 1981. It was a calculated decision by Weller as by then The Jam were superstars and his inclusion on the bill significantly raised the profile of the event. The Jam singer had long been dedicated to helping other artists and was at last able to use his profile to benefit others. In the event Weller shared the bill with Roger McGough, who was a Liverpool contemporary of one of Weller's favourite poets Adrian Henri (see 'Tonight At Noon'). The Poetry Olympics was Paul's first public appearance outside The Jam.

The opening chords of 'Saturday's Kids' are so distinctive that, just one beat in, fans would cheer as if a home team had scored the winner in injury time. They were first heard on John Peel's BBC radio show, broadcast on 5 November 1979, 11 days before *Setting Sons* was released. The Jam opened the Peel show with 'Thick As Thieves' followed by 'The Eton Rifles' (released two days earlier and not yet having charted). 'Saturday's Kids' was the third album track featured before the band rounded off the show with their previous single 'When You're Young', to ensure casual listeners would recognise at least one of the tracks and identify The Jam accordingly.

Despite being a firm live favourite, 'Saturday's Kids' never appeared on any live compilation, though a rough demo, recorded in London in July 1979, turns up on *Extras*. On it Paul sings lead and backing vocals, also contributing rudimentary guide bass guitar and drum parts which are nothing like the parts Bruce and Rick later recorded.

In November 1979 The Jam embarked on The Setting Sons Tour of the UK, for which they enlisted the help of Merton Parka Mick Talbot, who sat almost anonymously at the back of the stage playing keyboards on tracks such as 'The Eton Rifles' and 'Heatwave'. The tour kicked off on the 17th in Aylesbury and the band were supported by another act local to Woking, The Vapors.

During a break between The Jam's European tour in February and their third visit to America in April, Bruce Foxton had indulged in regular Thursday boys' nights out in and around Guildford with his old mates. Bruce was by then living in Brookwood, directly opposite the station, which is part-way between Woking and Guildford. On one of these occasions he happened upon a pub in Godalming known as Scratchers, which was well known for having band nights. On stage playing their first gig, having formed only weeks earlier, were The Vapors.

The Guildford-based band were playing a set they claimed to have written in only two days (which later would largely make up their debut album, *New Clear Days*, produced by Vic Coppersmith-Heaven). Foxton was genuinely impressed and, when given a copy of their demo tape, he agreed to play it to The Jam's manager John Weller. The two of them quickly offered The Vapors a joint management deal which in turn led to a record deal. In a matter of months The Vapors had an album on the way and found themselves supporting one of the country's biggest groups on a national tour.

Things happened quickly for The Vapors, who proved so popular on the tour that by February 1980 they had equalled The Jam with a number three UK hit single ('Turning Japanese'), even eclipsing them by taking it to number one in other parts of the world. Within a few short months they were embarking on their own UK and US tours and the single-minded Weller was not impressed. In typical fashion Weller (not unnaturally) demanded his father's sole attention and insisted John choose between The Jam or The Vapors. This proved an easy choice for Weller Sr. As it was, The Vapors failed to follow up their initial success and began fading from view before self-destructing in August 1981, the result of personal differences rather than the absence of the Foxton/Weller management team.

For The Jam, however, the November tour was a huge success and, swelled by an ever-growing audience, each venue was packed to the rafters. Having become well known for allowing fans into the afternoon sound check, the Setting Sons Tour was characterised by growing numbers milling around at the stage door as the band arrived in the afternoon. It became common to have as many as 500 people present during the sound checks. But this was yet another natural tie with their fans that the band had to relinquish eventually as the situation rapidly got out of control. Rick Buckler remembers that, although the band were happy to keep allowing fans into the sound checks for free, venue security would later find them hidden in all sorts of darkened corners, whether lurking behind curtains or locked in toilet cubicles. The aim was to stay undetected until the doors opened, whereupon they could emerge and blend into the crowd.

HEATWAVE (Holland/Dozier/Holland)
Recorded on 10 October 1979 at The Townhouse Studios, Shepherd's Bush, London
Produced by Vic Coppersmith-Heaven
Album track: Setting Sons

Towards the end of the recording sessions at The Townhouse Studios, The Jam (having been contracted to an album of a minimum length) only had one original idea left. In September the band had demoed an experimental track called 'Hey Mister', which later appeared on the album *Extras* in 1992. But having decided it simply didn't work on the album (some felt it was bad enough not to fit on any album), Paul, Bruce and Rick once again looked to their live set for a cover to include. The classic Martha and The Vandellas' hit '(Love Is Like A) Heatwave' had been covered by The Who in the sessions for their first album, and had been popular in The Jam's set since the early days at Michael's Club. The band often re-introduced the song on tour, despite their ever-growing catalogue of original material.

At times Weller had been unhappy with the sound of The Jam's studio albums, feeling that a lot of the raw live feel to the music had been engineered out, but once it had been agreed to include 'Heatwave' (a song that mirrored none of the sentiments of the other album tracks), Weller was determined to record it as he felt it should be, and that was live. On 10 October The Jam called in Merton Parka Mick Talbot and saxophonist Rudi from X Ray Spex and invited them to play on a 'live' version.

The five musicians lined up in the studio and, after a short rehearsal, recorded 'Heatwave' in just a few takes, each playing his instrument simultaneously. After a small amount of smoothing out by producer Vic Coppersmith-Heaven the track was ready, essentially done in one take and the live feel captured. The only other song recorded that day, the last of the sessions, was 'Private Hell'. Given the thought that went into the other songs on the album 'Heatwave' is an unusual inclusion and only serves to underline the pressure the band were under to produce a new album.

The *Setting Sons* package was illustrated with images of the world wars and memorialised patriotism in a fashion totally alien to punk. On the front cover is a picture of a Benjamin Clemens bronze entitled The St John's Ambulance Bearers, which can be found at London's Imperial War Museum, having been presented by the British Red Cross in 1919. The reference to the ambulance bearers is imaginative considering that organisation's classless origins. The photo was taken, incidentally, by Andrew Douglas, who went on to direct award-winning adverts for United Airlines, Nike and Adidas.

Polydor art director Bill Smith explains: 'The picture we used was a little softer than a black-and-white photograph and a bit more romantic. We also embossed it on the original pressings to add a little bite. There is also wry humour behind those images – the idea of the beach scene was supposed to be lighthearted.' The rear sleeve carries ironic English images of a bulldog sitting on a beach in foul weather, next to a Union Jack deck chair.

Due to time constraints the sleeve was printed up before the band had enough songs for the album. As a result, a track list was left off the original print run and a sticker manually added to each copy once the order of songs had been decided. This means that owners of the original release have a very rare copy indeed, and no doubt there are hundreds of fans now wishing they hadn't peeled the sticker off and stuck it on their scooters. The album sleeve won a Q magazine award in 2001 as one of the '100 Best Record Covers Of All Time', the only Jam album to feature on the list.

Setting Sons, which had been previewed by the number three hit single 'The Eton Rifles', also arrived in the charts at number three, eclipsing the previous success of *All Mod Cons* and establishing The Jam as one of the most popular bands of the late 1970s. They also won the Best Album, Best Group and Best Songwriter categories at the 1979 *NME* Readers' Awards.

In the space of 12 months The Jam had responded to the cancelled studio sessions in style, with two Top Ten long players both voted album of the year by *NME* readers. That coveted number one hit single still eluded them, however. But not for much longer.

GOING UNDERGROUND (Weller)

Recorded in January 1980 at The Townhouse Studios, Shepherd's Bush, London
Produced by Vic Coppersmith-Heaven
Double A-side released 7 March 1980; Polydor POSPJ 113; reached no 1 in UK chart
Double A-side: 'The Dreams Of Children'
B-side: 'Away From The Numbers', 'The Modern World', 'Down In The Tube Station At Midnight'

In February 1980 The Jam played four low-key warm-up gigs in Cambridge, Canterbury, Malvern and finally at The Woking YMCA (the latter a benefit gig for that organisation). As most of their equipment had been shipped off to America for the tour that was due to begin a week later, The Jam turned to Steve Brookes, who happily agreed to supply a free PA for their YMCA appearance.

All three band members still lived around the town and would continue to appear in local pubs or make unpaid appearances at school fetes and other local functions. The previous summer, Paul, Bruce and Rick had even turned up bleary-eyed one Saturday morning to present the prizes at the Old Woking Primary School, later retiring to The Kingfield Arms pub outside the gates, where they discussed their in-production album, *Setting Sons*, with a gathering of schoolboys. The band at that point were still describing it as a concept album and explained the theme in the public bar while the landlord turned a blind eye to the underage drinkers that made up their audience.

The following week the band set out on their fourth tour of America and, buoyed by the commercial success of 'The Eton Rifles' and *Setting Sons* in the UK, they found their American fan base also increasing to the point where they were now able to sell out the 3000-capacity New York Palladium. Despite a positive start, the trip once again proved a sour one as Polydor's US arm clashed with the band by releasing the unsuitable 'Heatwave' as a single in an attempt to win over an even larger American audience.

After yet another arduous month travelling around the States, the band had just finished a gig in Austin, Texas on 22 March when they received a late-night Trans-Atlantic phone call during the after-show drinks party at their hotel. By then it was already Sunday morning in England and the UK charts had been published. The message was that 'Going Underground' had entered at number one, and the party accordingly switched into high gear. The following morning, through a haze of hangovers, the band were facing a week off before picking up the tour for the final leg starting in New Jersey the following Friday.

But the band members had other ideas. Collectively the decision was taken (in under a minute, apparently) that The Jam would pack their bags and return home to England in order to perform 'Going Underground' on *Top Of The Pops*, which was recorded on Wednesday afternoons. They could have gone back to America in time to complete the tour but they had already had enough. Their fourth US tour was over and Britain's biggest band were staying at home.

When The Jam performed 'Going Underground' on *Top Of The Pops* they were sans Rickenbacker, probably because their kit was still in the process of being shipped home. Foxton, in any case, was now

creating his sound by using a Fender Precision Bass. Weller decided to demonstrate his growing interest in pop art by wearing a kitchen apron bearing a Heinz Tomato Soup logo (which he later referred to in the sleeve notes of *Dig The New Breed,* the band's final album), although this move unnerved the BBC, who were very strict about product endorsement. Weller had only been using it as a reference to the pop art cover of The Who album *The Who Sell Out*, which features Roger Daltrey holding a giant can of Heinz baked beans. But Weller was only joking, and mocking what he expected the reaction in some parts of the music press would be to his band's long awaited success: 'Number One single – have The Jam sold out?'

In the event The BBC refused to allow Paul to wear the apron, although Weller characteristically agreed only to turn it round and wear it back to front. But with the studio lights blazing the apron became virtually transparent and viewers could clearly see the logo, which meant Weller had effectively got his way. But he wasn't happy with what he perceived as Establishment bullies laying the law down so when the time came for the performance (which was mimed), Weller minced about and deliberately got his words wrong. Another typically humorous gesture from a man publicly becoming known as 'Old Misery Guts', after being labelled that by *Smash Hits* magazine. Paul was largely unaffected by this tag, even playing up to it by introducing a flexi disc, given away by *Smash Hits*, with the words, 'Hello, this is Paul Weller speaking, but don't let that stop you enjoying yourselves.'

Driven once again by Foxton's bass line, 'Going Underground' tackles the growing nuclear threat, referring to the invasion of Afghanistan by Russia in December 1979. Again written in the first person, Weller portrays himself as the proletariat instructed by the establishment to support their wishes (presumably by increasing taxes) and meekly towing the line.

In 2002, 22 years after The Jam released 'Going Underground', Paul Weller gave Virgin Radio's breakfast DJ Daryl Denham permission to rewrite the lyrics to his number one hit. The song was released as 'Go England' just prior to the 2002 World Cup campaign.

THE DREAMS OF CHILDREN (Weller)
Recorded in January 1980 at The Townhouse Studios, Shepherd's Bush, London
Produced by Vic Coppersmith-Heaven
Double A-side released 7 March 1980; Polydor POSPJ 113; reached no 1
in UK chart
Double A-side: 'Going Underground'
B-side: 'Away From The Numbers', 'The Modern World', 'Down In The Tube
Station At Midnight'

After the band had listened to the playback *of Setting Sons* (during
October 1979), Weller asked producer Coppersmith-Heaven to play
the entire album to him backwards. Backwards guitar had been a
technique Weller was interested in experimenting with since
listening to the mid-1960s psychedelic productions of Pink Floyd,
and in particular their lost guitar genius Syd Barrett. Weller
explained: 'There was this one little bit, a backwards guitar and
backwards vocal from part of 'Thick As Thieves' that I liked. 'The
Dreams Of Children' came from that and I more or less wrote it on
the spot.' The same part looping through the song creates the
psychedelic effect Paul was looking for.

The title 'The Dreams Of Children' had been inspired by Liverpool
writer Clive Barker's 1972 horror story *The Forbidden*, based on the
Faust Myth, in which The Candyman kills to preserve his reputation,
so he can still haunt the 'dreams of children'. Weller's lyric, however,
is only loosely based on that theme but does allude to disrupted
dreams.

The band members originally intended 'The Dreams Of Children'
to be a single, changing their direction once again after the power
trio of 'Strange Town', 'When You're Young' and 'The Eton Rifles'.
However, yet another minor printing error in France saw an A also
being placed next to the intended B-side 'Going Underground'. So
the disc accidentally became a double A-side and radio producers
concentrated on 'Going Underground', which carried what they
regarded as the traditional Jam power sound.

In many respects this was a pity, as Polydor were at last fully
behind The Jam and, capitalising on their ever-growing fan base,

deliberately delayed the single's release by a full week. This left fans clutching sales receipts after being forced to pre-order rather than collect and effectively gave the song an extra week of sales. When the disc finally arrived in the shops, a massive 200,000 were picked up, guaranteeing the band a number one hit, regardless of whether it was 'Going Underground' or 'The Dreams Of Children' on the A-side.

The record label also cleverly delivered the single to its national distributor in tranches, each large enough to ensure enough sales to keep it in the number one slot for three weeks running. That was the longest time any band had been at number one that year and was only bettered in October when The Police spent four weeks at the top with 'Don't Stand So Close To Me'. It was also the first time any band had entered the chart at number one since Slade's 'Merry Xmas Everybody' in 1973, and The Jam were confirmed as Britain's favourite band.

Capitalising on Jam hysteria, Polydor immediately re-released each of their previous singles and, such was the demand, six of them even made it back into the charts simultaneously. ('In The City' – 40, 'All Around The World' – 43, 'Strange Town' – 44, 'The Modern World' – 52, 'News Of The World' – 53 and 'David Watts' – 54.) It was the biggest chart success any band had had since The Beatles. All this only four years after the teenage Weller, Foxton and Buckler were performing Beatles covers in working men's Clubs and dreaming of a record deal.

In 1992 'The Dreams Of Children' became The Jam's first posthumous single, supported by live versions of 'Away From The Numbers' and 'The Modern World' on the flip, in order to promote the album *Extras*.

The summer of 1980 was quiet for The Jam, with the entire set-up taking a holiday and a break from band business. Since they had cut short the US tour the band had only had a smattering of live dates. Firstly there were two shows in early April at The Rainbow Theatre on London's Seven Sisters Road, which formed part of that venue's 50th anniversary celebrations. The Rainbow had by now become a Jam stronghold and thousands were locked out as fans, new and old, came to welcome the group back to the UK and hear 'Going Underground' played live. Ten days later the band played a hastily arranged gig at the Guildford Civic Hall, The Jam's home venue, and once again Guildford ground to a halt as the three local lads, still only in their early twenties, arrived in town to a heroes' welcome. The band then spent the next few months playing various festivals in Holland, France and Scotland, the latter becoming a mud bath characterised only by the violence that broke out. It was during this time that a handful of new songs were introduced, among them 'Pretty Green' and 'Start!'.

On 1 July The Jam departed for the first time to Japan, a country where they achieved almost instant success and are still idolised to this day. Each of their singles had been released in Japan and had been hugely successful. The land of the Rising Sun had provided the band with their biggest market outside Britain and the public there had waited a long time to experience The Jam's live sound.

Although the band members were just as fond of their Japanese public, they initially found that some cultural issues needed explaining. For a start, the Japanese audience considered it an insult to make a noise of any kind while a performer was on stage. On the face of it this seems reasonable enough when applied to media like theatre, opera and classical recitals. But for The Jam to be playing their 100mph brand of music to a sea of immobile faces (only breaking ranks at the end of each song to applaud and cheer and then return to absolute silence as the next song started) was disconcerting to say the least. 'I should be used to it by now,' Paul said in 1994, 'but it's hard to thrash away on guitar all night without getting any feedback. You think they don't like you, but they do really.'

But the band took it as the compliment it was meant to be and the tour, in stark contrast to America, was a complete success. After a one-day stopover for an ABC television performance in Los Angeles, The Jam made for home and the Guildford Civic Hall. But not before another row had broken out, once again with their record label Polydor. While the band were in Japan, Polydor executives had taken the decision to release 'Pretty Green' as The Jam's follow-up single to 'Going Underground', a hard act to follow for any song. But Weller

wasn't happy as he wanted 'Start!' (at that time entitled 'Two Minutes') to be the next single.

During the inevitable heated argument and ensuing stand-off Polydor hedged their bets and arranged for two separate sleeves to be designed and submitted to the printers so that the decision could be left to the last possible moment. But with his star firmly in the ascendant, Paul refused to give way and Polydor had to concede. 'Start!' was agreed on as the band's follow-up to 'Going Underground' and Paul was vindicated in August when the song gave the group their second consecutive number one hit.

START! (Weller)

Recorded in June 1980 at The Townhouse Studios, Shepherd's Bush, London
Produced by Vic Coppersmith-Heaven and The Jam
A-side released 23 August 1980; Polydor 2059 266; reached no 1 in UK chart
B-side: 'Liza Radley'

'Start!' has long been regarded as a song about short relationships, possibly even one-night stands. This could not be further from the truth. For that we have to travel to Spain, Barcelona to be exact, and to the Spanish Civil War (1936-39).

During the late 1970s Weller had been reading at a frenetic pace and one of his favourite authors, as previously noted, was George Orwell. In 1938 Orwell published *Homage to Catalonia*, which described his experiences in Barcelona as he joined the fight against fascism during Spain's civil war. In the first few chapters Orwell describes arriving in Barcelona for the first time and seeing his own vision of democratic socialism at work, which was an ideal the writer felt well worth fighting for. Weller instantly related to this: 'There is lots of talk of an 'egalitarian society' where all people are equal but this was it, actually in existence, which for me is something that is very hard to imagine, even though it was for a short time.'

Orwell goes on to describe how like-minded people travelled from all over the world with the same ideals as the writer himself. They could barely communicate with each other but all instinctively embraced this new socialist ideal and fought together to preserve it. And that, in a nutshell, is the story behind 'Start!'. This time Weller's adaptation of an Orwell story has improved along with his song-writing technique, and 'Start!' is far more astute than the rampaging 'Standards' from 1977.

If 'The Dreams Of Children' had been meant to divert the band away from their power trio of singles, then 'Start!' proposed an even more radical change of direction. Musically much has been made of the song's similarity to The Beatles' 'Taxman'. It's hard to deny that the first few notes of the bass line are extremely similar but Weller shrugs off the likeness. 'People weren't meant not to notice,' he said. 'If anything there is a little tribute in there but after the first few notes the bass line is very different to 'Taxman'.' Lyrically and melodically 'Start!' is completely different to George Harrison's opening track on *Revolver*.

Thanks to yet another pressing mistake in France, there are some very rare copies of 'Start!' in the UK which have The Village People's 'Can't Stop The Music' playing on the A-side instead of The Jam's number one classic. A similar problem led to some Dutch copies playing The Original Mirrors' 'Boys Don't Cry' on the A-side.

The Jam played 'Start!' during the BBC's *In Concert* series from the Hippodrome in Golders Green on 19 December 1981. The track was covered by the Beastie Boys for the Jam tribute album *Fire And Skill*.

LIZA RADLEY (Weller)
Recorded in June 1980 at The Townhouse Studios, Shepherd's Bush, London
Produced by Vic Coppersmith-Heaven and The Jam
B-side to 'Start!'

'Liza Radley' is another of Paul Weller's 'named' character songs. 'It is just a piece of nonsense really,' said Weller. 'Just me playing around being psychedelic, English and whimsical. Just images plucked out of nowhere.' Rick Buckler claims to have contributed a verse (the only lyrical contribution Rick made to any of the songs) but says he 'cannot remember which part'. A demo of 'Liza Radley' appears on *Extras*, less delicate than the final version and without the echoed vocal and soft bass line, which mirrors that of 'Start!'. Nor does it contain Bruce Foxton's subtle and imaginative contributions on accordion.

'Liza Radley' was played live but does appear on *The Sound of The Jam*, the 2002 hit compilation album. The song also appeared on *The Very Best Of The Jam*, which was the first time it had been released in its complete form since appearing as the B-side to 'Start!' in August 1980. The track must have been a major surprise to many fans who had not bought the single at the time.

Shortly after the release of the 'Start!'/'Liza Radley' single, *Melody Maker* came up with the idea of introducing Paul Weller to his musical hero Pete Townshend at The Who's offices in Soho. The idea was to send along a reporter to cover the meeting in the hope the encounter would make for good copy. Initially Weller was enthusiastic. Despite being the man of the moment, with two number one hit singles to his name, he had long cited Townshend as a major influence and felt a strange affinity to the guitarist. But at the meeting the two found they had little in common. In late 1980 Townshend was 36 years old, Weller 22 and, as their backgrounds were entirely different, their characters clashed.

Weller was brash and confrontational. 'If you lot [ie, The Who] want to carry on then change your set,' he told the guitar legend. Townshend, by contrast, was reflective and thoughtful. 'Paul Weller is a hero,' he later wrote, 'a British hero. There is no bitterness in his writing that isn't fully shared by his fans.' During the meeting they discussed politics, America and their musical influences, but Weller emerged unimpressed by the encounter. 'I disagreed with him about a lot of things,' he later said.

Melody Maker front-paged with the encounter but in fact the article was a disappointment and the transcript uninteresting. The music paper also managed to misunderstand Paul completely, running the article with the headline *The Punk And The Godfather*. But there was no punk and no godfather. No wonder Paul was continually at odds with the music press, given the tags and labels they had imposed on him throughout his career.

SIX

BOYS ABOUT TOWN

IN 1996 Paul was asked if he had a favourite teacher, to which he replied, 'Yeah – I had four of them, The Beatles.' Musically he drew inspiration from other guitarists like Pete Townshend and Wilko Johnson, but also added his contemporaries, The Sex Pistols and The Clash, into the equation.

By the time The Jam's second album was being written Weller had discovered literature in the shape of George Orwell and Ken Kesey, and their influence, particularly Orwell's, remained with him throughout the next three albums. Weller was able to trace Orwell's own influences back to Karl Marx, whose early vision of Democratic Socialism was one that both Orwell and Weller related to strongly.

SOUND AFFECTS

PRETTY GREEN (Weller)

Recorded in September 1980 at the Townhouse Studios, Shepherd's Bush, London
Produced by Vic Coppersmith-Heaven and The Jam
Album track: Sound Affects

Lyrically 'Pretty Green', the opening track on The Jam's fifth album *Sound Affects*, is a powerful strike at conservative capitalism and its obsession with money, especially during the song's middle-eight section, in which Paul suggests that the only real way power is measured by the 'pound or the fist'. A Marxist sentiment if ever there was one. But like Marx and Orwell, Weller identified with peaceful protest rather than violent confrontation.

The song's title relates to the pound note, which in 1980 (prior to the pound coin being introduced) was a paper note not unlike today's fiver, only green. In anatomising the dawn of Thatcherism and Britain's obsession with money, the song all but predicts the transformation of the working classes into council house-owning, microwave-using, satellite dish-displaying middle Englanders. The message in the song is clear. If you don't have any money you'd better make sure you get hold of some as this Government won't be looking out for you otherwise.

Musically 'Pretty Green' opens up with an instantly recognisable one-note bass line, the song having evolved from a Jam session Bruce and Rick were having in the studio, which Paul joined later and wrote a simple but effective set of lyrics for. As a 13-year-old schoolboy, radio presenter Peter Gordon understood the sentiment of 'Pretty Green' perfectly. Gordon: "Pretty Green' is very much a song which stated facts rather than provided answers. As always it is the truth in what Weller says that hits home. You either have to be strong or made of money to make it in this world and, while offering no solutions, Weller makes it clear that this is a situation he certainly does not condone.'

'Pretty Green' is one of the strongest tracks on the *Sound Affects* album, with a thundering base line, good precision drumming (helped by the use of echo) and stinging guitar. Polydor had initially wanted 'Pretty Green' to be a single and even went as far as having sleeve artwork made up, but Weller wanted 'Start!' to be the band's follow-up to 'Going Underground'. Consequently the song's only radio appearance was during The Jam's *In Concert* performance, broadcast by The BBC from the Golders Green Hippodrome on 19 December 1981. 'Pretty Green' is also included on the 2002 album *The Sound Of The Jam*.

MONDAY (Weller)

Recorded in September 1980 at the Townhouse Studios, Shepherd's Bush, London
Produced by Vic Coppersmith-Heaven and The Jam
Album track: Sound Affects

'Monday' is a wistful, psychedelic tune in the tradition of the Syd Barrett-influenced 'The Dreams Of Children' and 'Liza Radley'. Its lyric deals with self-doubt, shyness and a stormy relationship and is transparently autobiographical. Weller: 'The songs on *Setting Sons* are more like complete short stories. Whereas [the ones on] *Sound Affects* are based more on my own thoughts at the time.'

Certain evocative lyrics reveal Weller intent on expressing himself openly and insisting that love is nothing to be embarrassed about. It's a radical assertion given that very few 22-year-olds would admit such an emotion, especially to their friends. But the so-called hard man of pop was doing just that. The song itself ambles along, underpinned by a gently inventive bass line high in the mix. Echoed backing vocals, meanwhile, provide a haunting feel as Paul delivers an almost monotone lead vocal, contrasting with his trebly Rickenbacker.

By late 1980, and with everything going their way, Paul, Bruce and Rick had begun to learn how to work the press in their favour. Some of this change of heart came simply from the fact that they were now hugely popular and treated with respect wherever they were invited. No longer regarded as arrogant punks, the band had achieved a crossover and were taken seriously by the media in all its forms.

Invitations flooded in from all quarters and many were accepted, including a live appearance on the Saturday morning cult television show *Tiswas*, hosted by a fresh-faced Chris Tarrant. On 15 November, during the Sound Affects Tour, the band returned to London to play four high-profile concerts prior to heading off to Europe, so fans were surprised to see The Jam make an unscheduled appearance on the cult TV show. They played 'Start!' and followed that up with a mock custard pie fight with members of Sad Café, something Weller would never have considered a few years earlier.

After the show the band retired to the studio bar and decided to order taxis to ferry them to the Rainbow Theatre in time for the sound check. As they emerged they discovered that fans, having realised *Tiswas* was always broadcast live, had surrounded the building. As the band made for the cars hundreds broke through the security cordon (which amounted to a couple of guards) and swarmed around the cars, shaking and rocking them, a frightening experience for everyone concerned.

Rick Buckler remembers similar incidents, one of which could have had disastrous consequences. 'We were making for the tour bus on one occasion and a fan leant over and grabbed Paul's neck scarf at precisely the same time as someone else opposite got hold of the other end,' he remembers. 'Paul ended up nearly being strangled but luckily some of the road crew saw what had happened and jumped to the rescue. That could have been nasty. I remember another occasion in Glasgow. We had been on tour for a while and I had to drop into the town centre to buy some things. I was wandering about and suddenly got the feeling I was being watched and turned around to find about 30 people following me. But none of them would say anything. They were just staring at me, which is a bit disconcerting when you're in Boots picking up your toiletries.'

Being such naturally down to earth individuals, Paul, Rick and Bruce were often taken by surprise by the attention they received. As the group generally worked all the time, either in the studio or on tour, they were often unaware of the build-up in interest in them both personally and as a band. On one occasion the tour bus rolled into a town and they drove past a queue of people stretching down the street, as far as the eye could see. To begin with they were all a little deflated and one even conjectured that The Rolling Stones or some other major act must be playing the same night. Of course, the monster queue turned out to be theirs.

BUT I'M DIFFERENT NOW (Weller)

Recorded in September 1980 at the Townhouse Studios, Shepherd's Bush, London
Produced by Vic Coppersmith-Heaven and The Jam
Album track: Sound Affects

The first demo of 'But I'm Different Now' was recorded at the Stratford Place Studios in April 1980 and appears on the 1992 album *Extras*. That recording is obviously work in progress but Weller's guitar and vocal is virtually unchanged on the version later recorded for *Sound Affects*. The guide bass line Weller contributed is weak and Foxton later characteristically wrote his own parts, which would drive the song alongside Buckler's powerful drum performance. There are no drums on the demo; a tambourine taps out the percussion and Polydor studio engineer Pete Wilson contributes Hammond Organ.

Weller had spent much of April 1980 in the studio with Wilson. He was supposed to be demoing new material for *Sound Affects* but found himself unable to work properly without Foxton or Buckler, who were having a 'few days off'. During those sessions the only positive work towards the new album was on 'But I'm Different Now'; the rest of the time was used in other ways, Weller covering some of his own favourite songs with mixed results. Two Beatles track were recorded, a fantastic version of 'And Your Bird Can Sing', which later appeared on *Extras*, along with a lumpen copy of *Rain* which later turned up on disc five of the *Direction Creation Reaction* box set, released on 26 May 1997.

Paul was particularly pleased with the former. Weller: 'Yeah, that's a good one. In fact, we did loads of 1960s things at that time. We did a version of Sandie Shaw's 'Always Something There To Remind Me' and 'Stand By Me' with just me on guitar and bass and Pete Wilson on drums and organ. Those tapes have been lost, which might be a good thing really, because I can't remember how good they were.' He added, 'Whenever we weren't touring or making records I'd be demoing at Polydor. It felt like I was there all the time. The studio was in their old Stratford Place building, off Oxford Street. When we did those 60s tracks I was supposed to be demoing new songs for the *Sound Affects* album, but I only really had 'That's Entertainment' and a couple of others written. So Pete and I spent the rest of the time fucking about.'

As 1980 drew to a close *Sound Affects*, released on 28 November, was at number two in the UK album chart; ABBA's 'Super Trouper' had gone to number one on the 22nd and stayed there for nine weeks. To underline their popularity, The Jam dominated the *NME* Readers' Poll Awards by winning each of the ten categories they could be included in. Best single ('Going Underground'), best album (*Sound Affects*), best group, best male singer, best dressed LP (*Sound Affects*), most wonderful human being (Paul Weller) and best songwriter (Paul Weller), best bass guitarist, best drummer and best guitarist.

The band also won the best single category at the *Daily Mirror*
Rock and Pop Awards for 'Going Underground' – and unusually for
Paul, Bruce and Rick they actually attended. With a brass band
playing a 'hotel lobby' version of the hit single, the band made their
way up to collect the award from Dave Lee Travis. But on reaching
the stage, Bruce and Rick turned around to realise Paul had
disappeared without warning. Suitably embarrassed, Foxton and
Buckler were left to collect the award alone.

SET THE HOUSE ABLAZE (Weller)
Recorded in September 1980 at the Townhouse Studios, Shepherd's Bush, London
Produced by Vic Coppersmith-Heaven and The Jam
Album track: Sound Affects

For some people 'Set The House Ablaze' signalled the beginning of
the end of The Jam. In the lyric, Weller writes about having lost sight
of his ambition, which would appear to give credence to the idea.
But in fact the song comes in several parts, with the verses being an
anti-Fascist tirade mirroring George Orwell's pamphlet *The Lion and
the Unicorn*, published in 1941, and to a lesser extent his harrowing
novel *1984*. The Reichstag fire of 22 February 1933, widely regarded
as the catalyst for the rise of the Nazi party and its subsequent
domination of Europe, is reflected throughout the verses and chorus
of 'Set The House Ablaze', Weller's anti-neo Nazi rant.

The song's middle eight is borrowed from the theme of Geoffrey
Ashe's 1971 book *Camelot and the Vision of Albion*, a theme woven
throughout the album. Ashe suggested we had lost sight of our
purpose in life and that our material goals had been obscured by
spiritual goals that had clouded our perception, an idea Weller
repeats almost word for word in the lyric. He readily admitted
Ashe's influence on the album and added: 'There were also religious
overtones. On reflection the ideas and philosophies are quite
heady and hippyish, but that was just a phase I was going through
at the time.'

If, as a writer, Weller had been finding new socialist influences
in authors such as Orwell and Marx, then he was finding his

philosophical guidance from the likes of Geoffrey Ashe, who wrote extensively in the 1970s about the court of King Arthur. Towards the end of 'Set The House Ablaze' Weller uses oration inspired by the works of the early 19th century poet Percy Bysshe Shelley, extracts from whose poems *Call To Freedom* and *The Mask of Anarchy* appear printed on the rear sleeve of *Sound Affects*. This caused confusion among many Jam fans, who failed to connect Shelley's passive revolutionary references with the band. But Weller was only just discovering the poet and his real influence would show itself in The Jam's sixth and final album, *The Gift*.

Explaining 'Set The House Ablaze' in the *Sound Affects* songbook, Weller called for his young fans to 'stay alive and fresh', claiming that the last thing they should be 'at this time is closed minded'. 'Set The House Ablaze' was such a live favourite that a version of it recorded at the Hammersmith Palais on 14 December 1981 was included on the band's final album *Dig The New Breed*, which was intended to be a reflection of The Jam's live career.

THAT'S ENTERTAINMENT (Weller)

Recorded in September 1980 at the Townhouse Studios, Shepherd's Bush, London
Produced by Vic Coppersmith-Heaven and The Jam
Album track: Sound Affects
B-side: 'Down In The Tube Station At Midnight' (live)

'Coming home from the pub pissed and writing 'That's Entertainment' in ten minutes – Weller's finest song to date, hah!' is how Weller himself refers to the song in his sleeve notes for *Dig The New Breed*. 'That's Entertainment', by using candid language, creates a vista of the English way of life in 1980 and is widely regarded as Weller's finest attempt at articulating the society he is a part of and his day-to-day boredom with it.

But the lyric is apparently based on a poem called 'That's Entertainment' written by Paul Drew and submitted to Riot Stories for publication in their 1980 collection of poems *Mixed Up-Shook Up*. In 2003 Paul was asked on his official website if it was true 'that someone call Paul Drew wrote a poem, which the lyrics for 'That's Entertainment' are based on or am I completely mistaken?' Weller, unabashed by this suggestion of plagiarism, replied cheerfully: 'You are not mistaken at all!'

The visual image the lyric creates is used for the theme of the album cover, which is borrowed from a BBC Sound Effects album Paul found in the studio during the recording sessions. Weller simply substituted the small picture of each of the effects on the album with everyday urban images, many of which can be found in the 'That's Entertainment' lyric. The inner sleeve picture was taken at sunrise, an early morning Weller refers to in his *Dig The New Breed* sleeve notes.

Several demos of 'That's Entertainment' were recorded, one of which appears on the 1983 compilation album *Snap*, including a gentle drum part and experimental bass line, neither of which was used in the final version. The Jam also recorded a lively 'punk' version of 'That's Entertainment' which Buckler likened to the version Reef contributed to the tribute album *Fire And Skill* in 1999, but that effort has never been recovered. The final stripped-down version of 'That's Entertainment' has been described by some as Buckler's single biggest contribution to the art of drumming: knowing when not to drum and having the confidence not to.

When 'That's Entertainment' was initially released in Germany in 1981, The Jam were so popular in the UK that it sold enough copies on import alone, despite the release never being publicised in Britain, for it to reach number 21 in the UK charts. It went on to stay in the top 75 for a total of seven weeks.

'That's Entertainment' has remained popular, and synonymous with The Jam, for over 20 years and has been played live by many artists, the most recent being Busted, who performed it to massive cheers at the 2003 Prince's Trust Party In The Park concert in London's Hyde Park, broadcast live on national television.

DREAM TIME (Weller)
Recorded in September 1980 at the Townhouse Studios, Shepherd's Bush, London
Produced by Vic Coppersmith-Heaven and The Jam
Album track: Sound Affects

'Dream Time' is regarded by many as the best track on *Sound Affects*. Lyrically based around one of Weller's poems, the music was created by Bruce and Rick in the studio and then adapted to fit a melody Paul had in mind. It could easily have been a classic Jam single but, buried away on an album and never played during a radio session, the song is only known to the most ardent Jam fans. Surprisingly, too, 'Dream Time' has never appeared on any of the band's greatest hits compilations, which is a shame as it contains one of Buckler's best drum performances.

Written in the first person, Weller has his character once more on the run, despairing at modern-day pre-packaged lifestyles and trying to find a way out of the town he feels trapped in. Paul's character goes on to complain about whole lives being planned out by 'others', with even our love coming in frozen packs at the local supermarket.

MAN IN THE CORNER SHOP (Weller)
Recorded in September 1980 at the Townhouse Studios, Shepherd's Bush, London
Produced by Vic Coppersmith-Heaven and The Jam
Album track: Sound Affects

'Man In The Corner Shop' was debuted live on 14 February 1981, when The Jam played their first gig of the year, the first of three small warm-up gigs prior to setting off on a two-week tour of Europe to promote *Sound Affects*. In typical fashion the biggest band in Britain chose their hometown of Woking for all three gigs and made unannounced appearances at tiny venues around town. The gigs were billed as 'A special performance by The Jam's road crew'. But, needless to say, word went round town and each venue was packed with local fans who had been tipped off The Jam might actually be appearing instead. No one was disappointed.

The Cricketers in Woking is an ordinary pub and, although bands still play there to this day, all of them turn up to find there is no stage, no sound system and no lighting. They simply have to set their gear up in a small corner by the bar and get on with it. The Jam were no exception on Valentine's Night 1981. To avoid giving the game away too early, the band's road crew discreetly set up the band's equipment, leaving Paul, Bruce and Rick to turn up later for the impromptu performance. Unfortunately, violence erupted in the packed pub. Foxton: 'We had just finished playing and one of the girls watching picked a fight with my girlfriend Pat (now Mrs Foxton) and pulled a clump of her hair out. It was awful. All because she was my girlfriend. I only caught the tail end of it and my first reaction was to go for the girl's boyfriend. Well, I couldn't hit her, could I? But before I could get to him security jumped on me. After that it was just mayhem all round. Happy days.'

Two days later the group played a second benefit concert at the Woking YMCA (which raised nearly £1000 for the association), followed by a fund-raising gig at Sheerwater Youth Club, which regularly allowed the band to rehearse for free in their early days and even lent them the club minibus on occasion. The gigs were characteristic of Paul, Bruce and Rick's shunning of the superstar status they were afforded. Foxton: 'It was always only about the music for us, and being in touch with the audience. The more popular The Jam became the harder it was for us to do. But whenever we could we would go back and play tiny venues again, just for fun.'

These regular acts of benevolence have gone largely unnoticed by Woking's Borough Council. No reference to The Jam or any acknowledgement of their achievement can be found anywhere in the town. Even Woking's multi-million pound live music venue is inappropriately named The H G Wells Centre. Fans from all over the world regularly make the pilgrimage to Woking and find nothing of any interest apart from a few landmark venues such as Michael's Club, which is regularly photographed. (It is no longer a music venue, however, having had its license revoked in the late 1970s as a result of the amount of times the Police had to visit.)

Lyrically 'Man In The Corner Shop' cleverly illustrates the difference between small businesses and large ones. In the song, the owner of the local corner shop sells cigars to the boss of the nearby factory and wonders what it must be like to run such a large business. But, for his part, the factory boss is also wondering what it must be like to run his own business, even if it's only a small shop on the corner, hinting at the possibility that, for both of them, 'the grass is always greener...' In summary, Weller places both characters in church together on a Sunday, illustrating that we are all the same before God, whatever our job titles might indicate to others.

A clever song but never a particularly popular one, it was never played live at any of the BBC sessions. Nor has it appeared on any compilation album, though it does make an appearance as the sixteenth track on *The Jam Live*, a collection of their live performances.

MUSIC FOR THE LAST COUPLE (Weller/Foxton/Buckler)
Recorded in September 1980 at the Townhouse Studios, Shepherd's Bush, London
Produced by Vic Coppersmith-Heaven and The Jam
Album track: Sound Affects

'Music For The Last Couple' is one of many Jam songs that started out as a musical 'Jam' between the band members, but it is also the first one to be recognised as such. Following the success of *All Mod Cons* in 1978, The Jam would write virtually all their later songs while in the studio and record them almost immediately. As a result, many Jam songs were conceived from a musical idea Bruce and Rick were working on which Paul then joined in on, either writing lyrics to suit or re-working existing lyrics to fit the melody.

With some tracks on *Sound Affects* this technique is obvious. 'Pretty Green', 'Monday', 'Dream Time' and 'Scrape Away' are all examples, but all have Weller lyrics so became Weller songs. Buckler: 'Things like 'Pretty Green' grew out of Paul picking up on a rhythmic idea that Bruce and I were messing about with one day. Or else we'd experiment with some of Bruce's bass lines, to link sections for two

different songs which weren't quite working and turn them into one that did.' 'Music For The Last Couple', with only one line in the way of lyrics, is the only track with a joint writing credit. Weller explained in the *Sound Affects* songbook, published in 1980, that the band were in the studio playing around with 'this little lick' and the song developed from there.

As the *Sound Affects* sessions stumbled on, more friction between band and record label surfaced. The Jam had agreed to a UK tour starting on 26 October and running until the middle of December. Once again writing in the studio, the band felt they didn't have enough material to complete the album in time, so Weller wanted to return in the new year to round the project off. Polydor, on the other hand, were having a poor financial year in 1980 and, recognising that a new Jam album would be a 'banker' for them, wanted it out before Christmas. They felt Weller was deliberately stalling the sessions and called the band's A&R man, Dennis Munday, into the managing director's office. Munday: 'I was asked straight, "Is he playing games with us?"' Munday assured Polydor that the only problem was a lack of material and the band were simply having trouble writing the album to a deadline.

In a bizarre twist, Munday was then asked to approach Godley and Creme (whom he was also working with at the time) and ask them to write some songs for The Jam. Munday refused to make such an approach. He understood how Paul, Bruce and Rick would react to the suggestion and made a mental note never to mention it to them. Godley and Creme, for their part, later wrote and released a song called 'Dreamtime', a title which had obvious similarities to that of a track on *Sound Affects*.

In the event, *Sound Affects* was completed with time to spare and the group used up the remaining studio time recording little sound *effects* to scatter between the tracks. That was when Buckler recorded the sounds, including a fly he found buzzing at a window, that can be heard at the start of 'Music For The Last Couple'.

BOY ABOUT TOWN (Weller)

Recorded in September 1980 at the Townhouse Studios, Shepherd's Bush, London
Produced by Vic Coppersmith-Heaven and The Jam
Album track: Sound Affects

A two-minute pop classic, 'Boy About Town' speaks directly to the band's core audience and is a dynamic mod anthem reflecting everyday working-class life. If Weller was uncomfortable with his growing status as the voice of a generation, then this was yet to be reflected in his songwriting.

Paul was no fool, however, fully understanding how his political convictions didn't endear him to his record company, commenting in 1981: 'The music industry isn't worried about politics, it doesn't affect them. Their only objective is to sell records and it makes life much easier for them if you're singing about cars and girls.' And he was also aware of his limitations as a pop star: 'A pop song ain't exactly going to change the world but it can act as a vehicle for thoughts and carry those thoughts worldwide.'

But he failed to appreciate that they could only be carried to those who understood what he was trying to say. As an observational writer, Weller usually only tackled subjects in 'his own street', and that meant nothing to those in America and many other parts of the world. A fact that goes some way to explaining why The Jam became heroes to their own kind of people – working-class Englishmen – but failed to achieve the worldwide success their music deserved, apart from in Japan, where they were afforded superstar status.

SCRAPE AWAY (Weller)

Recorded in September 1980 at the Townhouse Studios, Shepherd's Bush, London
Produced by Vic Coppersmith-Heaven
Album track: Sound Affects

'Scrape Away' emerged from a Jam session between Foxton and Buckler, which Weller picked up on by adding a striking psychedelic guitar riff and haunting melody. The track contains arguably one of

the best drum tracks ever recorded; its clever, off-beat pattern is original and imaginative and sits perfectly with Foxton's gently ascending bass line. But drummer Rick Buckler rarely gets the credit he deserves. The track's failure to be played during any live radio sessions or to appear on any 'best of' compilations leaves this hidden gem largely unheard.

Lyrically we are taken back to the band's fourth album *Setting Sons* and the three young idealists who grow up with changing and conflicting convictions about the world in which they live. That album's 'Burning Sky' saw a letter from the 'capitalist' (Steve Brookes?) written to the revolutionary dreamer (Dave Waller?), warning him to wake up and discover the real world. 'Scrape Away' is an acidic, scathing reply from the revolutionary, dismissing his friend's advice and providing some sound reasoning of his own. Suggesting his businessman friend has dried up and given in, Weller's character insists that his own 'feeling real' should not be dismissed as 'dreaming'. Instead of making a real difference to the world, he regards his friend's existence as a means of merely scraping his way through life.

Sound Affects may well have been Paul Weller's favourite Jam album to date; in it he managed to reflect Orwell's (and Shelley's) argument that the 'central problem of how to prevent power from being abused remains unsolved', an admission Orwell made in 1940 when summarising his book *Homage to Catalonia*. But the band were frustrated by Vic Coppersmith-Heaven's slow pace and in the end the album had to be recut several times in an attempt to compensate for the flat production. Denis Munday agreed that the final mixes weren't up to standard. That, coupled with the decision to enter the studio without any complete songs, just 'scraps and ideas', pushed the total cost of the album to over £120,000.

Weller wanted to remix the album a few more times but by then there was neither the money or the time. So *Sound Affects* was left as it was. It was the last time Coppersmith-Heaven worked with The Jam; he was replaced on every subsequent Jam record by Polydor sound engineer Pete Wilson. However, *Sound Affects* was The Jam's most successful album in America, selling over 150,000 copies on release, more than it initially sold in the UK.

FUNERAL PYRE (Words: Paul Weller, Music: The Jam)
Recorded in April 1981 at the Townhouse Studios, Shepherd's Bush
Produced by Pete Wilson and The Jam
A-side released 29 May 1981; Polydor POSP 257; reached no 4 in UK chart
B-side: 'Disguises'

'Funeral Pyre' is yet another Jam song created by Foxton and Buckler
by experimenting in the studio with drum and bass riffs, and is widely
regarded as Rick's most memorable drum performance. Fast and furious,
Buckler doesn't step off the pace for a moment. Also, it's another Jam
track that opens up with an instantly recognisable bass line. It's no surprise that 'Funeral Pyre' is listed with a joint writing credit. In fact, the
only real surprise is that there aren't more of them, as this form of
songwriting was apparently standard during Jam studio sessions.

'Funeral Pyre' was released a full ten months after the previous
single 'Start!' and seven months after *Sound Affects* had shot to
number two in the charts. It was also the first Jam record produced
by Polydor studio engineer Pete Wilson, and the change in sound
Wilson brought to the desk was immediately noticeable. Lyrically the
song once again reflects Weller's sympathy with Orwell, Marx and
Shelley's vision of Democratic Socialism, launching a stinging attack
on what he regarded as the selfishness and conceit of those in power,
at that time Thatcher's Conservative government.

There were many similarities between Thatcher and Lord
Liverpool, the Tory leader who ruled Britain for 15 years during
Shelley's most productive period. Liverpool was Thatcher's favourite
Prime Minister and provided a blueprint for her own vision of
conservatism. For his part, Weller was able to identify closely with
Shelley, using his own emotive language in the lyric to illustrate how
the strong (either financially or physically) crush the weak, a truism
apparent in all forms of nature.

For the video, the band returned to Woking and the sandpits close
to the town where H G Wells had located his Martian invasion.
Using hundreds of local kids and a vast bonfire, the film created an
evocative image of normal people being led into the flames. Filmed
at dusk for maximum effect, production was halted on several

occasions when the wind changed, blowing hot ash high into the air over the band, with small pieces landing directly on Buckler's drum skins, searing straight through.

To coincide with the release of 'Funeral Pyre' the band set off on a UK tour starting, after two warm-up gigs in Sweden, on 17 June at The Rainbow Theatre in London. It's tempting to regard this period as the beginning of the end of The Jam. By now Paul's girlfriend Gill had become part of the band's set-up and was running their office, located at Nomis Studios in west London's Sinclair Road. But Gill also joined the band on the road so, just as in the past, all Jam business ceased when they were away on tour. Although they had at least invested in an answering machine by this time.

Though popular, Gill's presence usually meant she and Paul would spend all their free time together. As Bruce and Rick rarely took their partners on tour, apart from the occasional trip to Japan and America, they relaxed in other ways, often out and about in order to sample the 'local culture'. Weller, by contrast, never left his hotel, and even coaxing him out of his room wasn't easy. Buckler: 'What with all the attention surrounding Paul he couldn't go anywhere without being mobbed, so he didn't go anywhere, simple as that. It was easier for Bruce and myself and in places like Japan we would go out and about to have a look around, but Paul never came.'

The second sign of the beginning of the end was The Jam's actual show. Polydor's A&R man Dennis Munday had reservations from the very beginning of the tour. 'It got to the stage where leaping up and down had become a bit passé,' he said. Although it was an integral part of the band's visual performance, nobody else was doing it any more as it was stuff for teenagers, not for one of continent's biggest bands. Jumping up and down at the Marquee Club works well, but Paul and Bruce jumping about and tearing around on a 100' stage didn't work, and nor did the sight of Paul's dad introducing the band on stage.'

This was something Weller Sr had done since his son's very first gig and it was an important part of the show for both of them. But a teenage Weller being introduced by his dad had a warm old-fashioned feel to it, while a 23-year-old superstar, hero and icon to many, being virtually led out on stage by his old man looked odd to many casual observers. Longtime Jam fans felt the need to justify this to newcomers by describing it as 'tradition'.

Thirdly, the early part of 1981 had seen a vast change in the music scene as punks turned into New Romantics. The Jam's style began to look old very quickly, despite the major success they had had over the previous 12 months. The New Romantic movement was spearheaded by old punk Adam Ant, who spent five weeks at number one in May 1981 with 'Stand And Deliver', followed by another four with 'Prince Charming' a few months later. Initially, Weller was complimentary of the dandies, saying of Adam and The Ants: 'They've got a bit of style and do it with a bit of class,' leaving Jam fans wondering what was next in line for their favourite band. But Weller wasn't averse to doing a 'U' turn, later saying: 'People like Adam Ant and Depeche Mode have totally lost sight of pop and it's as if punk never happened. I think music should have some kind of sensibility, some kind of consciousness, instead of being party to this crap people like Adam want to bring back.'

Despite the song's enormous popularity live, 'Funeral Pyre' failed to reach number one in the UK charts, stalling instead at number four (the first time The Jam had failed to make number one since 'The Eton Rifles' in 1979). Adam Ant, of course, was occupying the top spot instead.

DISGUISES (Townshend)
Recorded in April 1981 at the Townhouse Studios, Shepherd's Bush
Produced by Pete Wilson and The Jam
B-side to 'Funeral Pyre'

In the months prior to releasing 'Funeral Pyre' and its flip, 'Disguises', Weller had become a regular visitor to clubs such as Le Beat Route in Soho, where jazz-fusion, soul and funk were all on the playlists. Paul was also a regular at the Club For Heroes, run by former punk turned New Romantic Steve Strange. Club For Heroes mainly played Glam Rock in the shape of Bowie and Lou Reed, but black music was also an integral part of the scene, as were the emerging New Romantic groups.

One night during the summer of 1981, Weller ran into Pete Townshend (original writer of 'Disguises') and Thin Lizzy star Phil Lynott (whom The Jam had supported in Croydon as schoolboys six years earlier) at the club. Townshend explains the scene: 'Steve Strange had dimmed the lights and a bunch of bedraggled rock stars, including Paul Weller, were huddled around a table attempting to form sentences while people rushed around getting us all drinks. About an hour later I woke up in hospital, discovering that I had over-imbibed to the extent of nearly killing myself.'

In fact, the Who guitarist had been experimenting with heroin and Lynott, a hardened user, had accidentally injected him with a near-fatal shot in the club's toilets. The anti-drug Weller claimed he was 'so pissed' he could hardly remember the incident; however, he wisely chose to distance himself from that scene in the future. Lynott, for his part, failed to heed the warning. He died on 4 January 1986 of the physical deterioration brought on by the ravages of drug abuse, including heroin addiction, at only 36 years of age.

It's a well documented fact that Weller is an avid collector of bootlegs and pirated cassettes of his 1960s heroes. He later revealed that the whole arrangement of The Jam's 1981 cover of 'Disguises' was built around a repeat-echo guitar sound pinched from Townshend's original solo demo of the song, which Paul had discovered in a New York specialist shop.

ABSOLUTE BEGINNERS (Weller)

Recorded in August 1981 at the Townhouse Studios, Shepherd's Bush
Produced by Pete Wilson and The Jam
A-side released 16 October 1981; Polydor POSP 350; reached no 4 in UK chart
B-side: 'Tales From The Riverbank'

By the summer of 1981, described by Weller as a 'horrible year for songs', The Jam were taking a well-earned breather. With no new album planned and therefore little to promote, Paul, Bruce and Rick were able to slow down, take time off and pick and choose their gigs, which they did only to showcase their two singles that year and the release of *Sound Affects* in Japan. By now The Jam were big enough to fill venues like Wembley Arena but Weller wasn't having any of it: 'I've been to those places as a punter and they have always been shit gigs with shit sound.'

With plenty of space in the diary Weller spent some time exploring new musical scenes, notably the New Romantic movement gathering pace across Europe. Weller also started to enjoy other contemporary bands, describing Madness in 1981 as 'inspiring' and listing The Beat ('Mirror In The Bathroom') and Department S ('Is Vic There?') as personal favourites.

Weller personally had had a difficult year and found himself increasingly at odds with his audience. He had never seen himself as a punk and always advocated anti-violence, as so many of his songs confirm. The odd loss of temper aside, Weller was largely a peaceful individual and always saw himself more as a white English Soul Boy than he did an angry young punk. Jam fans, on the other hand, are pretty much the music world's equivalent to Millwall fans and, looking out at their audience of skinheads, punks and London mods, the band were witnessing violence breaking out at their shows with increasing regularity.

One of the worst examples of this came on 26 February 1981, when the band visited the Pavilion Baltard in Paris as part of a European promotional tour of *Sound Affects*. As usual, an army of Jam fans had travelled from England to support the band. During the gig, in what seemed to be an orchestrated event, hundreds of French skinheads started a riot and attacked the English fans with knives and broken bottles. Over 100 people were eventually arrested and dozens hospitalised. After calm had been restored, The Jam returned to the stage with Weller branding the French 'animals' and igniting patriotic fervour by tying a Union Jack to his microphone stand. The incident has since passed into legend (if everybody who claimed to be there actually was, then the whole of Paris would have come to a standstill), but the musicians themselves were appalled.

It became increasingly obvious to Weller that The Jam's barbed and 'blokish' guitar sound would have to change if the group was to be recognised for its soul and Motown roots rather than as a swaggering lads' band. Surprisingly, it was a New Romantic group that provided the answer for Weller, when, on 18 July 1981, Spandau Ballet released 'Chant No 1 (I Don't Need This Pressure On)', which Paul considered 'a genuine English soul record'. Weller now felt he could combine his descriptive lyrics with his love of soul music and create his own genuinely English soul records. He also revealed that he had been listening to Michael Jackson's *Off The Wall* and was greatly impressed by the guitar styles on the album. Weller responded to 'Chant No 1' by immediately writing the horn-driven 'Absolute Beginners'. It was the start of Weller's transition into 'Blue Eyed Soul Boy' and – for real this time – the beginning of the end for The Jam.

'Absolute Beginners' is the title of a 1958 book written by Colin MacInnes about youth culture in postwar London, where the style was mod but the music was jazz. The book articulated the peaceful youth revolution Weller craved and would later provide the blueprint for his post-Jam project, The Style Council. Ironically, Paul hadn't read the book when he wrote 'Absolute Beginners' and had originally called the song 'Skirt'. But, having had the book outlined to him, its title meant enough to him to use it.

'Absolute Beginners' debuted on the BBC's Studio B15 Live radio show on 25 October 1981. It was also the first of a three-track set The Jam played live at Mandagsborsen in Sweden which features on the *Complete Jam* DVD. These are the only live versions of the song available.

'Absolute Beginners' came in a sleeve decorated with a depressing urban image, using a photograph taken by Rick Buckler from the tour coach as the band travelled to a gig in Leicester.

TALES FROM THE RIVERBANK (Weller)
Recorded in August 1981 at the Townhouse Studios, Shepherd's Bush
Produced by Pete Wilson and The Jam
B-side to 'Absolute Beginners'

A few years after apologising for his suburban roots in 'Sounds From The Street', Weller was back in the Woking countryside, spiritually at least, extolling the virtues of 'pastel fields' and trying to spread 'hope into our hearts' down by the riverbank he played along as a child. The riverbank near Stanley Road, Woking (close to Weller's childhood home) is in fact the Basingstoke Canal, but don't let that spoil a good story for you. The song creates images of long summer evenings and twinkling water, reviving our spirits and providing a welcome relief from city life.

'Tales From The Riverbank', which took its name from a children's TV show detailing the adventures of Hammy the Hamster and others, was one of the few Jam songs Weller continued to play in his acoustic set during his tours of the mid-1990s. But the band itself rarely played the track live in its recorded format, although they did perform it at later gigs with a brass section on stage. The song debuted with a brass section during the BBC's Studio B15 Live radio show on 25 October 1981. Such was The Jam's change in musical style (yet again), the show's presenter seemed confused and asked immediately after the track: 'What label, gentlemen?' To which the band replied in unison: 'None at all.' Weller then went on to say: 'It's music, that's all it is; we don't want to get into that categorisation thing' – illustrating that the singer was still trying to rid his band of the tags imposed upon them by certain sections of the music press.

Another song played live during that BBC session was Arthur Conley's 'Sweet Soul Music', suggesting The Jam, despite the diversity of their music, were still very close to their soul roots.

Earlier versions of 'Tales From The Riverbank', 'Not Far At All' and 'We've Only Started' (all musically very similar), later appeared on *Extras*, revealing that 'Tales' had started life as a typically energetic Jam song that might well have returned the band to the number one slot. But once again they refused to go for the easy option, preferring to change their sound and converting 'Not Far At All' into the slower, more wistful track it became, also changing its name to 'Tales From The Riverbank', rewriting the lyrics and relegating it to a B-side. Weller: 'The song makes me think of Woking and is written about my childhood.' To many fans, 'Tales' equals 'That's Entertainment' as one of The Jam's most enduring songs. A later

version including a brass section, originally recorded for *The Gift*, appears as track two on *Extras*.

On 23 October (two days prior to the B15 Live session), the band reconvened to appear as surprise guests at a Gang Of Four benefit show at The Rainbow Theatre in London. In a gig supporting the Campaign for Nuclear Disarmament (CND), the band played a short 'impromptu' set, including a version of Sandy Shaw's 'Long Live Love', which had joined 'Sweet Soul Music' in The Jam's new live set.

They followed up next day with an appearance on the back of a lorry at a CND rally in London. But there were no new songs performed as, without a horn section, the band were unable to play their new single 'Absolute Beginners'. The following week The Jam booked into Beatles producer George Martin's AIR Studio in Oxford Street to start work on what would become their final album, *The Gift*. It was during those sessions that Weller finally met his boyhood hero Paul McCartney. Together they posed for Linda McCartney, whose double-portrait would later appear in *Smash Hits* magazine.

Also during the session, The Jam took a break to play four more CND benefit gigs, two at the Michael Sobell Centre and two at the Hammersmith Palais, this time recruiting Keith Thomas on saxophone and Steve Nichol on trumpet/piano and performing what was essentially a 1960s 'soul revue'. The set included covers of Chairmen Of The Board's 'Give Me Just A Little More Time' and Eddie Floyd's 'Big Bird' (which later appeared on *Dig The New Breed*). With their new brass section, The Jam were evolving yet again.

Weller, to his credit, was continuing to use his high profile to promote other young acts, even to the point of inviting unknown dance troupe Bananarama to support The Jam during these benefit gigs. Jam fans, used to hearing stomping Northern Soul tunes provided by the band's touring DJs, stared in disbelief at the three girls dancing around to a backing tape. Bananarama were jeered off stage amid a barrage of abuse, much to Weller's disgust. His frustration with his narrow-minded audiences was by now reaching boiling point, but his belief in Bananarama was vindicated when two months later they topped the charts with their Funboy Three collaboration, 'It Ain't What You Do (it's the way that you do it)'.

At the tail end of 1981, The Jam won their third of an unprecedented four consecutive Best Band Awards in the *NME* readers' poll, while Weller picked up his third of four consecutive Best Songwriter Awards.

TOWN CALLED MALICE (Weller)
Recorded in December 1981 at AIR Studios, Oxford Street, London
Produced by Pete Wilson and The Jam
A-side released 13 February 1982; Polydor POSP 400; reached no 1 in UK chart
Double A-side: 'Precious'

In February 1982 The Jam had not topped the charts for 18 months and, despite the fact that the two singles they had released since the 1980 hit 'Start!' had both reached number 4 ('Funeral Pyre' and 'Absolute Beginners'), they once again needed to make a comeback. In 1978 the band had returned in style with the seminal *All Mod Cons*. This time, three and a half years later, they again managed to produce something special. 'Town Called Malice' crashed into the charts at number one on 13 February and remained there for three weeks, while simultaneously enjoying comprehensive chart success all over the world.

The song's title is an obvious allusion to Nevil Shute's popular novel *A Town Called Alice*, but nothing else of Shute's makes it onto the track. Instead, Weller presents his defining image of everyday urban English life. The real inspiration comes from Paul's old friend Dave Waller, whose method of descriptive urban imagery is mirrored in 'Town Called Malice'. The images could have reflected any suburban town, but in fact it was The Jam's hometown of Woking that provided the backdrop.

In 1982 the Unigate Dairy on Goldsworth Road was on the verge of closing, with the town's milkmen making way for the hypermarkets and their wall-to-wall plastic milk cartons. Also, 1982 was a time of high unemployment in the area and Weller draws on this, giving his townsfolk the choice of 'beer or the kids' new gear' as families are forced to make cutbacks. The whole thing is set against a classic bass line and a stomping Motown beat borrowed from The Supremes' 1966 gem 'You Can't Hurry Love', written by Holland/Dozier/Holland (and inspiring Phil Collins to rework The Supremes' song itself in November 1982).

Squire guitarist Enzo Esposito remembers that, despite the chart success of 'Town Called Malice', Paul was never totally happy with the end result. Enzo: 'Paul wanted it to have a slower, more soulful tempo, more like he plays it these days. I think he was happy with the song but just felt it was recorded with a faster tempo than he would have liked at the time.'

But The Jam were back, and bigger than ever. 'Town Called Malice' was in fact released as a double A-side with 'Precious' and the band were immediately asked to perform both tracks on the same edition of *Top Of The Pops*. In doing so they became the first act since The Beatles performed 'Day Tripper' and 'We Can Work It Out' to play two songs back-to-back on the show. It was official: The Jam were, to many people, as popular as The Beatles, and Weller felt he had achieved his childhood dream.

Unlike 1981, The Jam set out on a gruelling world tour, starting on 12 March at the Guildhall in Portsmouth, taking in the whole of the UK, parts of Europe, America, Canada and Japan before returning to London on 26 June to play at Loftus Road in Shepherd's Bush. The tour was a major success and The Jam sold out in every town, but the yobbish culture of the band's audience increasingly depressed Weller, who was by now determined to lighten up and enjoy the lifestyle advocated by Colin MacInnes in his book *Absolute Beginners*. In the video for 'Town Called Malice' the band flashed up a series of subliminal messages, one of them reading: 'If we ain't getting through to you then you obviously ain't listening.'

PRECIOUS (Weller)

Recorded in December 1981 at AIR Studios, Oxford Street, London
Produced by Pete Wilson and The Jam
A-side released 13 February 1982; Polydor POSP 400; reached no 1 in UK chart
Double A-side: 'Town Called Malice'

Combined with his inherent love of Motown and Northern Soul, Paul Weller was also taking an interest in funk, especially the horn-driven funk he saw as a natural progression of English soul in the Spandau Ballet mould. Freeez were one of the early jazz-funk bands, hitting the charts in 1981 after Beggars Banquet re-released their 1980 album *Southern Freeez*. The title track's chart success paved the way for other jazz-funk bands that summer. One of these was a group called Pigbag, whose instrumental 'Papa's Got a Brand New Pigbag' stormed the clubs that summer just as The Jam were looking around for a new direction. Now, with 'Precious', they experimented with a jazz-funk bassline and horns, an approach very similar to the Pigbag hit, leaving no one with any doubt about the inspiration behind the track.

The integration of horns into The Jam's musical framework was for the first time working well, and Weller's conversion to dance music was clearly well under way. But his foot-stomping, head-punching audience remained unconvinced. Soul and eighties funk were his new direction, but Weller was aware the band's continuing chart success was largely due to fans keeping their collections going, while new fans were proving hard to attract. After all, everybody now knew who The Jam were, and if you didn't like 'Going Underground' you wouldn't be listening to anything else they had to offer. But The Jam were now musically miles beyond 'Going Underground'. Despite Foxton and Buckler continuing to contribute many of the musical ideas, Weller rightly recognised that it would be just as difficult for The Jam to suddenly offer up a jazz-funk record as it would be for long-established acts like The Rolling Stones. Realising this, the writing was now firmly on the wall.

Pigbag's 'Papa's Got A Brand New Pigbag' finally entered the UK charts, reaching number three in April 1982. But by then The Jam's

double A-side had been in and out of the number one slot, while 'Precious' was still riding high in the album charts on *The Gift*, leaving the uninitiated believing that Pigbag had copied their favourite band when in fact it was the other way round.

One of the first songs to be recorded during *The Gift* sessions, lyrically 'Precious' provides evidence of its writer's state of mind: he reveals that he is simply unable to express himself in the way he would wish, and as a result finds himself 'trapped in sorrow'. Weller tries to find a way round it but decides instead 'that's how I am'.

For those wondering where the name of The Jam's final album, Dig The New Breed, came from (and what it means), the answer can be found connected to Precious. Pigbag's 'Papa's Got A Brand New Pigbag' is obviously lifted from James Brown's 1965 R and B classic 'Papa's Got A Brand New Bag', and that track includes the line 'He ain't too hip now but I can dig the new breed babe.'

SEVEN

RUNNING ON THE SPOT

THE weight of expectation now sat heavily on Paul Weller's 23-year-old shoulders. The pressure began to show and, unhappy with the studio sessions for the band's latest album, Weller finally cracked, collapsing during a rare break and suffering a mini-breakdown. He'd also been drinking heavily and contracted a painful dose of shingles. 'Cracking up over *The Gift* LP, I wanted it perfect but settled for good, oh well!!' was how Paul described the experience in his sleeve notes for *Dig The New Breed*.

Evidently, as 1981 became 1982 Paul Weller was a troubled man. But at least he paid heed to the warning signs. 'This is fucking mad,' he commented. 'I'm too young for all this.' And with that he quit drinking and embarked on a healthier lifestyle.

THE GIFT

HAPPY TOGETHER (Weller)
Recorded in October 1981 at AIR Studios, Oxford Street, London
Produced by Pete Wilson
Album track: The Gift

'Now for those of you watching in black and white, this one is in Technicolor', advises the voice in BBC English. Foxton then screams 'Ba-a-a-by' in Woking English and The Jam's sixth studio album comes alive with yet another inventive bass riff.

After the experiments of the funk-inspired 'Precious' and horn-laden 'Absolute Beginners', core Jam fans were relieved to find the eagerly awaited new album opening up with the classic Jam sound. 'Happy Together' is, if nothing else, pure Jam and another safe number one, had it ever been considered as a single.

In fact, 'Happy Together' is a shining highlight of an otherwise disorganised album. Written by Weller in late 1981, the song reflects on relationships and the destructive influence drink and drugs can have on them. Weller had spent the latter part of the year in turmoil, feeling weighed down by the dual pressures of his songwriting responsibilities and the expectations of both press and fans, who hung on the 23-year-old's every word. Adding to the pressure was 'Absolute Beginners'' failure to reach number one; despite the single selling over 300,000 copies, Polydor considered it a failure. Weller clearly wasn't much fun to live with during this period and at one time even moved out of the flat he shared with Gill, opting to spend a few days in a hotel instead.

But Weller soon effected a reconciliation and, as The Jam entered the studio to record their sixth album, he had completely cleaned up his act. Weller: 'Rock can destroy you if you let it. I've given up drinking and I don't take drugs any more.' The events leading up to the sessions clearly improved his own personal relationships, or at least his attitude towards them, as he suggests in *The Gift*'s opening track.

'Happy Together' provided early evidence of a new switch in Weller's songwriting. Whereas in the past he wrote and sang mainly observational songs (with a few personal asides cropping up on *Sound Affects*), now Weller was writing introspectively. He was no longer embarrassed about revealing his personal thoughts and feelings, and this new-found candour presented itself regularly throughout the album, although in some cases widening the gulf between the singer and his audience. About 90 per cent of The Jam's natural fan base was comprised of working-class, white teenage males. As Weller had also been a working-class white teenage male his audience related to his every word and almost every early Jam song meant something to someone. Almost like a mod agony aunt, Weller provided observation, answers and evidence that his anxious teen listeners were not alone.

With the release of *The Gift* it was obvious Weller was growing up. But his fan base wasn't necessarily growing up with him. Lyrically some of the album's songs, particularly the rambling tirades against Thatcherism, were lost on many, although fans could still stomp along to classic Jam sounds such as 'Happy Together' without necessarily relating to the lyric.

'Happy Together' was a firm live favourite. Introduced by its rumbling bass line, its stomping Northern Soul beat could be heard throughout the UK tour in early 1982, although the song never made it onto either radio or TV. Nor does it appear on any compilation album, live or otherwise, leaving it as yet another hidden gem, tucked away on a studio album.

GHOSTS (Weller)
Recorded in October 1981 at AIR Studios, Oxford Street, London
Produced by Pete Wilson
Album track: The Gift

Providing instant relief from the heavy thundering Jam sound, 'Ghosts' was listed as track two on *The Gift*. Once again Weller writes introspectively, recognising the need to do some soul-searching and to be unafraid of what we find. In a passionate piece of abbreviated psychoanalysis, the songwriter encourages us to shed the disguises we wrap around our emotions and reveal all the good we have deep inside us. Emotive and easy to understand, 'Ghosts' urges us to find direction, lose our prejudice, open up, share the good things we keep hidden for fear of ridicule and to 'lift up our lonely hearts'.

It's a parable and one that wasn't lost on young Jam fans. Broadcaster Peter Gordon: 'I understood 'Ghosts' straight away. Here was my favourite songwriter asserting the need for people to open up and be brave, to admit to themselves that, with some thought and honesty, things can get better. In my enclosed world of school and rampant adolescence, the light suddenly went on. If we allow insecurity to hold us back we will miss out on all the beauty in this world.'

Jam fan Nikki Potter, who was only five years old when *The Gift* was released, recognises the sentiment 21 years later. 'To me 'Ghosts' is about someone who is reluctant or scared to reveal themselves fully, for fear of rejection or ridicule. Maybe that applies to all of us in one way or another. The moral does encourage us to be more open and accept ourselves but that isn't easy when we don't know what is expected of us. You want to be able to have goals and focus in life but when this is clouded by fear, the task is a lot more difficult. 'Ghosts' illustrates that sentiment perfectly.'

In many ways 'Ghosts' shares its theme with 'Monday', where we were encouraged not to be 'embarrassed about love'. Gentle sentiment from a songwriter dismissed by many as overtly political and insensitive. In December 1982, The Jam opened their last television appearance (on the first edition of the music television programme *The Tube*) with 'Ghosts'. Foxton begins the performance with his haunting bass line, accompanied by a delicate trumpet to add to the atmosphere. Underpinned by Buckler's simple drumbeat, Weller delivers an almost monotone vocal; unusually for a Jam song, 'Ghosts' stays on the same beat throughout, without lifting for either chorus or bridge. The technique forces the listen to focus on the lyric, as if to emphasise the message.

To promote the album, the band embarked on a UK tour, starting at The Guildhall in Portsmouth on 12 March 1982, the day *The Gift* was released. With the name borrowed from Kraftwerk's 1977 album *Trans Europe Express*, The Jam's Trans-Global Unity Express Tour was due to take them all over Britain and Europe before setting out for America and Japan. The band visualised a Continental mission in which they could spread their gospel, picking up followers along the way.

In his tour programme notes Weller was characteristically direct and uncompromising. 'I hope this tour is a fucking shake-up. I hope it is the knife to slice through the increasing apathy. Most music is at the moment pure showbiz [a direct reference to the New Romantic movement of 1982] and pure crap. If I thought all that a group could accomplish was appearing on *Top Of The Pops* I'd fucking jack it in tomorrow. We've all got so much inside us, we've just gotta let it come through. And forget your prejudices forced upon us by social conditioning. Forget them and find your own values. I want my music to reach people emotionally, to show 'em just how much power we have inside us.'

The tour, which was featured on the *Trans-Global Unity Express* video, reveals Weller playing awkwardly at times and without any real conviction. As a group the band weren't at their best and as individuals demonstrated none of the unity called for by the album they were touring. Weller was still off the booze and would follow each show with a cup of tea before sloping off on his own. Buckler had developed a circle of friends among the road crew and sometimes even travelled with them between gigs as it was 'more fun', while Foxton was the only musician outwardly enjoying himself and looking for a night out. Surprisingly, he was often the only band member present at the after-show parties.

The Jam's support band, Rudi, were surprised by the situation. Brian Young revealed in John Reed's book *My Ever Changing Moods*, 'We thought they would be good mates but the three of them hardly even spoke to each other throughout the tour.' There was never any animosity, however, just a straightforward, business-like relationship. Young also told John Reed that Weller had surrounded himself with 'yes men' and had his own entourage with him on tour.

Weller was adamant about the tour's 'message' but few members of the music press seemed to understand what it was. Unity... anti-war... pro-unions... enjoy life... depression... All were themes suggested by the song titles. But Weller's relationship with the music press had deteriorated to the point of open hostility, and the inevitable outcome was poor reviews. 'A Jam gig is a fairly joyless spectacle,' wrote Barney Hoskyns in the *NME*. But that fact wasn't lost on Weller himself. He could see all too clearly, thanks to the mod army jumping up and down and chanting like a Millwall football crowd between songs, that a Jam gig had little to do with the music these days.

JUST WHO IS THE 5 O'CLOCK HERO (Weller)

Recorded on 6 January 1982 at AIR Studios, Oxford Street, London
Produced by Pete Wilson
Album track: The Gift
Single A-side released on 11 June 1982 in Holland (Polydor 2229 254), Germany
(metronome 0030-561), Spain (Polydor 2059 515), Sweden (Polydor 2141 558)
and Australia/New Zealand on 12" (Polydor 2141 558) b/w 'War' plus 'The Great
Depression'

Paul Weller had no doubt about who his heroes were. 'The real
heroes in this country are obviously the geezers who have to go out
and do a nine to five job,' he explained. 'So the nurses and the
miners are the real heroes because they keep this country going – not
the pop stars.'

Contrary to popular belief, 'Just Who Is The 5 O'Clock Hero' was
never released as a single in Britain. 'Going Underground', 'Town
Called Malice' and 'That's Entertainment' were the only Jam singles
up until 1982 to be released in Holland. The success of those songs,
plus the sell-out concerts The Jam played on the European leg of
their Trans-Global Unity Express Tour, encouraged Polydor to release
a second single from the *The Gift* once news leaked of the band's
impending break-up in July 1982. Such was the demand for the
single in Great Britain that, despite the song having already been
released as an album track, UK sales for 'Just Who Is The 5 O'Clock
Hero' took it to number eight in the UK charts, selling more copies
than any other import up to that time.

The song provides the perfect example of the direction Weller
intended for the band and equally proves that the rhythm section
were more than up to the task. Buckler's inventive and original
soul-inflected drum pattern underpins the song brilliantly, while
Foxton's bass line is as natural and fluid as ever. But Weller appeared
unhappy with the finished product, feeling the final recording was
too fast to capture the soul feeling he intended for the song.

Enzo Esposito: "5 O'Clock Hero' is another song like 'Town Called
Malice' that I think Paul wanted to have with a much slower soulful
tempo, and it would have sounded much better. But I know what it

is like when you are in a band and someone else just won't agree to small changes like that. In Squire we have this great soulful song but our drummer just doesn't like it and doesn't want to do it. But we are not a professional band so it doesn't really matter to us. But in The Jam's case all the time these songs kept coming out faster than Paul would have liked, and he felt unable to persuade the others to go along with his ideas, then that was the beginning of the end for them.'

Of course, Esposito's account only serves to underline the fact that The Jam were very much a band and not just Weller's backing group, as some would suggest. On the other hand it was obvious that if Weller couldn't get his feelings across – especially to Buckler, who is a particularly strong and stubborn character – then he was bound to be unhappy in his work. To add to his disgruntled mood, the New Romantics were gaining ground and Weller was frustrated to find that, at the time 'Just Who Is The 5 O'Clock Hero' was trickling into the UK, Adam Ant was at number one again with the vacuous 'Goody Two Shoes'. Other acts at number one during that time included Irene Cara ('Fame'), Musical Youth ('Pass The Duchie') and even The Damned's Captain Sensible with the inane 'Happy Talk'. And Weller didn't like any of it.

On 24 February 1982, just after the recording sessions for *The Gift* had been completed, The Jam appeared at the Polytechnic of Central London during a series of gigs for the 'JOBS not YOPS' campaign. Through the Manpower Services Commission (MSC), important initiatives were taken in the 1970s to develop schemes for unemployed school-leavers, such as the Youth Opportunities Scheme (YOPS) in 1978, which was later replaced by the youth training scheme (YTS). The intention of YOPS was to modernise the apprenticeship system and to provide places for all 16- and 17-year-old out-of-work school leavers to improve their 'employability'.

The scheme was deeply unpopular, for, unlike the apprenticeship system, trainees had no real guarantee of a job at the end of their training. The idea was dismissed by many as a way of securing cheap labour with no long-term commitment from employers. Weller was one of those vociferously opposed to the YOPS scheme and the song

'Just Who Is The 5 O'Clock Hero' reflected his views, proving instantly popular when it was debuted during the protest concert.

TRANS-GLOBAL EXPRESS (Weller)

Recorded in January 1982 at AIR Studios, Oxford Street, London
Produced by Pete Wilson
Album track: The Gift

The central theme of most of Paul Weller's output is of a man at odds with what he sees around him and not being able to 'join the gang'. Initially the gang is the left-wing 'art school' clique that was punk. Later he defended punk by rounding on what he perceived as the establishment censorship of The Pistols ('Standards'), while still attacking those who, in his estimation, treated The Jam as outsiders ('The Modern World'). On *All Mod Cons* the music business was in for a broadside, although the album mellowed lyrically – after Mr Clean had been given his bitter warning – into an evocative image of contemporary England. By the time *Setting Sons* was being written, Weller had found his ground and stood firmly behind his Orwellian convictions.

But, as noted earlier, to understand Orwell's rationale it's necessary to take a look at his own literary influences. Step forward Percy Bysshe Shelley. In its lyric 'Trans-Global Express' reflects the sentiments running throughout Shelley's work: namely, unity, hope and belief. It also reflects Shelley's call for the proletariat to join together and oppose oppression, while borrowing a sentiment from The O'Jays' 1972 hit 'Love Train', which advocated that people all over the world should board a global 'love train' headed for peace and freedom.

In Weller's stark lyric, he advocates that people all over the world should join his (peaceful) revolutionary train and wonders what the world would be like if everybody went on strike. Not just the British Leyland workers, but everybody. Who would earn the profits and pay for the bombs then, he asks. British Leyland was the car company crippled by a series of strikes in the 1970s led by militant shop steward Derek 'Red' Robinson, who became a household name by calling out the workers on 44 separate occasions in 1975 alone. British Leyland was nationalised by the Labour government in 1977, then privatised by Thatcher's Tory government in 1983, eventually leading to its closure in 1991.

But for all Paul's conviction he was an easy target for criticism. Regularly dismissed as a 'champagne socialist', he was labelled a fashion-conscious young pop star who made a great deal of money from his socialist views by writing songs about them. But the same criticism had been applied, in effect, to Shelley and Orwell. In any case, Paul was comfortable with his lifestyle. He shunned excess, lived a normal understated life and saw nothing wrong with being a wealthy young Democratic Socialist. He did, after all, invest a lot in providing opportunities for other young people.

Musically, 'Trans-Global Express' is cluttered and disorganised but neatly borrows a riff from World Column's steaming Northern Soul track 'So Is The Sun'. Weller is clumsy with his lyrics at times, some of the lines suggesting that the song was forced and hurried, the incoherence and lack of melody serving only to confirm that. 'Trans-Global Express' made no radio or TV appearances and hasn't appeared on any of The Jam compilation albums

RUNNING ON THE SPOT (Weller)

Recorded on 6 January 1982 at AIR Studios, Oxford Street, London
Produced by Pete Wilson
Album track: The Gift

'Running On The Spot' is another classic Jam song, both lyrically and musically. With a powerful ascending intro, the song explodes into life with Weller's echoed vocal 'I was hoping we would make real progress', which kicks off a lyric that could relate as much to society in general as to The Jam and their fans. Some saw it as another call for soul-searching, to take a closer look at our motives in order to find out why we weren't improving as individuals, as Weller had been insisting we must for several years. Looking around at his fans,

Paul must have wondered why so many of them weren't hearing his peace and love message, and why they 'get all violent when the boat gets rocked'.

Broadcaster Peter Gordon was clear about the message in 'Running On The Spot': 'I think it is one of Weller's sad songs; he can only be observational and reflective but can offer no real positive solutions, such as are common in a lot of other Jam songs. In this one he seems to be saying "Well, if everyone else has given up I might as well give up too."'

Weller felt the image of running on the spot without making any progress was such a powerful one, he decided to reflect that message on the album's sleeve by having photographs taken of all three band members running on the spot on the roof of AIR Studios. Shortly before *The Gift* was released, Paul was still agonising over the sleeve design in minute detail. Dennis Munday recalls the problem and told Steve Malins in his biography, *Paul Weller*: 'I can only think of about two occasions when he actually asked for something that did cost a lot of money. One of those was when he asked to change the sleeve to *The Gift* whilst it was actually being printed. The original version had a jagged line around the three photographs. He came in one morning, very early, and he was clearly agitated. He said, "Look, I really don't like it." So I said fine, take it off. We had to destroy about 75,000 copies. He didn't demand a change, he just asked whether it was possible, and it was.'

CIRCUS (Foxton)

Recorded in October 1981 at AIR Studios, Oxford Street, London
Produced by Pete Wilson
Album track: The Gift

'Circus' is a funk instrumental written by Foxton in the studio as the recording sessions commenced in October 1981, and was the first track on *The Gift* to be recorded. AIR Studios overlooked London's Oxford Circus, providing inspiration for the song's title (it was not, as many fans believed, a reference to the song's 'Big Top' cabaret feel). The track has since been used on several television programmes, notably by the BBC during their coverage of the 1996 European Cup.

THE PLANNER'S DREAM GOES WRONG (Weller)

Recorded on 12 January 1982 at AIR Studios, Oxford Street, London
Produced by Pete Wilson
Album track: The Gift

'The Planner's Dream Goes Wrong' is generally regarded as one of The Jam's least popular tracks. It does illustrate, however, not only Weller's desire to experiment musically but also the band's ability to tackle diverse genres. It was a brave move but not one that Jam fans warmed to, and as a result the song was rarely played live. It has also never appeared on any 'best of' collections and remains tucked away on a musically varied album as testament to the skill of the musicians, if nothing else.

Lyrically Weller tackles the subject of town planning and urban development, notably high-rise flats dressed up as luxury apartments. Echoing a regular Weller theme, first surfacing in 'Bricks And Mortar' in 1977, the song illustrates the conditions the working classes are forced to live in, the reality of which was urine-stained hallways, litter and broken-down lifts. Vastly different from the image presented by the town planners in their glossy brochures. With little else going for the song, Paul at least manages to highlight the contrast between the lifestyles of the planners and those they plan for by creating the image of a wealthy town planner sitting in his country house, laying out plans for how he believes the rest of us should exist, 14 floors from the ground.

The calypso drumming was an unusual feature in a Jam track; in fact, it was the only occasion the steelpan was used. Playing for The Jam in the studio was the legendary calypso drummer Russ Henderson who had been approached one day in 1965 by social worker Rhaune Laslett and asked to perform at a small event she was planning in the streets of Notting Hill. Henderson agreed, told all his friends (who turned up in large numbers) and started playing in Ladbroke Grove. Henderson's band subsequently walked along Bayswater with a growing number of followers and the now world-famous Notting Hill Carnival was born.

CARNATION (Weller)

Recorded on 8 January 1982 at AIR Studios, Oxford Street, London
Produced by Pete Wilson
Album track: The Gift

Following the clumsy 'Planner's Dream', The Jam were quickly back to their best with a beautiful, haunting ballad. Starting with a lazy drum roll, 'Carnation', like so many Jam songs, is underpinned by the drum part and bass line.

Lyrically 'Carnation' tackles greed and Weller's dissatisfaction with the society we have created for ourselves. Written in the first person, Paul has us hating his character and wondering if he is portraying his own feelings. Using emotive language, he represents an insensitive, selfish individual without regard for others. But in a final twist Weller gives us something to think about by suggesting that greed, fear and hate are in all of us; the character could be any one of us at times. Clearly influenced by Ken Kesey, who provided much inspiration during Weller's early songwriting career, Paul describes 'machinery roaring to his empty sound', machinery being a Kesey term for society's governing or ruling classes.

Although the theme of 'Carnation' is similar to many Jam songs, its lyric is possibly one of the cleverest of them all. Gone is the usual stark urban language conjuring images of cities, streets, towns and tube stations. These are replaced by images of cold-hearted greed and the need for introspection. 'Carnation' has lyrics to make you think twice, and anything that does that must be a good thing.

'Carnation' was a regular staple in The Jam's live set and featured on both the Transglobal Unity Express and The Beat Surrender tours. A live version from the Transglobal Unity Express Tour features on 1993's *Live Jam* album and the song was included on the definitive collection *The Sound Of The Jam* in 2002. In 1999 Liam Gallagher and Steve Craddock, of Oasis and Ocean Colour Scene respectively, recorded a haunting psychedelic version of 'Carnation', included on the tribute album *Fire And Skill* and also released as a single on 23 September 1999 and reaching number 6 in the UK charts.

THE GIFT (Weller)
Recorded on 11 January 1982 at AIR Studios, Oxford Street, London
Produced by Pete Wilson
Album track: The Gift

Despite being the band's only rock-solid number one album, *The Gift* still attracted criticism from the music press, with the *NME* commenting that 'Weller's ambition is to face the pains and injustices of contemporary class society and yet remain positive which, times being what they are, is almost impossible. The stress of the effort pulls *The Gift* to pieces and it ends up a collection of false starts.' In America, meanwhile, *The Gift* was slammed as 'The Jam's most undernourished album'.

By and large Jam fans appear to agree; in almost every fan poll of favourite top ten Jam tracks only 'Town Called Malice' regularly appears from the band's final recording year. Almost every vote goes for tracks produced during the band's middle period between 1979 and 1980 (*All Mod Cons* to *Sound Affects*).

The Gift was one of the first songs written for the final album and was included in The Jam's live set from December 1981. It opened their BBC *In Concert* series, broadcast live on 19 December from the Hippodrome in London. That performance was introduced by Gary Crowley, who asked for a 'Magic hand for a magic band, it's Paul, Bruce and Rick – The Jam.' 'The Gift' was also the last song The Jam ever played together, performing it for the final time during their last encore in Brighton on 12 December 1982.

THE GREAT DEPRESSION (Weller)
Recorded in January 1982 at AIR Studios, Oxford Street, London
Produced by Pete Wilson
B-side to 'Just Who Is The 5 O'Clock Hero'

At the tail end of 1981, Polydor and The Jam had considered releasing a collection of soul covers, as The Jam's set had been sprinkled with soul classics throughout their career. But the planned EP was shelved after the band performed four CND benefit concerts with a set including a handful of soul tunes and a few similarly inspired new Jam songs, including 'The Great Depression'.

With the idea of the soul EP abandoned, 'The Great Depression' made its only appearance tucked away on the B-side of import single 'Just Who Is The 5 O'Clock Hero'. The song was an attempt to bring a new soulful feel to The Jam's music. During the benefit concerts, however, the stomping masses roared in unison when the band played the likes of 'Going Underground' and 'The Eton Rifles' but shuffled around awkwardly to 'The Great Depression' and Eddie Floyd's 'Big Bird'. Weller was fighting a losing battle.

'The Great Depression' is a good example of the direction The Jam were taking. Its inclusion of horns and busy arrangements, and with its marching Northern Soul melody, the song overtly borrows sections from The Temptations' Motown hit 'My Girl'. Unbelievably, Polydor allowed the sleeve notes for the boxed set of The Jam's *Singles Collection*, released in 2001, to advise fans that the song would have been better placed in the hands of Paul Weller's follow-up project The Style Council. Weller certainly disagreed with such ill-informed opinions at the time, as The Jam included 'The Great Depression' among the eight songs played during the band's final live television appearance on *The Tube*.

Fortunately, Polydor finally noticed the bizarre attitude of their sleeve-note writers to the band's rhythm section and, after a series of complaints, put a stop to it. *The Singles Collection* sleeve notes were by no means the only offenders. In the booklet accompanying *Direction Creation Reaction*, a collection of the entire Jam catalogue, Pat Gilbert couldn't help himself and described Foxton's 'Carnaby Street' and

'London Traffic' as coming 'perilously close to cementing the band's reputation as blinkered little Englanders' and 'lacking a lyric of maturity' respectively. The same writer was soon dismissing Bruce's 'Don't Tell Them You're Sane' as a 'middling Foxton contribution'.

Paulo Hewitt picks up the baton in a later section by surmising that Foxton's 'News Of The World', despite its selling in much greater numbers than Weller's previous effort 'The Modern World', was not the 'return to form the band and audience wished for'. And followed that up by unnecessarily pointing out that most of the songs on The Jam's proposed third album, which was scrapped as they were not 'up to scratch', were 'penned by Bruce'. Many of them were in fact Weller efforts. Buckler managed to avoid criticism in these notes, although he received only one passing mention in the entire section for his 'power drums'.

But with the anti-Foxton/Buckler contingent in full flow on their product packaging, maybe such phrasing was to be expected. It didn't end there. On The Jam's *Greatest Hits* album, Matteo Sedazzari contributes the sleeve notes and insists that 'Bruce Foxton and Rick Buckler were the strong rhythmic piece of the band but whose musical interests differed from that of Paul Weller. In order not to embarrass themselves they ended their career with their heads held high.' Sedazzari had failed to recognise The Jam's integral dynamic, but Polydor still sent it to print.

Other sleeve notes are equally scathing, with Foxton's 'The Night' being described in *The Singles Collection* as 'only notable for the introduction of the harmonica to The Jam sound', which in fact was introduced a year earlier on 'The Midnight Hour', the last track on *This Is The Modern World*. In the same booklet, Foxton's 'News Of The World' is waved aside as 'winging it in a cloud of bluster'. Regardless of whether any of these observations are valid or not, such remarks should have been left to independent reviewers, not included in the sleeve notes of the band's own product. A bewildering development, it has cast a shadow over Jam history.

The Jam played another secret gig at the Guildford Civic Hall (this was to celebrate Weller's parents' 25th wedding anniversary) before embarking on a world tour to promote *The Gift*. When the band returned from Japan they were due to play two CND benefit concerts at Loftus Road, the home of Queen's Park Rangers in west London, but the shows were cancelled at the last minute, giving the band a month off.

Weller used the unplanned break to take a well-earned holiday with girlfriend Gill and to reflect on the events of the previous 12 months. Now sober (indeed, tee-total), his mood was dour and serious. His fan base seemed unable to understand The Jam's musical direction and appeared unwilling to share the singer's vision of soul. The previous year had been a difficult time both personally and professionally, and he had not enjoyed touring in the spring of 1982 either. And the prospect of agreeing new deals to churn out traditional Jam sounds didn't appeal to him. But Polydor demanded it, the fans demanded it and a sizeable staff of engineers, road crew, security men, drivers and merchandising contractors all relied upon it for their living.

The 24-year-old Weller lay on the beach in Italy unhappy and under siege. The thought of another tour in front of some elements of The Jam's audience – namely the ones down the front causing all the trouble – horrified him. He wanted to be the white Marvin Gaye but realised that the sort of audience The Jam had would not appreciate it, nor would his record company embrace it. Things only got worse when Paul received news during August that his former school friend, poetic inspiration and partner in his publishing company Riot Stories, Dave Waller, had been found dead as a result of a drugs overdose in a shabby Woking hotel.

With the benefit of hindsight it's easy to understand why Weller had to leave The Jam. He was never a punk and all his life's influences were rooted in soul and Motown. All his songs are anti-violent yet were misinterpreted; many have humour, much of it misunderstood; and his political vision is one of peaceful reform rather than the revolution so often attributed to him. Weller's own vision of mod was one of individualism and self-expression, yet the sight of thousands of uniformed kids turning up at the gigs frustrated him.

Weller wanted his music and lyrics to mean something and the concerts to be musical experiences. Instead, many of them degenerated into violent mayhem. Paul's decision on that Italian beach to leave The Jam had nothing to do with Bruce and Rick's suggested lack of musical dexterity, as has been erroneously suggested in the past. Paul's decision to leave The Jam was because they had become a lads' band with a lad fanbase, despite much of their music being subtle and cultured.

There were no fallouts, no rows and no 'bitter pill'. Weller simply understood that he would never be regarded as a serious soul artist in a lads' band. And the image of The Jam jumping up and down playing youth anthems into their thirties, with thousands of kids in parkas chanting 'We are the mods' back at them, wasn't one that any of them relished.

Weller later confirmed this when in 1986 he told *Go Go* fanzine: 'I was getting more and more frustrated with The Jam towards the end. The following we had was all-the-lads-together types and I didn't like that aspect.' By the time Paul caught the Orient Express home from Italy, he had firmly made up his mind to leave the band. As far as he was concerned it was all over.

THE BITTEREST PILL (I EVER HAD TO SWALLOW) (Weller)

Recorded in August 1982 at the Maison Rouge Studio in Fulham
Produced by Pete Wilson and The Jam
A-side released 10 September 1982; Polydor POSP 505; reached no 2 in UK chart
B-side: 'Pity Poor Alfie'/'Fever'

'The Bitterest Pill (I Ever Had To Swallow)' was written, or at least started, by Weller during his Italian sojourn in the summer of 1982. Weller: 'I saw a ghost once, when I was on holiday in Italy. I was petrified, so I got up and wrote the third verse to 'The Bitterest Pill'.'

At the time he was wrestling with his decision to leave the band. He kept that decision quiet from all but his father once he had returned from Italy, but thought that once the decision was made it would become effective immediately. Instead, he had to be reminded that he still had agreements to record two more singles and a seventh album, so with studio time booked the band had to keep working. But Weller was adamant there would be no further album, so a compromise was reached by releasing a live LP (*Dig The New Breed*), meaning that no new LP needed to be written and recorded but Polydor still got their seventh Jam album.

But two new singles were required, and the following month was therefore perhaps the most productive Weller had ever experienced. In that period he finished off 'The Bitterest Pill (I Ever Had To Swallow)' and wrote 'A Solid Bond In Your Heart', 'Beat Surrender' and 'Dr Love'. The first two were immediately regarded as potential singles and the latter donated to Bananarama for their debut album. But Weller commented at the time that he wanted to keep 'A Solid Bond In Your Heart' for 'the future', still giving no clue that his future was without The Jam. Clearly Weller was already planning his next project.

'Bitterest Pill' was arguably a mistake and didn't suit The Jam's natural style. Fans were bemused by yet another change in musical direction and very few outside the Weller camp (for whom he could do no wrong) warmed to the song. It reached number two in the charts purely as a result of the band's vast fan base keeping their collections up to date and, in retrospect, The Jam should have bowed out in style with 'A Solid Bond in Your Heart' followed by 'Beat Surrender'. But it wasn't to be and The Jam are stuck with this mediocre offering towards the end of their discography.

There are two versions of 'The Bitterest Pill (I Ever Had To Swallow)', both including The Belle Stars' Jenny McKeown on backing vocals. The initial demo was scrapped at a cost to the band of nearly £10,000 (the second expensive change Weller asked Dennis Munday for) in favour of an alternative version which sounds much the same, both of them lacking 'feel'. The original version appears on disc five (odds and sods) of *Direction Reaction Creation*, the definitive Jam box set.

PITY POOR ALFIE / FEVER (Weller/Davenport/Cooley)
Recorded in August 1982 at the Maison Rouge Studio in Fulham
Produced by Pete Wilson and The Jam
B-side to 'The Bitterest Pill (I Ever Had To Swallow)'

Disappointed by 'The Bitterest Pill (I Ever Had To Swallow)', fans did find some compensation in its high-quality B-side 'Pity Poor Alfie/Fever', a track which represented The Jam at their very best during that final year. Finding such an invaluable B-side on a Jam single surprised nobody; the only surprise was that 'Alfie' wasn't granted the A-side status it deserved. Fans could only speculate that yet another printing/pressing error at the factory had been responsible for this apparent error in judgment. Surely it must have been a mistake?

Although lyrically muddled and unclear, the song is The Jam's last character song and tells the tale of a suicidal, or perhaps drug-crazed, young man. The initial demo is a swing version which appears on disc five of The Jam's definitive collection *Direction Creation Reaction*. Fans' disdain for the track, or confusion at its style, led to a rethink and 'Alfie' was later re-recorded with a rousing Northern Soul beat running through it – also a horn section apparently borrowed from the theme tune of the hit cop show *The Sweeney*. The track then neatly segues into a version of 'Fever', the 1956 hit for jazz singer Peggy Lee, penned by John Davenport and Eddie Cooley, which had been part of The Jam's live set. Its inclusion on the B-side says as much about Weller's eclectic musical tastes as it does about the lack of material he had for the final Jam offerings.

Once Weller had decided he was definitely leaving The Jam, he felt the best time to inform his band mates would be the next time he saw them, which was when they arrived at the Maison Rouge Studios in Fulham for the 'Beat Surrender' sessions. As Bruce and Rick arrived at the studio, Paul's dad told them Paul wanted a band meeting in the reception area. Bruce immediately feared the worst. Foxton: 'Before we went in there I realised something was up. Meetings weren't something we had ever done before. Usually when things

needed discussing we just chatted about them in the studio, at rehearsals or even on tour. No one had ever called a meeting before.'

With all three band members and John Weller present, Paul simply sat down and told the others he wanted to leave the band. Rick Buckler recalls the atmosphere and notes that everybody tried to talk Paul out of it, but he remained adamant. Buckler: 'No one wanted the band to finish. Nobody at the record label and neither myself, Bruce or John. Paul was the only one who wanted to move on.'

Foxton's immediate reaction was to suggest Paul took some time off and pursue other projects without actually abandoning The Jam, thus leaving the door open for a return in a 'year or so'. But Weller was determined to leave and once he had found the courage to blurt out the news, he was not going to be dissuaded. For Paul it was time to move on. For a while Bruce and Rick remained hopeful that Weller would change his mind, since they still believed The Jam had some mileage left, especially as they finally seemed to be making progress in America. But as youngsters they had always agreed that if one of them wanted to leave the others would call it a day too. With Paul gone, The Jam were gone.

On 20 September 1982 The Jam set out on a mini-tour to promote their new single. The Solid Bond In Your Heart Tour confused many as 'Solid Bond In Your Heart' was not the new single; 'Bitterest Pill' was, and that had taken a critical hammering. Starting at the Leacliff Pavilion, the band set out across country before crossing the water to the Channel Islands, France, Belgium and Holland. The impending split was kept a closely guarded secret and the band jettisoned their horn section in favour of a keyboard player and backing singers Afrodiziac. The tour went well but the pressure of being Paul Weller was starting to take its toll; the singer became ill, leading to the cancellation of some key shows.

The band had managed to keep the impending break-up a secret throughout the summer and well into autumn. News finally leaked out, however, allegedly via a member of The Questions, the band signed to Weller's Respond label and who were supporting The Jam on their end-of-year Beat Surrender Tour. The tour had been booked before Weller's decision to split the band, so no one realised it would be a farewell tour when it was first promoted. Instead, Paul had planned to announce the split during The Jam's live television performance on *The Tube*. *Sounds* ran the story, however, and it was soon echoed by *Record Mirror* and the London *Evening Standard*, leading to an official statement, via a hand-written note, on 30 October.

> 'Personal address to all our fans – At the end of this year, The Jam will be officially splitting up as I feel we have achieved all we can together as a group. I mean this both musically and commercially, I'd hate us to end up old and embarrassing like so many other groups do. I want us to finish with dignity. The longer a group continues, the more frightening the thought of ever ending it becomes and that's why so many of them carry on until it becomes meaningless. I've never wanted The Jam to get to that stage. What we (and you) have built up has meant something and for me that is honesty, passion, energy and youth. I want it to stay that way... Thank you for all the faith you have shown us and for building such a strong force of feeling that all three of us have felt and been touched by. Here's to the future, in love and friendship, Paul Weller.'

Weller immediately agreed to an interview published in *Melody Maker* on 6 November 1982, during which he explained that he wanted to preserve the legacy of his band and that by continuing with The Jam he recognised the risk of spoiling that legacy. By then he wanted to write songs free from the weight of expectation that came with being in the biggest band in the country, and he implied that if his future songs failed then he would not want to spoil The Jam in the process.

Weller insisted he wanted to break up The Jam because he cared about the band. 'It's not because I want to embark on a solo venture and I don't need Bruce and Rick or any of that old bollocks,' he told *Melody Maker*. At no time during the last year of The Jam did Paul, Bruce and Rick show any animosity towards each other, with Weller insisting that they 'always got on really well, probably better as we've

grown older.' But no sooner had the split been announced than others close to the singer waded into the fray. Paul's mother Ann, quoted by Steve Malins: 'Yeah, well, they [Foxton and Buckler] should have done more. They were always resting when Paul was hard at it.'

John Reed, while researching his book *My Ever Changing Moods*, noticed a similar sentiment. 'What is really fascinating' he wrote, 'is the degree of bickering, back-biting and plain immaturity which seems to have emerged.' Read saw for himself how those close to Weller were quick to dismiss Foxton and Buckler. Read got the impression that the pair were deemed 'untouchable' but could see for himself that the actual split was 'by all accounts relatively civilised.'

BEAT SURRENDER (Weller)

Recorded in October 1982 at the Maison Rouge Studios, Fulham
Produced by Pete Wilson
A-side released 26 November 1982; Polydor POSPX 540; reached no 1 in UK chart
B-side: 'Shopping'/'Move On Up'/'Stoned Out Of My Mind'/'War'

With its title apparently a variation of Anita ('Ring My Bell') Ward's 1979 soul hit 'Sweet Surrender', The Jam bowed out with their fourth and last number one hit single. 'Beat Surrender' entered the charts at number one, the third time the band had achieved that feat (after 'Going Underground' and 'Town Called Malice') and listed by the BBC as a record at that time. Their only number one not to enter the charts at the summit was 'Start!', which took an extra week to replace David Bowie's 'Ashes to Ashes' in the top spot.

'Beat Surrender' was released as public grieving at the passing of The Jam was at its height and the Carnaby Street-led 'Save The Jam Campaign' was gathering pace. Despite this there would be no turning back and the country's biggest band had written and recorded together for the last time.

The first and last time 'Beat Surrender' was performed live on television was on 5 November 1982, when The Jam made their final live television appearance on the first edition of Channel Four's *The*

Tube. Hosted by Paula Yates, Jools Holland and Muriel Gray, *The Tube* went on to become a cult TV show. The Jam's appearance on its debut programme secured its credibility from the start, with Channel Four experiencing record viewing figures for a show of its type. Jam fans tuned in to witness, and record, the band's farewell performance, and prior to the show Muriel Gray was given the task of interviewing Weller in his dressing room. He claimed he had no immediate plans to form another band, though his Style Council project would be announced only weeks later.

During the emotional performance, The Jam started with a slow, horn-driven version of 'Ghosts' followed by quality versions of 'In The Crowd', 'The Modern World', Curtis Mayfield's 'Move On Up' and 'The Great Depression' before Weller introduced 'Beat Surrender' as the band's final single. Viewers were given a glimpse of Paul's future musical intentions, with the band flanked by a horn section, tambourine-playing backing singers (complete with traditional African dress) and a keyboard player. The big band image was unusual as for years The Jam had played live as a power trio, but any suggestion that Foxton and Buckler weren't able adapt to such a line-up is quashed by the performance here. The Jam had never looked more comfortable or sounded better. The final song the band played on live television was 'Precious', once again at odds with later suggestions that Weller was unhappy with the rhythm section parts of the track.

Weller's future musical projects included developing his own new label, Respond Records, which he intended to use to discover and promote new young artists. One of these artists was 18-year-old singer Tracy Young, who later became known for having a minor hit with The Questions-penned song 'The House That Jack Built'. Weller decided to use Tracy's backing vocal on The Jam's final hit single but more for the exposure it would give her than for the benefit of the song. 'We don't actually need you to do backing vocals,' Weller shamelessly told her, 'but it will be good exposure for you.' In the same spirit, Paul invited Tracy to appear with the band on *Top Of The Pops*, where the two singers danced around out of time on a platform behind Rick and Bruce, who had taken up positions at the front of the stage. Weller looked awkward shuffling around without his guitar and for some Jam fans enough was enough.

Musically, 'The Bitterest Pill (I Ever Had To Swallow)' aside, The Jam were bowing out in style but fans were still bemused by Weller's attitude. Peter Gordon: 'I felt that Paul was distancing himself from what was happening, and that was disappointing. It was The Jam's last single, a rallying cry, a snapshot of everything the band stood for and was proud of. And yet Weller wasn't interested. He certainly didn't look too interested.'

The single's sleeve featured Paul's girlfriend Gill holding a white flag of surrender, while the sleeve notes introduced The Boy Wonder, a nom de plume for Paul himself.

SHOPPING (Weller)

MOVE ON UP (Mayfield)

STONED OUT OF MY MIND (Record/Acklin)

WAR (Whitfield/Strong)

Recorded in October 1982 at the Maison Rouge Studios, Fulham, London
Produced by Pete Wilson
B-side to 'Beat Surrender'

Sharing side one with 'Beat Surrender' was Weller's last ever Jam song. A clear indication of his future direction, 'Shopping' is a slow-paced, dreamy jazz tune. For its lyrical inspiration the writer puts himself in the first person again and drifts up and down a suburban high street, echoing the theme of many previous Jam songs, 'Private Hell', 'Boy About Town' and 'Dream Time' to name but a few. This time the subject attempts to find his own fashion but as usual fails to fit in with the 'in crowd', an introspective element obvious in much of Weller's songwriting.

Musically Paul draws on his new jazz influences culled from the 'Absolute Beginners' culture, in the shape of Blue Note artists like James Taylor and Jimmy Smith. It's not one of The Jam's best and in their last studio session the powerful Rick Buckler drum patterns, that had underpinned all The Jam's best work, are notable only for their absence. On 'Shopping' Buckler plays a slow and effective jazz snare with brushes.

In terms of their recording career The Jam had come full circle. They started out as a schoolboy R and B/soul covers band and took in a wide range of influences throughout their career, before ending it with three consummate soul covers. First out of the box was 'Move On Up', a classic Curtis Mayfield track which The Jam had played regularly throughout their live career.

Weller had always been inspired by Mayfield's positive approach to lyric writing and this was reflected in most of The Jam's catalogue; he once commented: 'The words are really important to my songs. I think it's sad that words have become a bit unfashionable, no one's that bothered about lyrics. A lot of records which I really like – dance records – which have a lot of good grooves in them and are great to dance to, the words always let them down. They're often not even good pop lyrics, or good love songs, usually they are just inane. Kool and The Gang are brilliant. I think you should try and use all the song, every bit of it. Motown did it. They kept the groove but they still had good lyrics. In the seventies people like Curtis Mayfield managed to do it with positive political lyrics.'

Mayfield's 'Move On Up' was as upbeat as they come and, as The Jam disintegrated, Weller made sure young fans had a positive message to take with them. Weller deliberately included the track in The Jam's last ever live television performance in an attempt to encourage fans to remain positive about the split. For some the band had almost become a way of life and the 'Save The Jam' campaigns were by now in full flow.

Next up was 'Stoned Out Of My Mind', a hit song written in 1973 by the Chi Lites' Eugene Record and R and B singer Barbara Acklin, who had previously written the smash hit 'Have You Seen Her'. Weller had long been a fan and The Jam's version, complete with a Frisco flute solo, is clearly a supper-club jazz pastiche. Once again, Rick demonstrates his versatility with a brilliant performance with the brushes, skilfully underpinning Foxton's inventive bass lines. The use of horns gives the song a slight *Starsky and Hutch* feel.

Last but by no means least is The Jam's rousing version of Norman Whitfield and Barrett Strong's 'War', which gave Edwin Starr a big hit in 1970 on the Tamla Motown label. Whitfield and Strong had been responsible for a series of hits in the 1960s such as 'Papa Was a Rolling Stone' and 'I Heard It Through The Grapevine'. Weller, being a big fan of their work, felt their anti-war anthem was the perfect way to demonstrate The Jam's support of the growing CND movement – and to round off the band's studio career.

EIGHT

... SO SHALL IT BE IN THE END

AS the band played out their final moments, the extent of Weller's personal celebrity became even more apparent. The sycophants appeared in droves, with books about The Jam, written by Weller fans and/or personal friends, supposedly providing the inside story but reducing the roles of Foxton and Buckler to mere bit parts. One of the group's originators, Steve Brookes, barely got a mention at all. Weller, to his credit, makes only the occasional comment on the split: 'It's sad, but as you drift apart you lose contact with people,' he later said. 'I haven't seen Rick and Bruce for some time. You move in different circles and make new friends, it's a fact of life.'

It's only Weller, however, who moves in new circles, maintaining little significant contact with anyone except Steve Brookes and Enzo Esposito. Brookes and Weller have managed to put their differences behind them, having reunited in 1994 after 13 years when Steve was invited to a surprise birthday party for Weller. Brookes tells the story: 'My wife and I arrived after the party was underway but before Paul had got there. Before long word went round he was about to arrive and everybody broke into "Happy birthday to you" as he came in. When he saw me it took a few seconds for him to recognise me and when he did he flung his arms around me, which threw me for a moment. He had won the Ivor Novello Award for songwriting earlier that day and had already started celebrating. We spent most of the evening talking about old times and have stayed in touch ever since.'

Most of Foxton's friends are the same people he socialised with during his printing apprenticeship in Woking before The Jam signed a record deal, while Buckler remains friendly with many of his old Woking mates and members of The Jam's entourage.

As The Jam dissolved, comments by Polydor A&R man Dennis Munday were typical of the prevailing attitude: 'I don't think Paul could go anywhere further with The Jam. I think that's what *The Gift* proved, that there wasn't anywhere else to go. Bruce and Rick just weren't good enough to transpose out of The Jam into The Style Council.' With judgments like that, it's hardly surprising that Polydor failed to even consider issuing recording contracts to Foxton and Buckler. Munday again: 'Paul realised he was good enough for soul but that the others couldn't follow. I would love to hear The Style Council play 'Beat Surrender'.' Munday seems to be suggesting that The Style Council was in some way a step up from The Jam and that only Paul was good enough to make it. The fact that The Style Council had nothing like the success of The Jam highlights a flaw in his theory.

Such comments are typical of the Weller camp but, significantly, never come from Paul himself. In fact, Weller failed to make his 'soul classic', only coming close in 1984 with his single 'You're The Best Thing'. Considering Munday's comments, it could equally be noted that some of the better Style Council tracks, such as 'Shout To The Top' and 'My Ever Changing Moods', could have been even better had Bruce and Rick played on them. All this must remain conjecture, however. What's certain is that The Jam devolved, not because Bruce and Rick weren't equal to Paul's change in musical direction, but largely because Weller was disillusioned by the thuggish and narrow-minded element in the band's audience.

In fact, Weller's view had been vindicated when the band toured Britain and Europe for the final time in late 1982. Violence among the audiences was a regular feature. Starting on 25 November at The Glasgow Apollo, the Beat Surrender Tour hadn't been planned as a farewell tour. That was the reason for the relatively small and unusual locations included in the itinerary; it's hard to imagine the Poole Arts Centre or the Afan Lido in Port Talbot hosting farewell gigs for the country's most popular group otherwise. But there were large venues on the list, too, such as Birmingham's Bingley Hall (a Jam stronghold) and their home venue of Guildford Civic Hall.

Such was the demand to see The Jam one final time that Weller agreed to one big London gig at Wembley Arena on 1 December, a venue he hated but which would give as many fans as possible a chance to see the band. Weller had miscalculated The Jam's popularity, however; the Arena sold out within minutes, leading to a second date being added for the following night. Once announced, this too sold out within minutes, as did a third date. In the end The Jam stayed at Wembley for five nights, only leaving in order to honour a pre-arranged date at The Pavilion in Bridlington Spa. At many venues around the country, notably the first date in Glasgow, the band received an emotional standing ovation as they walked on stage. Tension was apparent everywhere, however, and fighting among the crowd periodically broke out.

The worst of this came in Brighton, at the band's farewell gig. What was intended as a musical celebration of The Jam's career, with early tracks such as 'In The City' and 'The Modern World' reappearing on the set list, instead turned into a succession of ugly, violent scenes. At one point Foxton stopped playing to lecture the troublemakers from the stage, while Weller merely sat on his amplifier, staring into space. The mood was sour and it was a relief for everyone when it was over.

The last track The Jam ever played together was 'The Gift', after which the venue fell silent, fans shuffled through the exits and The Jam were gone. The band themselves were in no mood to party and made their separate ways home to Woking, meeting again a week later for the group's annual Christmas party at the Greyhound in Fulham, the scene of many of their London appearances five years earlier. Every year the band had booked the Greyhound for their Christmas get-together, but in 1982 the atmosphere resembled a wake rather than a festive event.

Rick Buckler woke up the following morning without a job. A month later, however, he was the first member of The Jam to emerge from the ashes. His first decision was to start looking around for songwriters to work with. Not that this was too difficult, as unsolicited demo tapes dropped through his door on a daily basis. One of these came from Ray Simone, who in turn suggested his Master Switch band mate Jimmy Edwards. This wasn't the first time the singer had been recommended so Rick asked Ray to arrange a meeting.

Until this time Jimmy had been working with bands such as The Pretenders, Sham 69 and the song-writing duo Godley and Creme, who had assisted him in his solo career. Edwards and Buckler formed an immediate bond and agreed to put a band together; Time UK was created. The following few months were occupied by song-writing, the search for professional representation and a record deal, plus the small matter of finding the remaining band members. Word went out and the subsequent auditioning process brought in guitarist Danny Kustow from the Tom Robinson Band and Nick South of both the Yoko Ono Band and Steve Marriott's All Stars. Later, Kustow returned to TRB and was replaced by Fletcher Christian.

In April 1983, Rick and Jimmy took the band out on a minor tour and the reviews were very good. So good that they were approached by Red Bus Records, who offered to release the debut single 'The Cabaret'. Unfortunately, a mix-up by the promotional team led to a prime-time TV appearance being aired three weeks after the record had slipped out of the charts, denying the band vital promotion that might have led to a Top Ten hit. This, coupled with Buckler being refused access to The Jam Fan Club, led to hundreds of thousands of would-be fans not even knowing about the release. Nearly 60,000 copies were sold, enough these days to take it to number one, but not quite enough in 1983.

Despite the setbacks, the success of 'The Cabaret' caught the attention of major record label Arista, who signed the band up and released their following singles, the Tony Visconti-produced 'Playground of Privilege' and 'You Won't Stop'. Moderate success followed, particularly on the live scene, but as public interest in New Wave-type guitar bands gave way to the New Romantic movement, so popular in the mid-1980s, the band members started pursuing other projects. Christian moved to a New York studio after finding work as a sound engineer and South emigrated to Los Angeles, marrying the daughter of former Labour chancellor Tony Crosland in the process. Ray Simone moved into the merchandising side of the business, Jimmy Edwards had a studio built in Surrey which he used to help underprivileged children and to produce charity records, and Rick bought Arkentide Recording Studios in Islington, north London, though that business ground to a halt during the recession of the early 1990s.

Rick has turned his back on the music business and now lives with his wife Leslie (his girlfriend during the days of The Jam) on the outskirts of Woking with their two children. He remains proud of the legacy he helped create but, when asked about his future musical ambitions, replies with a smile: 'I've done all the drumming I want to do, it's time to leave it to others.' There have been suggestions that Rick sits by the phone waiting for a call to say that The Jam are reforming, but this is patently untrue. He doesn't rule out playing again with his old band mates but feels it's extremely unlikely and would certainly never initiate such an idea. Symbolically, his famous white roto toms lie rotting at the bottom of his garden, where Rick nailed them to a tree for his children to play with when they were younger.

No sooner had The Jam ended than Bruce Foxton was offered a solo deal with Arista Records, his debut single 'Freak' reaching number 22 in the UK charts. It was a promising start, and his subsequent album *Touch Sensitive* also charted well. But Bruce found the record company were in too much of a hurry to cash in on his reputation. As a result some of the songs on the album, by his own admission, aren't as good as they might have been. Foxton: 'Whatever I gave Arista they just said, "Yeah, go ahead, put it on the album," when what they should have said was, "Well, it's not very good is it?" They just wanted to cash in while the interest was still out there. Half of it I'm really proud of, but I just wish I had taken more time over it now.'

These days (ever since 1990, in fact) Bruce is a member of Stiff Little Fingers. SLF regularly tour Britain and America, with Jam fans always turning out in large numbers. The band's latest album, *Guitar and Drum*, is regarded by some critics as the best work they have ever done. Foxton now lives on the outskirts of Guildford with his wife Pat (who was also his girlfriend during the Jam's career), and for a man with such a high musical profile many people are amazed to find him dropping into local pubs around his hometown for a night out with old friends. The oft-reported animosity he is supposed to bear towards his old band is hard to substantiate; Bruce is always happy to chat with fans and sign autographs, apparently unaffected, albeit surprised and flattered, by the attention he receives.

Like Rick, Bruce doesn't rule out the possibility of The Jam playing together again but would never initiate such a project himself. Neither man feels any of the bitterness towards Weller that is suggested by those close to the singer. Bruce has even, on occasion, forwarded on the odd message of goodwill. Foxton: '*Wild Wood* is one of my favourite albums. When I first heard it I sent a note to Paul's studio with my best wishes and telling him I thought it was a great album.'

Within weeks of The Jam's final gig, Paul Weller had formed The Style Council with Mick Talbot, formerly of The Merton Parkas, who had done session work with The Jam during 1979 and 1980. Without ever matching the success The Jam achieved, The Style Council produced a catalogue of good tunes throughout the 1980s. But with his core audience out of touch with Weller's new style of music, Polydor took the commercial decision in 1989 not to release the album *Modernism: A New Decade*. And with that The Style Council disbanded.

Weller then spent two years without either a band or a record deal but in 1991 picked up his guitar again and started writing new tunes. The subsequent album *Paul Weller* received only muted praise, but his follow-up single, the aptly named *Into Tomorrow*, put Weller back in the Top 40. In late 1993 Weller cemented his comeback with the album *Wild Wood*, which sold over 100,000 copies within two weeks of its release, taking it to number two in the UK charts. Two years later he released the million-selling album *Stanley Road* to critical acclaim all round.

Throughout the 1980s and 90s The Jam's musical legacy has been seen as an influence on hundreds of bands, some as successful as The Smiths, Stone Roses (who were originally called English Rose after The Jam song), Ocean Colour Scene, Oasis and Blur. Polydor A&R man Dennis Munday claims he saw this coming: 'I reckon two or three bands come up every decade who have an effect on pop and rock music which lasts forever – the Jam are one of those bands. And I like to think I recognised it almost immediately – unlike a lot of people at Polydor, who I'm certain never thought the band had any longevity.'

Seen in retrospect, there's little doubt that the material released by The Jam in their heyday, and still available today, counts as one of the strongest, and most consistently stimulating, back-catalogues in rock.

APPENDIX 1

UK SINGLES

Polydor 2058 866 **IN THE CITY/TAKIN' MY LOVE** *(4/77: no 40)*

Polydor 2058 903 **ALL AROUND THE WORLD/CARNABY STREET** *(7/77: no 13)*

Polydor 2058 945 **THE MODERN WORLD** [censored]/**SWEET SOUL MUSIC** (live)/**BACK IN MY ARMS AGAIN** (live)/**BRICKS AND MORTAR** (part)(live) *(10/77: no 36)*

Polydor 2058 995 **NEWS OF THE WORLD/AUNTIES AND UNCLES (IMPULSIVE YOUTHS) /INNOCENT MAN** *(2/78: no 27)*

Polydor 2059 054 **DAVID WATTS/'A' BOMB IN WARDOUR STREET** *(8/78: no 25)*

Polydor POSP 8 **DOWN IN THE TUBE STATION AT MIDNIGHT** [edit]/**SO SAD ABOUT US/THE NIGHT** *(10/78: no 15)*

Polydor POSP 34 **STRANGE TOWN/THE BUTTERFLY COLLECTOR** *(3/79: no 15)*

Polydor POSP 69 **WHEN YOU'RE YOUNG/SMITHERS-JONES** *(8/79: no 17)*

Polydor POSP 83 **THE ETON RIFLES/SEE-SAW** *(10/79: no 3)*

Polydor POSP 113 **GOING UNDERGROUND/THE DREAMS OF CHILDREN** *(3/80:no 1)*

Polydor POSPJ 113 **GOING UNDERGROUND/THE DREAMS OF CHILDREN/ AWAY FROM THE NUMBERS** (live)/**THE MODERN WORLD** (live)/**DOWN IN THE TUBE STATION AT MIDNIGHT** (live) [limited edition of 100,000] *3/80*

Polydor 2059 266 **START!/LIZA RADLEY** *(8/80: no 1)*

Polydor POSP 257 **FUNERAL PYRE/DISGUISES** *(5/81: no 4)*

Polydor POSP 350 **ABSOLUTE BEGINNERS/TALES FROM THE RIVERBANK** *(limited edition of 100,000 with lyric sheet – 10/81: no 4)*

Polydor POSP 400 **TOWN CALLED MALICE/PRECIOUS** *(2/82: no 1)*

Polydor POSPX 400 **TOWN CALLED MALICE** (live)/**PRECIOUS** (extended) *(12", 2/82)*

Polydor POSP 505 **THE BITTEREST PILL (I EVER HAD TO SWALLOW)/PITY POOR ALFIE/FEVER** *(9/82: no 2)*

Polydor POSP 540 **BEAT SURRENDER/SHOPPING** *(11/82: no 1)*

Polydor POSPJ 540 **BEAT SURRENDER/SHOPPING/MOVE ON UP/STONED OUT OF MY MIND/WAR** *(limited edition double-pack – 11/82)*

Polydor POSPX 540 **BEAT SURRENDER/SHOPPING/MOVE ON UP/STONED OUT OF MY MIND/WAR** *(12": 11/82)*

Polydor POSP 482 **THAT'S ENTERTAINMENT/DOWN IN THE TUBE STATION AT MIDNIGHT** (live) *(1/83: no 21, import 1/81)*

Polydor POSP 483 **JUST WHO IS THE 5 O'CLOCK HERO/WAR/THE GREAT DEPRESSION** *(1/83: no 8, import 6/82)*

Polydor SNAPL 45 **LIVE EP: Move On Up/Get Yourself Together/The Great Depression** *(9/83)*

[serial number unknown] **BUT I'M DIFFERENT NOW** (limited edition EP given away with first pressing of Snap!) *(9/83)*

Old Gold OG 9895 **BEAT SURRENDER/THE BITTEREST PILL (I EVER HAD TO SWALLOW)** *(12/89)*

Old Gold OG 9894 **TOWN CALLED MALICE/ABSOLUTE BEGINNERS** *(3/90)*

Old Gold OG 9896 **THE ETON RIFLES/DOWN IN THE TUBE STATION AT MIDNIGHT** *(3/90)*

Old Gold OG 9897 **GOING UNDERGROUND/START!** *(3/90)*

Strangefruit SFPS 080 **THE PEEL SESSIONS: In The City/Art School/I've Changed My Address/The Modern World** *(12": 7/90)*

Strangefruit SFPSMC 080 **THE PEEL SESSIONS** *(cassette, 7/90)*

Strangefruit SFPSCD 080 **THE PEEL SESSIONS** *(CD, 7/90)*

Polydor PO 155 **THAT'S ENTERTAINMENT/DOWN IN THE TUBE STATION AT MIDNIGHT** *(6/91)*

Polydor POCS 155 **THAT'S ENTERTAINMENT/DOWN IN THE TUBE STATION AT MIDNIGHT** (live) *(cassette, 6/91)*

Polydor PZ 155 **THAT'S ENTERTAINMENT/DOWN IN THE TUBE STATION AT MIDNIGHT** (live)/**TOWN CALLED MALICE** (live) *(12", 6/91)*

Polydor PZCD 155 **THAT'S ENTERTAINMENT/DOWN IN THE TUBE STATION AT MIDNIGHT** (live)/**TOWN CALLED MALICE** (live) *(CD, 6/91)*

Polydor PO 199 **THE DREAMS OF CHILDREN/AWAY FROM THE NUMBERS** (live)/**THE MODERN WORLD** (live) *(3/92)*

Polydor PZ 199 **THE DREAMS OF CHILDREN/AWAY FROM THE NUMBERS** (live)/**THE MODERN WORLD** (live) *(12", 3/92)*

Polydor PZCD 199 **THE DREAMS OF CHILDREN/AWAY FROM THE NUMBERS** (live)/**THE MODERN WORLD** (live) *(CD, 3/92)*

nb: all The Jam singles up to 'Going Underground' were re-released in May 1980 and again in January 1983.

US SINGLES

Polydor PD 14442 **IN THE CITY/TAKIN' MY LOVE** *(1977)*

Polydor PD 14462 **I NEED YOU (FOR SOMEONE)/IN THE CITY** *(1978)*

Polydor PD 14553 **THE BUTTERFLY COLLECTOR/STRANGE TOWN** *(black or yellow vinyl, 1979)*

Polydor PD 14556 **MR. CLEAN/DOWN IN THE TUBE STATION AT MIDNIGHT** *(1979)*

Polydor PD 2051 **THE ETON RIFLES/SMITHERS-JONES** *(promo only, 1979)*

Polydor PD 2074 **HEATWAVE/SATURDAY'S KIDS** *(1979)*

Polydor PD 2155 **START! /WHEN YOU'RE YOUNG** *(picture sleeve, 1980)*

Polydor PRO 145 **GOING UNDERGROUND/THE DREAMS OF CHILDREN**
(given away with initial copies of Sound Affects, 1980)

Polydor PX 1-503 **THE JAM: Absolute Beginners/Tales From The Riverbank/
Funeral Pyre/Disguises/Liza Radley** *(12" EP, picture sleeve, 1981; no 176)*

Polydor PD 2206 **TOWN CALLED MALICE/PRECIOUS** *(1982)*

Polydor PX 1-506 **THE BITTEREST PILL (I EVER HAD TO SWALLOW)/PITY
POOR ALFIE/FEVER/THE GREAT DEPRESSION/WAR** *(12", picture sleeve,
1982; no 135)*

Polydor CX 1-506 **THE BITTEREST PILL (I EVER HAD TO SWALLOW)/PITY
POOR ALFIE/FEVER/THE GREAT DEPRESSION/WAR** *(cassette, 1982)*

Polydor 810 751-1 **BEAT SURRENDER/SHOPPING/MOVE ON UP/STONED
OUT OF MY MIND/WAR** (version) *(12", picture sleeve, 1982; no 171)*

Polydor 810 751-4 **BEAT SURRENDER/SHOPPING/MOVE ON UP/STONED
OUT OF MY MIND/WAR** (version) *(cassette, 1982)*

S/Fruit DEI 8350-2 **THE PEEL SESSIONS: same as UK** *(CD, 1990)*

nb: 7" promos with both sides playing the A-side exist for all singles with the PD
prefix, and are generally much easier to find than the official releases.

OTHER US RELEASES

Polydor PRO 078 **MR CLEAN** [censored]**/ENGLISH ROSE/TO BE SOMEONE
(DIDN'T WE HAVE A NICE TIME)** *(12" promo, 1979)*

Polydor PRO 149 **MONDAY/THAT'S ENTERTAINMENT/PRETTY GREEN/START!**
(12" promo, 1980)

Polydor PRO 180 **TOWN CALLED MALICE/TOWN CALLED MALICE**
(12" promo, 1982)

Polydor SACD 491 **JAM COVERS: And Your Bird Can Sing/I Got You (I Feel Good)/Move On Up/Disguises/So Sad About Us/Stoned Out Of My Mind** *(CD promo, 1992)*

UK ALBUMS

Polydor 2383 447 **IN THE CITY: Art School / I've Changed My Address/ Slow Down / I Got By In Time / Away From The Numbers / Batman Theme / In The City / Sounds From The Street / Non-Stop Dancing / Time For Truth / Takin' My Love / Bricks And Mortar** *(5/77: no 20)*

Polydor 2383 475 **THIS IS THE MODERN WORLD: The Modern World / London Traffic / Standards / Life From A Window / The Combine / Don't Tell Them You're Sane / In The Street Today / London Girl / I Need You (For Someone) / Here Comes the Weekend / Tonight At Noon / In The Midnight Hour** *(11/77: no 22)*

Polydor POLD 5008 **ALL MOD CONS: All Mod Cons / To Be Someone (Didn't We Have A Nice Time) / Mr. Clean / David Watts / English Rose / In The Crowd / Billy Hunt / It's Too Bad / Fly / The Place I Love / 'A' Bomb In Wardour Street / Down In The Tube Station At Midnight** *(11/78: no 6)*

Polydor POLD 5028 **SETTING SONS: Girl On The Phone / Thick As Thieves / Private Hell / Little Boy Soldiers / Wasteland / Burning Sky / Smithers-Jones / Saturday's Kids / The Eton Rifles / Heatwave** *(11/79: no 4)*

Polydor 2683 074 **IN THE CITY/THIS IS THE MODERN WORLD** *(reissue of 1st and 2nd album as a double-pack, 8/80)*

Polydor POLD 5035 **SOUND AFFECTS: Pretty Green / Monday / But I'm Different Now / Set The House Ablaze / Start! / That's Entertainment / Dream Time / Man In The Corner Shop / Music For The Last Couple / Boy About Town / Scrape Away** *(11/80: no 2)*

Polydor POLD 5055 **THE GIFT: Happy Together / Ghosts / Precious / Just Who Is The 5 O'Clock Hero / Trans-Global Express / Running On The Spot / Circus / The Planner's Dream Goes Wrong / Carnation / Town Called Malice / The Gift** *(early copies in candy-striped bag, 3/82: no 1)*

Polydor POLD 5075 **DIG THE NEW BREED: In The City / All Mod Cons / To Be Someone / It's Too Bad / Start! / Big Bird / Set The House Ablaze / Ghosts**

/ Standards / In The Crowd / Going Underground / The Dreams Of
Children / That's Entertainment / Private Hell *(live, 12/82: no 2)*

Polydor SPECLP 27 **IN THE CITY** *(reissue, 8/83)*

Polydor SNAP 1 **SNAP!: In The City** / Away From The Numbers / All Around
The World / The Modern World [censored] / News Of The World / Billy
Hunt / English Rose / Mr. Clean / David Watts / 'A' Bomb In Wardour
Street / Down In The Tube Station At Midnight / Strange Town / The
Butterfly Collector / When You're Young / Smithers-Jones / Thick As
Thieves / The Eton Rifles / Going Underground / The Dreams Of Children
/ That's Entertainment (demo) / Start! [/ Man In The Corner Shop] /
Funeral Pyre (remix) / Absolute Beginners / Tales From The Riverbank /
Town Called Malice / Precious / The Bitterest Pill (I Ever Had To Swallow)
/ **Beat Surrender** *(two LPs, 9/83: no 2)*

Polydor SPECLP 66 **THIS IS THE MODERN WORLD** *(reissue, 3/84)*

Polydor SPECLP 107 **DIG THE NEW BREED** *(reissue, 6/87)*

Polydor 823 284-1 **SOUND AFFECTS** *(reissue, 4/90)*

Polydor 815 537-1 **SNAP!** *(reissue, 6/90)*

Polydor 810 041-1 **DIG THE NEW BREED** *(reissue, 6/90)*

Polydor 823 285-1 **THE GIFT** *(reissue, 6/90)*

Polydor 817 124-1 **IN THE CITY** *(reissue, 7/90)*

Polydor 823 281-1 **THIS IS THE MODERN WORLD** *(reissue, 7/90)*

Polydor 831 314-1 **SETTING SONS** *(reissue, 11/90)*

Polydor 849 554-1 **GREATEST HITS: In The City** / All Around The World / The
Modern World [censored] / News Of The World / David Watts / Down In
The Tube Station At Midnight / Strange Town / When You're Young / The
Eton Rifles / Going Underground / Start! / That's Entertainment / Funeral
Pyre / Absolute Beginners / Town Called Malice / Precious / Just Who Is
The 5 O'Clock Hero / The Bitterest Pill (I Ever Had To Swallow) / **Beat
Surrender** *(7/91: no 2)*

Polydor 513 177-1 **EXTRAS: The Dreams Of Children** / Tales From The

Riverbank / Liza Radley (demo) / Move On Up / Shopping / Smithers-Jones / Pop Art Poem / Boy About Town (live) / A Solid Bond In Your Heart / No One In The World / And Your Bird Can Sing / Burning Sky (demo) / Thick As Thieves (demo) / Disguises / Get Yourself Together / The Butterfly Collector / The Great Depression / Stoned Out Of My Mind / Pity Poor Alfie / Fever / But I'm Different Now (demo) / I Got You (I Feel Good) / Hey Mister / Saturdays Kids (demo) / We've Only Started / So Sad About Us / The Eton Rifles (demo) *(limited edition, two LPs, 4/92: no 15)*

Polydor 519 667-1 **LIVE JAM:** The Modern World / Billy Hunt / Thick As Thieves / Burning Sky / Mr. Clean / Smithers-Jones / Little Boy Soldiers / The Eton Rifles / Away From The Numbers / Down In The Tube Station At Midnight / Strange Town / When You're Young / 'A' Bomb In Wardour Street / Pretty Green / Boy About Town / Man In The Corner Shop / David Watts / Funeral Pyre / Move On Up / Carnation / The Butterfly Collector / Precious / Town Called Malice / Heatwave *(two LPs: 10/93)*

Polydor 531 493-1 **THE JAM COLLECTION :** Away From The Numbers / I Got By In Time / I Need You (For Someone) / To Be Someone (Didn't We Have A Nice Time) / Mr. Clean / English Rose / In The Crowd / It's Too Bad / The Butterfly Collector / Thick As Thieves / Private Hell / Wasteland / Burning Sky / Saturday's Kids / Liza Radley / Pretty Green / Monday / Man in the Corner Shop / Boy About Town / Tales From The Riverbank / Ghosts / Just Who Is The 5 O'clock Hero / Carnation / The Great / Depression / Shopping *(two LPs, 7/96: no 58)*

UK CASSETTES

Polydor 3170 447 **IN THE CITY** *(5/77)*

Polydor 3170 475 **THIS IS THE MODERN WORLD** *(11/77)*

Polydor POLDC 5008 **ALL MOD CONS** *(11/78)*

Polydor POLDC 5028 **SETTING SONS** *(11/79)*

Polydor POLDC 5035 **SOUND AFFECTS** *(11/80)*

Polydor POLDC 5055 **THE GIFT** *(3/82)*

Polydor POLDC 5075 **DIG THE NEW BREED** *(12/82)*

Polydor 3574 088 **IN THE CITY/THIS IS THE MODERN WORLD** *(reissue of 1st and 2nd albums as a double cassette, 2/83)*

Polydor 3574 098 **ALL MOD CONS/SETTING SONS** *(reissue of 3rd and 4th albums as a double cassette, 2/83)*

Polydor TWOMC 1 **SOUND AFFECTS/THE GIFT** *(reissue of 5th and 6th albums as a double cassette, 6/83)*

Polydor SPECMC 27 **IN THE CITY** *(reissue, 8/83)*

Polydor SNAPC 1 **SNAP!** *(limited edition with live EP tracks, 9/83)*

Polydor SPECMC 66 **THIS IS THE MODERN WORLD** *(reissue, 3/84)*

Polydor SPECMC 107 **DIG THE NEW BREED** *(reissue, 6/87)*

Polydor 823 284-4 **SOUND AFFECTS** *(reissue, 4/90)*

Polydor 815 537-4 **SNAP!** *(reissue, 6/90)*

Polydor 810 041-4 **DIG THE NEW BREED** *(reissue, 6/90)*

Polydor 823 285-4 **THE GIFT** *(reissue, 6/90)*

Polydor 817 124-4 **IN THE CITY** *(reissue, 7/90)*

Polydor 823 281-4 **THIS IS THE MODERN WORLD** *(reissue, 7/90)*

Polydor 831 314-4 **SETTING SONS** *(reissue, 11/90)*

Polydor 847 730-4 **IN THE CITY/THIS IS THE MODERN WORLD** *(reissue of 1st and 2nd albums as a double cassette, 1/91)*

Polydor 849 554-4 **GREATEST HITS** *(7/91)*

Polydor 513 177-4 **EXTRAS** *(4/92)*

Pickwick PWKMC 4129 **WASTELAND: News Of The World/Burning Sky/ Saturday's Kids/Art School/In The Street, Today/Non-Stop Dancing/ Wasteland/In The City/Strange Town/Standards/'A' Bomb In Wardour**

Street/In The Crowd/London Girl/David Watts/I Got By In Time/All Around The World *(10/92)*

Karussell 550 006-4 **BEAT SURRENDER: Beat Surrender/Town Called Malice/ Pretty Green/That's Entertainment/The Gift/Carnaby Street/Batman Theme/In The City/All Mod Cons/The Modern World/When You're Young/Funeral Pyre/Private Hell/In The Midnight Hour** *(6/93)*

Polydor 519 667-4 **LIVE JAM** (10/93) **The Modern World/Billy Hunt/Thick As Thieves/Burning Sky/Mr. Clean/Smithers-Jones/Little Boy Soldiers/The Eton Rifles/Away From The Numbers/Down In The Tube Station/Strange Town/When You're Young/'A' Bomb in Wardour Street/Pretty Green/Boy About Town/Man in the Corner Shop/David Watts/Funeral Pyre/Move On Up/Carnation/The Butterfly Collector/Precious/Town Called Malice/ Heatwave** *(re-released May 2003)*

Polydor 531 493-4 **THE JAM COLLECTION** *(7/96)*

Polydor 821 712-2 **COMPACT SNAP!: In The City/All Around The World/The Modern World** [censored]**/News Of The World/David Watts/'A' Bomb In Wardour Street/Down In The Tube Station At Midnight** [edit]**/Strange Town/When You're Young/Smithers-Jones/The Eton Rifles** [edit]**/ Going Underground/The Dreams Of Children** [edit]**/That's Entertainment** (demo)**/ Start!** [edit]**/ Funeral Pyre** (remix)**/Absolute Beginners/Town Called Malice/ Precious** [edit]**/The Bitterest Pill (I Ever Had To Swallow)/Beat Surrender** *(9/84)*

Polydor 831 314-2 **SETTING SONS** *(3/87)*

Polydor 823 282-2 **ALL MOD CONS** *(5/87)*

Polydor 823 284-2 **SOUND AFFECTS** *(4/88, possibly withdrawn)*

Polydor 823 284-2 **SOUND AFFECTS** *(reissue, 4/90)*

Polydor 815 537-2 **COMPACT SNAP!** *(reissue, 6/90)*

Polydor 810 041-2 **DIG THE NEW BREED** *(6/90)*

Polydor 823 285-2 **THE GIFT** *(6/90)*

Polydor 817 124-2 **IN THE CITY** *(7/90)*

Polydor 823 281-2 **THIS IS THE MODERN WORLD** *(7/90)*

Polydor 847 730-2 **IN THE CITY/THIS IS THE MODERN WORLD** *(reissue of 1st and 2nd albums on one CD, 1/91)*

Polydor 849 554-2 **GREATEST HITS** *(7/91)*

Polydor 513 177-2 **EXTRAS** *(4/92)*

Pickwick PWKS 4129 **WASTELAND** *(10/92)*

Karussell 550 006-2 **BEAT SURRENDER** *(6/93)*

Polydor 519 667-2 **LIVE JAM** *(10/93)*

Startrax **ALL THE CHOICE CUTS** *(1994)*

Polydor 531493-2 **THE JAM COLLECTION** Away From The Numbers/I Got By In Time/I Need You (For Someone)/To Be Someone (Didn't We Have A Nice Time)/Mr. Clean/English Rose/In The Crowd/It's Too Bad/The Butterfly Collector/Thick As Thieves/Private Hell/Wasteland/Burning Sky/Saturday's Kids/Liza Radley/Pretty Green/Monday/Man In The Corner Shop/Boy About Town/Tales From The Riverbank/Ghosts/Just Who Is The 5 O'clock Hero/Carnation/The Great Depression/Shopping *(7/96)*

Polydor CD5371432 **DIRECTION REACTION CREATION:** In The City/Takin' My Love/Art School/I've Changed My Address/Slow Down/I Got By In Time/Away From The Numbers/Batman Theme/Sounds From The Street/Non-Stop Dancing/ Time For Truth/Bricks And Mortar/All Around The World/Carnaby Street/The Modern World/London Traffic/ Standards/Life From A Window/The Combine/ Don't Tell Them You're Sane/In The Street Today/London Girl/I Need You For Someone/ Here Comes The Weekend/Tonight At Noon/In The Midnight Hour /News Of The World/Aunties And Uncles (Impulsive Youths)/Innocent Man/David Watts/'A' Bomb In Wardour Street/Down In The Tube Station At Midnight/So Sad About Us/The Night/All Mod Cons/To Be Someone/ Mr. Clean/English Rose/In The Crowd/Billy Hunt/It's Too Bad/ Fly/The Place I Love/Strange Town/The Butterfly Collector/When You're Young/ Smithers-Jones/ The Eton Rifles/See-Saw/Girl On The Phone/Thick As

Thieves/Private Hell/Little Boy Soldiers/ Wasteland/Burning Sky/Smithers-Jones/Saturday's Kids/Heatwave/Going Underground/ The Dreams Of Children/Start!/Liza Radley/Pretty Green/Monday/But I'm Different Now/ Set The House Ablaze/That's Entertainment/Dream Time/Man In The Corner Shop/Music For The Last Couple/Boy About Town/Scrape Away/ Funeral Pyre/Disguises/Absolute Beginners/Tales From The Riverbank/ Town Called Malice/Precious (12" version)/ Happy Together/Ghosts/Just Who Is The 5 O'clock Hero/Trans-Global Express/ Running On The Spot/Circus/The Planner's Dream Goes Wrong/Carnation/The Gift/ The Great Depression/The Bitterest Pill (I Ever Had To Swallow)/Pity Poor Alfie/Fever/Beat Surrender/Shopping/Move On Up/Stoned Out Of My Mind/War/In The City/Time For Truth/Sounds From The Street/So Sad About Us/Worlds Apart/Billy Hunt (Alternative Version)/It's Too Bad/To Be Someone/David Watts/Best Of Both Worlds/That's Entertainment/ Rain/Dream Time/Dead End Street/Stand By Me/Every Little Bit Hurts/ Tales From The Riverbank (alternative version)/Walking In Heavens Sunshine/Precious/Pity Poor Alfie (swing version)/The Bitterest Pill (I Ever Had To Swallow) (first version)/A Solid Bond In Your Heart
(five CDs; 5/97: no 8)

Polydor 589 781-2 **THE SOUND OF THE JAM** In The City/Away From The Numbers/The Modern World (uncensored)/David Watts (album version)/ Down In The Tube Station At Midnight (single version)/It's Too Bad/To Be Someone (Didn't We Have A Nice Time)/Mr. Clean/English Rose/The Butterfly Collector/The Eton Rifles (album version)/Private Hell/Thick As Thieves/Smithers-Jones (album version – strings)/Saturday's Kids/Going Underground/Start! (alternative version)/Liza Radley/Pretty Green/Boy About Town/That's Entertainment (previously unreleased version)/Tales From The Riverbank/Town Called Malice/Ghosts/Carnation/Beat Surrender
(5/02: no 3)

Polydor 589 9382 **THE JAM AT THE BBC**
disc one
In The City/Art School/I've Changed My Address/Modern World
(John Peel – recorded 26.4.1977, transmitted 2.5.1977)
All Around The World/London Girl/Bricks & Mortar/Carnaby Street
(John Peel – recorded 19.7.1977, transmitted 25.7.1977)
Billy Hunt/In The Street Today/The Combine/Sounds From The Street/ Don't Tell Them You're Sane/Modern World/'A' Bomb In Wardour Street/ News Of The World/Here Come The Weekend/All Around The World
('In Concert' 1.6.1978, Paris Cinema, Regent Street)

disc two
Thick As Thieves/The Eton Rifles/Saturday's Kids/When You're Young
(John Peel – recorded 29.10.79, transmitted 5.11.1979)
Absolute Beginners/Tales From The Riverbank/Funeral Pyre/Sweet Soul Music
('Studio B15' live 25.10.1981)
The Gift/Down In The Tube Station At Midnight/Ghosts/Absolute Beginners/Tales From The Riverbank/Precious/Town Called Malice/In The Crowd/Circus/Pretty Green/Start/Boy About Town
('In Concert' 19.12.1981, Golders Green Hippodrome)

bonus disc
Girl On The Phone/To Be Someone/It's Too Bad/Burning Sky/Away From The Numbers/Smithers-Jones/Modern World/Mr Clean/The Butterfly Collector/Private Hell/Thick As Thieves/When You're Young/Strange Town/Eton Rifles/Down In The Tube Station At Midnight/Saturday's Kids/All Mod Cons/David Watts
('In Concert' – 4.12.1979 Rainbow Theatre, London)

US ALBUMS

Polydor PD 1-6110 **IN THE CITY**: same as UK *(1977)*

Polydor PD 1-6129 **THIS IS THE MODERN WORLD: The Modern World/All Around The World/I Need You (For Someone)/London Traffic/Standards/ Life From A Window/In The Midnight Hour/In The Street, Today/London Girl/Here Comes The Weekend/The Combine/Tonight At Noon/Don't Tell Them You're Sane** *(1977)*

Polydor PD 1-6188 **ALL MOD CONS**: originally same as UK *(1978)* but reissued in 1979 with The Butterfly Collector replacing Billy Hunt

Polydor PD 1-6249 **SETTING SONS: Burning Sky/Saturday's Kids/The Eton Rifles/Heatwave/Girl On The Phone/Strange Town/Thick As Thieves/ Private Hell/Little Boy Soldiers/ Wasteland** *(1979: no 137)*

Polydor PD 1-6315 **SOUND AFFECTS: Start!/Pretty Green/Monday/But I'm Different No w/Set The House Ablaze/That's Entertainment/Dream Time/ Man In The Corner Shop/Music For The Last Couple/Boy About Town/ Scrape Away** *(1980: no 72)*

Polydor PD 1-6344 **THE GIFT**: same as UK *(1982: no 82)*

Polydor PD 1-6365 **DIG THE NEW BREED**: same as UK *(live, 1982: no 131)*

Polydor 815 537-1 **SNAP!**: same as UK *(two LPs, 1983)*

US CASSETTES

Polydor CT 1-6110 **IN THE CITY** *(1977)*

Polydor CT 1-6129 **THIS IS THE MODERN WORLD** *(1977)*

Polydor CT 1-6188 **ALL MOD CONS** *(1978, reissued 1979)*

Polydor CT 1-6249 **SETTING SONS** *(1979)*

Polydor CT 1-6315 **SOUND AFFECTS** *(1980)*

Polydor CT 1-6344 **THE GIFT** *(1982)*

Polydor CT 1-6365 **DIG THE NEW BREED** *(1982)*

Polydor 815 537-4 **SNAP!** *(1983)*

Polydor 849 554-4 **GREATEST HITS**: same as UK *(1991)*

Polydor 513 177-4 **EXTRAS**: same as UK *(1992)*

Polydor 519 667-4 **LIVE JAM**: same as UK *(1994)*

US CDS

Polydor 821 712- 2 **COMPACT SNAP!**: same as UK *(1984)*

Polydor 849 554- 2 **GREATEST HITS** *(1991)*

Polydor 513 177- 2 **EXTRAS** *(1992)*

Polydor 519 667- 2 **LIVE JAM** *(1994)*

nb: the CD reissues of the original LPs were the same as the UK versions (see UK discography)

JAM The SOUNDS FROM THE STREET

DVD

Polydor – **The Complete Jam – Jam On Film** *(two discs)*

Live TV – **So It Goes/Marc Bolan/Revolver/The Old Grey Whistle Test/ Something Else/Newcastle City Hall/Something Else/Mandagsborsen/ Popkrant/The Tube**

The Singles – **In The City/Art School/News of the World/Strange Town/ Butterfly Collector/ When You're Young/Going Underground/Dreams of Children/Start!/That's Entertainment/Funeral Pyre/Absolute Beginners/ Town Called Malice/Precious/Just Who Is The Five O'Clock Hero/The Bitterest Pill**

FAN CLUB RELEASES

Fan Club **WHEN YOU'RE YOUNG** (live) *(12/80)*

Fan Club **TALES FROM THE RIVERBANK** (version) *(12/81)*

MAGAZINE FLEXI DISCS

Sounds **GOOD FOR NOTHING** *(includes Art School, free flexi EP, 1977)*

Flexipop 002 **POP ART POEM/BOY ABOUT TOWN** (version) *(blue, yellow or green flexi, free with Flexipop magazine, 2/81)*

MM PAOLO 100 **MOVE ON UP** (live) *(free flexi with Melody Maker, 11/82)*

The Jam – **interview disc**

PJAM 1 **INTERVIEW WITH PAUL WELLER AND BRUCE FOXTON** *(limited edition of 1200, picture disc with insert, 1983)*

APPENDIX 2

PAUL WELLER, STEVE BROOKES, RICK BUCKLER

26 January 1974 – Michael's Club, Woking
2 February 1974 – Michael's Club, Woking
16 February 1974 – Michael's Club, Woking
2 March 1974 – Michael's Club, Woking
16 March 1974 – Michael's Club, Woking
30 March 1974 – Michael's Club, Woking
7 April 1974 – Woking Working Men's Club, Woking
13 April 1974 – Michael's Club, Woking
26 April 1974 – Michael's Club, Woking
27 April 1974 – Michael's Club, Woking
3 May 1974 – Michael's Club, Woking
4 May 1974 – Michael's Club, Woking
10 May 1974 – Michael's Club, Woking
17 May 1974 – Michael's Club, Woking
4 May 1974 – Michael's Club, Woking
26 May 1974 – Parkside Club, Frimley
31 May 1974 – Michael's Club, Woking
1 June 1974 – British Legion Club, Ripley
7 June 1974 – Michael's Club, Woking
9 June 1974 – Michael's Club, Woking
14 June 1974 – Michael's Club, Woking
15 June 1974 – Sheerwater Fete, Sheerwater Youth Club, Woking
21 June 1974 – Michael's Club, Woking
28 June 1974 – Michael's Club, Woking
29 June 1974 – West End Club, Woking
5 July 1974 – Michael's Club, Woking
6 July 1974 – Woking Working Men's Club, Woking
7 July 1974 – Bunters Club, Guildford
12 July 1974 – Michael's Club, Woking
13 July 1974 – Woking Working Men's Club, Woking
19 July 1974 – Michael's Club, Woking
21 July 1974 – Bunters Club, Guildford
26 July 1974 – Michael's Club, Woking
27 July 1974 – Parkside Club, Frimley
28 July 1974 – Michael's Club, Woking
2 August 1974 – Michael's Club, Woking
3 August 1974 – Woking Working Men's Club, Woking
17 August 1974 – Michael's Club, Woking

23 August 1974 – Michael's Club, Woking
26 August 1974 – Parkside Club, Frimley
30 August 1974 – Michael's Club, Woking

PAUL WELLER, STEVE BROOKES, RICK BUCKLER, BRUCE FOXTON

6 September 1974 – Michael's Club, Woking
13 September 1974 – Michael's Club, Woking
14 September 1974 – British Army Cannon Club
20 September 1974 – Michael's Club, Woking
21 September 1974 – Parkside Club, Frimley
27 September 1974 – Michael's Club, Woking
28 September 1974 – British Legion Club, Leatherhead
2 October 1974 – Gaiety Bar, Blackdown, Aldershot, Hants
4 October 1974 – Michael's Club, Woking
5 October 1974 – Bunters Club, Guildford [cancelled]
6 October 1974 – Michael's Club, Woking
12 October 1974 – Michael's Club, Woking
13 October 1974 – British Legion Club, Hindhead
19 October 1974 – Michael's Club, Woking
20 October 1974 – Darts Club Party, Basingstoke, Hants
25 October 1974 – Michael's Club, Woking
26 October 1974 – Gladstone Club, Reading
27 October 1974 – The Greyhound, Park Lane, Croydon, Surrey
1 November 1974 – Michael's Club, Woking
2 November 1974 – Woking Working Men's Club, Woking
8 November 1974 – Michael's Club ,Woking
10 November 1974 – Michael's Club, Woking
15 November 1974 – Michael's Club, Woking
17 November 1974 – HM Prison, Coldingly
20 November 1974 – Gaiety Bar, Blackdown, Aldershot, Hants
22 November 1974 – Michael's Club, Woking
29 November 1974 – Michael's Club, Woking
30 November 1974 – Sheerwater Community Centre, Woking
1 December 1974 – Michael's Club, Woking
4 December 1974 – Tumbledown Dick, Farnborough Road, Farnborough, Hants
6 December 1974 – Michael's Club, Woking
13 December 1974 – Michael's Club, Woking
14 December 1974 – Lancing Bagnal Dance
15 December 1974 – The Hatch
16 December 1974 – The Winning Post, Chertsey Road, Twickenham, Middlesex
18 December 1974 – Tumbledown Dick, Farnborough Road, Farnborough, Hants
19 December 1974 – Highlands School
20 December 1974 – Michael's Club, Woking
21 December 1974 – Woking Working Men's Club, Woking
26 December 1974 – Hare And Hill Club, Ottershaw
29 December 1974 – Michael's Club, Woking
31 December 1974 – Woking Liberal Club, Woking

3 January 1975 – Fleet Country Club, Fleet, Hants
4 January 1975 – Leatherhead FC, Leatherhead
5 January 1975 – Woking Working Men's club, Woking
10 January 1975 – Michael's Club, Woking
11 January 1975 – Woking Liberal Club
15 January 1975 – Tumbledown Dick, Farnborough Road, Farnborough, Hants
17 January 1975 – Michael's Club, Woking
18 January 1975 – Stoughton Working Men's Club, Guildford
24 January 1975 – Michael's Club, Woking
25 January 1975 – West End Club, Woking
30 January 1975 – Michael's Club, Woking
1 February 1975 – Ivy League Club
2 February 1975 – Woking Working Men's Club, Woking
5 February 1975 – Tumbledown Dick, Farnborough Road, Farnborough, Hants
7 February 1975 – Michael's Club, Woking
8 February 1975 – Queens Hotel, Farnborough
9 February 1975 – Woking Liberal Club
14 February 1975 – Michael's Club, Woking
15 February 1975 – Sheerwater Community Centre, Woking
21 February 1975 – Michael's Club, Woking
22 February 1975 – British Legion Club, Hindhead
23 February 1975 – Michael's Club, Woking
28 February 1975 – Michael's Club, Woking
2 March 1975 – Byfleet Social Club, Byfleet
7 March 1975 – Michael's Club, Woking
8 March 1975 – Hounslow, Middx
9 March 1975 – Michael's Club, Woking
14 March 1975 – Aldershot Cricket Club
15 March 1975 – Bison Club, Hounslow
19 March 1975 – Tumbledown Dick, Farnborough Road, Farnborough, Hants
21 March 1975 – Michael's Club, Woking
23 March 1975 – Woking Liberal Club, Woking
28 March 1975 – Michael's Club, Woking
29 March 1975 – Sheerwater Community Centre, Woking
31 March 1975 – Queens Hotel, Farnborough, Hants
4 April 1975 – Michael's Club, Woking
6 April 1975 – Woking Working Men's Club, Woking
9 April 1975 – Tumbledown Dick, Farnborough Road, Farnborough, Hants
11 April 1975 – Michael's Club, Woking
13 April 1975 – New Haw Club, New Haw
18 April 1975 – Michael's Club, Woking
20 April 1975 – Michael's Club, Woking
21 April 1975 – Chelsea FC, Stamford Bridge, Fulham Road, London SW6
26 April 1975 – Peabody Club, Farnborough
2 May 1975 – Tumbledown Dick, Farnborough Road, Farnborough, Hants
3 May 1975 – Woking Working Men's Club, Woking
4 May 1975 – Sheerwater Community Centre, Woking
16 May 1975 – Michael's Club, Woking
17 May 1975 – Sheerwater Community Centre, Woking

23 May 1975 – Woking Football Club, Woking
25 May 1975 – Michael's Club, Woking
31 May 1975 – Hounslow Club
1 June 1975 – Woking Working Men's Club, Woking
6 June 1975 – Lightwater Social Club
7 June 1975 – Bison Club, Hounslow
13 June 1975 – Michael's Club, Woking
15 June 1975 – Michael's Club, Woking
8 June 1975 – Tumbledown Dick, Farnborough Road, Farnborough, Hants
20 June 1975 – Tumbledown Dick, Farnborough Road, Farnborough, Hants
21 June 1975 – Michael's Club, Woking
22 June 1975 – Michael's Club, Woking
28 June 1975 – West End Club
29 June 1975 – Michael's Club, Woking
5 July 1975 – The Greyhound, 175 Fulham Palace Road, London
6 July 1975 – The Greyhound, Park Lane, Croydon, Surrey
9 July 1975 – Tumbledown Dick, Farnborough Road, Farnborough, Hants
11 July 1975 – Tumbledown Dick, Farnborough Road, Farnborough, Hants
12 July 1975 – Sheerwater Youth Club, Woking
13 July 1975 – Michael's Club, Woking
20 July 1975 – Michael's Club, Woking
25 July 1975 – Michael's Club, Woking
20 September 1975 – The Greyhound, 175 Fulham Palace Road, London
26 September 1975 – Michael's Club, Woking

PAUL WELLER, BRUCE FOXTON, RICK BUCKLER

26 December 1975 – Tumbledown Dick, Farnborough Road, Farnborough, Hants
11 January 1976 – The Greyhound, 175 Fulham Palace Road, London
8 March 1976 – venue not known
20 March 1976 – The Greyhound, 175 Fulham Palace Road, London
8 May 1976 – Hope and Anchor, Islington, London
6 June 1976 – The Windsor Castle, Harrow Road, London
7 June 1976 – The Kensington, Russell Gardens, London W14
17 June 1976 – The Greyhound, 175 Fulham Palace Road, London
29 June 1976 – Hope and Anchor, Islington, London
5 July 1976 – The Windsor Castle, Harrow Road, London
autumn 1976 – Canley Teacher Training College, nr Coventry [exact date unknown]
8 September 1976 – Upstairs At Ronnie Scotts, 47 Frith Street, London W1
17 September 1976 – The Greyhound, Fulham, London
16 October 1976 – Rock On, 1-3 Soho Market, Newport Court, London WC2
21 October 1976 – Queensway Hall, Dunstable, Bedfordshire
9 November 1976 – 100 Club, 100 Oxford Street, London W1
16 November 1976 – 100 Club, 100 Oxford Street, London W1
23 November 1976 – Upstairs At Ronnie Scotts, 47 Frith Street, London W1
14 December 1976 – 100 Club, 100 Oxford Street, London W1
28 December 1976 – 100 Club, 100 Oxford Street, London W1
11 January 1977 – 100 Club, 100 Oxford Street, London W1

22 January 1977 – The Marquee, 90 Wardour Street, London W1
25 January 1977 – 100 Club, 100 Oxford Street, London W1
3 February 1977 – The Nags Head, 63 London Road, High Wycombe, Bucks
7 February 1977 – The Nashville, North End Road, London W14
19 February 1977 – The Hunt Hotel, Leighton Buzzard, Bucks
21 February 1977 – The Nashville, North End Road, London W14
24 February 1977 – The Roxy Club, 41-43 Neal Street, London WC2
25 February 1977 – The Greyhound, 175 Fulham Palace Road, Fulham, London
26 February 1977 – The Hunt Hotel, Leighton Buzzard, Bucks
1 March 1977 – The Railway Hotel, High Street, Putney, London
2 March 1977 – The Red Cow, 157 Hammersmith Road, Hammersmith, London
5 March 1977 – Leicester Polytechnic, Leicestershire
9 March 1977 – The Red Cow, 157 Hammersmith Road, Hammersmith, London
11 March 1977 – Kent University, Keynes College, Canterbury, Kent
15 March 1977 – The Hope And Anchor, Upper Street, Islington, London
16 March 1977 – The Red Cow, 157 Hammersmith Road, Hammersmith, London
18 March 1977 – Southbank Polytechnic, London
22 March 1977 – The Roxy Club, 41-43 Neal Street, London WC2
23 March 1977 – The Red Cow, 157 Hammersmith Road, Hammersmith, London
24 March 1977 – The Rochester Castle, 145 Stoke Newington High Street, London
25 March 1977 – Royal College Of Art, Kensington Gore, London
28 March 1977 – Paris Punk Festival, Palais De Glace, Paris, France
29 March 1977 – 100 Club, 100 Oxford Street, London W1
30 March 1977 – The Red Cow, 157 Hammersmith Road, Hammersmith, London
31 March 1977 – The Rochester Castle, 145 Stoke Newington High Street, London
1 April 1977 – Leeds Polytechnic, Leeds, York
5 April 1977 – The Nashville, North End Road, London W14
6 April 1977 – The Hope And Anchor, Upper Street, Islington, London
7 April 1977 – The Manor Ballroom, Ipswich, Suffolk
12 April 1977 – The Nashville, North End Road, London W14
15 April 1977 – The Embassy Cinema, Hove, Brighton, Sussex
16 April 1977 – The Rochester Castle, 145 Stoke Newington High Street, London
17 April 1977 – The Roundhouse, Chalk Farm Road, London NW1
20 April 1977 – The Roundabout Club, Newport, Gwent
22 April 1977 – North London Polytechnic, Price Of Wales Road, London NW5
23 April 1977 – The Marquee, 90 Wardour Street, London W1
26 April 1977 – Dingwalls, Camden Lock, Chalk Farm Road, London NW1
28 April 1977 – The Hope and Anchor, Upper Street, Islington, London
29 April 1977 – Royal College Of Art, Kensington Gore, London
3 May 1977 – Dingwalls, Camden Lock, Chalk Farm Road, London NW1
5 May 1977 – Oaks Hotel, Barlow Moor Road, Chorlton, Manchester
7 May 1977 – The Playhouse Theatre, 18-22 Greenside Place, Edinburgh
8 May 1977 – Rainbow Theatre, 232 Seven Sisters Road, London N4
12 May 1977 – The Nags Head, 63 London Road, High Wycombe, Bucks
4 June 1977 – The Nags Head, 63 London Road, High Wycombe, Bucks
7 June 1977 – Barbarells, 41 Cumberland Street, Birmingham
8 June 1977 – The Winning Post, Chertsey Road, Twickenham, Middlesex
9 June 1977 – The Winter Gardens, Eastbourne, Sussex
10 June 1977 – The Corn Exchange, Wheeler Street, Cambridge, Cambs

11 June 1977 – Bristol Polytechnic, Bristol

12 June 1977 – Chelsea FC, Stamford Bridge, Fulham Road, London SW6

14 June 1977 – Locarno Ballroom, Portsmouth, Hants

15 June 1977 – The Village Bowl Discotheque, Glen Fern Road, Bournemouth, Dorset

16 June 1977 – Leeds Town Hall, Leeds, York

17 June 1977 – Seaburn Hall, Whitburn Road, Seaburn, Sunderland

18 June 1977 – Poplar Civic Hall, Bow Road, London E3 (afternoon appearance)

18 June 1977 – University College London Union, Gower Street, London WC1

19 June 1977 – The Electric Circus, Collyhurst Street, Manchester

20 June 1977 – The Outlook, Doncaster

21 June 1977 – The Top Rank, Cardiff

22 June 1977 – The Lafayette, Wolverhampton

23 June 1977 – The Polytechnic, Huddersfield, York

24 June 1977 – The Brunel Rooms, Swindon, Wilts

25 June 1977 – The Winter Gardens, Malvern

26 June 1977 – The Greyhound, Park Lane, Croydon, Surrey

27 June 1977 – Battersea Town Hall, London

28 June 1977 – The Drill Hall, Lincoln, Lincs

29 June 1977 – The Cats Whiskers, York,

30 June 1977 – Rebecca's, Birmingham

1 July 1977 – The Mayfair, Newgate Street, Newcastle Upon Tyne

2 July 1977 – Middleton Civic Hall, Middleton, Manchester

5 July 1977 – The Top Rank, Plymouth

7 July 1977 – Mr Digby's Thomas Street, Birkenhead, Cheshire

8 July 1977 – The Town Hall, Linthorpe Road, Middlesborough, Cleveland

9 July 1977 – The California Ballroom, Whipsnade Road, Dunstable, Beds

10 July 1977 – Top Rank, Sheffield, York

13 July 1977 – Shuffles, Glasgow

14 July 1977 – Maniqui Hall, Meadow Street, Falkirk

15 July 1977 – Clouds, Edinburgh

16 July 1977 – Eric's Club, Matthew Street, Liverpool

17 July 1977 – Maxim's Disco, Barrow

22 July 1977 – West Runton Pavilion, Cromer

23 July 1977 – The Town Hall, High Wycombe, Bucks

24 July 1977 – The Odeon, Queen Charlotte Street, Hammersmith, London W6

6 August 1977 – Punk Rock Festival, The Bullring, Mont De Marson, France

10 September 1977 – The Nashville, North End Road, London W14

11 September 1977 – 100 Club, 100 Oxford Street, London W1

17 September 1977 – Chelmsford City FC, Chelmsford, Essex (afternoon appearance)

17 September 1977 – The Roxy Theatre Harlesden, London NW10

23 September 1977 – Malmo, Sweden

24 September 1977 – Ronneby, Sweden

30 September 1977 – Paradiso, Amsterdam Netherlands

8 October 1977 – Whisky-A-Go-Go, 8901 Sunset Boulevard, Hollywood Los Angeles. USA

9 October 1977 – Whisky-A-Go-Go, 8901 Sunset Boulevard, Hollywood, Los Angeles, USA

10 October 1977 – The Rat, 528 Commonwealth Avenue, Boston, Massachusetts, USA

13 October 1977 – The Rat, 528 Commonwealth Avenue, Boston, Massachusetts, USA

15 October 1977 – CBGB Theatre, 315 Bowery At Bleeker Street, New York, USA

16 October 1977 – CBGB Theatre, 315 Bowery At Bleeker Street, New York, USA

17 November 1977 – The Polytechnic, Huddersfield, York
18 November 1977 – The Mayfair, Newgate Street, Newcastle Upon Tyne
19 November 1977 – Leeds University, Riley Smith Hall, Lifton Place, Leeds, York
20 November 1977 – The Empire Theatre, Lime Street, Liverpool
22 November 1977 – The Top Rank, Cardiff
24 November 1977 – Leicester University, Leicester
25 November 1977 – Kings Hall, Derby
26 November 1977 – Friars, Maxwell Vale Hall, The Civic Centre, Aylesbury, Bucks
27 November 1977 – The Top Rank, Sheffield, York
28 November 1977 – The Top Rank, Birmingham
29 November 1977 – The Ardwick Centre, Manchester
30 November 1977 – The Apollo Theatre, Renfield Street, Glasgow
2 December 1977 – Bracknell Sports Centre, Bracknell, Berks
3 December 1977 – The Civic Hall, St Peters Square, Wolverhampton
4 December 1977 – The Locarno, Bristol
5 December 1977 – The Village Bowl Discotheque, Glen Fern Road, Bournemouth, Dorset
7 December 1977 – The Top Rank, Brighton, Sussex
8 December 1977 – The Locarno, Coventry
9 December 1977 – The Odeon Cinema, Canterbury, Kent
11 December 1977 – The Greyhound, Park Lane, Croydon, Surrey
14 December 1977 – The University of Lancaster, Lancaster
15 December 1977 – Victoria Hall, Hanley, Stoke On Trent
16 December 1977 – The Corn Exchange, Wheeler Street, Cambridge, Cambs
18 December 1977 – Hammersmith Odeon, London W6
13 February 1978 – Brussels, Belguim
14 February 1978 – Sportehall, Paris, France
24 February 1978 – The Marquee, 90 Wardour Street, London W1
25 February 1978 – The Marquee, 90 Wardour Street, London W1
27 February 1978 – 100 Club, 100 Oxford Street, London W1
2 March 1978 – The Music Machine, Camden High Street, Camden Town, London NW1
16 March 1978 – University of Bridgeport, Harvey Hubbles Gymnasium, Bridgeport, Connecticut, USA
18 March 1978 – The Tower Theatre, 69th Street and Ludlow, Upper Darby, Philadelphia, Pennsylvania, USA
19 March 1978 – The Agricultural Hall, 17th and Chew Streets, Allenton Fairgrounds, Allentown, Pennsylvania, USA
20 March 1978 – Four Acres Club, River Road, Marcy, Utica, USA
21 March 1978 – The Colonial, 301 Yonge Street, Toronto, Ontario, Canada
22 March 1978 – The Colonial, 301 Yonge Street, Toronta, Ontario, Canada
24 March 1978 – Hammond Civic Centre, 5825 Sohl Street, Hammond, Indiana, USA
25 March 1978 – Richfield Coliseum, 2923 Streetsboro Road, Richfield, Cleveland, Ohio, USA
26 March 1978 – Civic Centre, 14th and Main Street, Wheeling, West Virginia, USA
27 March 1978 – The Coliseum, 4000 Parnell Avenue, Fort Wayne, Indiana, USA
29 March 1978 – The Paradise Club, 967 Commonwealth Avenue, Boston, Massachusetts, USA
30 March 1978 – CBGB Theatre, 66th and 2nd Avenue, New York, USA
31 March 1978 – CBGB Theatre, 66th and 2nd Avenue, New York, USA
2 April 1978 – The Rupp Arena, 430 West Vine Street, Lexington, Kentucky, USA
3 April 1978 – Ricco One, 317 West Main, St Louis, Missouri, USA

4 April 1978 – Bunky's, 3 North Park Street, Madison, Wisconsin, USA

5 April 1978 – BJ's Concert Club, 1401 South Gratiot Avenue, Mount Clemens, Detroit, Michigan, USA

6 April 1978 – Bogarts, 2621 Vine Street, Cincinnati, Ohio, USA

7 April 1978 – Riviera Theatre, 4746 North Racine, Chicago, Illinois, USA

11 April 1978 – Celebrity Theatre, 440 North 32nd Street, Phoenix, Arizona, USA

12 April 1978 – Celebrity Theatre, 440 North 32nd Street, Phoenix, Arizona, USA

14 April 1978 – The Starwood, 8151 Santa Monica Boulevard, Santa Monica, California, USA

15 April 1978 – Winterland Ballroom, Post and Steiner Streets, San Francisco, California, USA

16 April 1978 – Exhibition Hall, 255 Almedan Boulevard, San Jose, California, USA

1 June 1978 – BBC Paris Theatre, Lower Regent Street, London W1

12 June 1978 – King George's Hall, Blackburn, Lancs

13 June 1978 – Victoria Hall, Keighley, Yorks

14 June 1978 – The Pier, Colwyn Bay

15 June 1978 – Barbarellas, 41 Cumberland Street, Birmingham

16 June 1978 – Barbarellas, 41 Cumberland Street, Birmingham

17 June 1978 – Friars, Maxwell Vale Hall, The Civic Centre, Aylesbury, Bucks

18 June 1978 – The Lyceum Ballroom, Wellington Street, The Strand, London WC2

30 July 1978 – The Civic Hall, Guildford, Surrey

31 July 1978 – The Town Hall, Torquay

1 August 1978 – The Fiesta, Plymouth

2 August 1978 – The Village Bowl Discotheque, Glen Fern Road, Bournemouth, Dorset

4 August 1978 – The Brunel Rooms, Swindon, Wilts

13 August 1978 – Bilzen Festival, Bilzen, Limburg, Belguim

28 August 1978 – 18th National Jazz & Blues Festival, The Showgrounds, Richfield Road, Reading, Berks

27 August 1978 – Groningen Festival, Holland

20 October 1978 – The Top Hat Club, Dublin Ireland

21 October 1978 – Leisureland, Galway Bay, Ireland

1 November 1978 – The Empire Theatre, Lime Street, Liverpool

2 November 1978 – Du Montford Hall, Granville Road, Leicester, Leics

3 November 1978 – St George's Hall, Bridge Street, Bradford, York

4 November 1978 – The City Hall, Newcastle Upon Tyne

5 November 1978 – The Apollo Theatre, Renfield Street, Glasgow

6 November 1978 – The Capitol, 434 Union Street, Aberdeen

7 November 1978 – The University of St Andrews, Fife

10 November 1978 – The Sheffield City Polytechnic, Nelson Mandella Building, Pond Street, Sheffield, York

12 November 1978 – Leeds University, Riley Smith Hall, Lifton Place, Leeds

13 November 1978 – The Apollo Theatre, Manchester

14 November 1978 – The Odeon Theatre, New Street, Birmingham

15 November 1978 – The Coventry Theatre, Coventry

17 November 1978 – The Corn Exchange, Wheeler Street, Cambridge, Cambs

18 November 1978 – The ABC Cinema, Great Yarmouth, Norfolk

20 November 1978 – Cardiff University, Cardiff

21 November 1978 – The Dome, 29 New Road, Brighton, Sussex

22 November 1978 – University of Kent, Keynes College, Canterbury, Kent

24 November 1978 – The Guildhall, Portsmouth, Hants

26 November 1978 – Colston Hall, Bristol

29 November 1978 – Wembley Arena, Wembley, Middx
7 December 1978 – University of Kent, Keynes College, Canterbury, Kent
21 December 1978 – The Music Machine, Camden High Street, Camden Town, London NW1
16 February 1979 – Reading University, Reading, Berks
20 February 1979 – Berlin, Germany
21 February 1979 – The Star Club, 39 Grosse Freiheit, Hamburg, Germany
22 February 1979 – The Star Club, 39 Grosse Freiheit, Hamburg, Germany
23 February 1979 – Wiesbaden, Germany
26 February 1979 – Paris, France
27 February 1979 – Reims, France
28 February 1979 – The Royale, Leon, France
4 March 1979 – Marseilles, France
6 March 1979 – Brussels, Belguim
10 April 1979 – The Rex Theatre, 635 Danforth Avenue, Toronto, Ontario, Canada
12 April 1979 – Paradise Theatre, 967 Commonwealth Avenue, Boston, USA
13 April 1979 – Tower Theatre, Philadelphia, USA
14 April 1979 – The New York Palladium, 126 East 14th Street, New York, USA
16 April 1979 – Agora Ballroom, Cleveland, Ohio, USA
17 April 1979 – Punch And Judy Theatre, Detroit, Michigan, USA
20 April 1979 – San Francisco, USA
21 April 1979 – University Of California, Los Angeles, Royce Hall, Los Angeles, USA
24 April 1979 – Commodore, Vancouver, Canada
4 May 1979 – Sheffield University, Sheffield, York
5 May 1979 – Sheffield University, Sheffield, York
6 May 1979 – Newcastle City Hall, Newcastle Upon Tyne
8 May 1979 – Salford University, Salford, Manchester
10 May 1979 – Rainbow Theatre, 232 Seven Sisters Road, London N4
11 May 1979 – Rainbow Theatre, 232 Seven Sisters Road, London N4
12 May 1979 – Student Union Auditorium, Loughborough University, Leics
14 May 1979 – Exeter University, Exeter
15 May 1979 – Liverpool University, Liverpool
16 May 1979 – Liverpool University, Liverpool
18 May 1979 – Strathclyde University, 90 John Street, Glasgow
19 May 1979 – Strathclyde University, 90 John Street, Glasgow
21 May 1979 – Colston Hall, Colston Street, Bristol
22 May 1979 – The Odeon Cinema, New Street, Birmingham
24 May 1979 – The Portsmouth Guildhall, Portsmouth, Hants
9 June 1979 – Saddleworth Arts Festival, Church Fields, Uppermill, Saddleworth, Lancs
2 November 1979 – The Marquee, 90 Wardour Street, London W1
3 November 1979 – The Nashville, North End Road, London W14
17 November 1979 – Friars, Maxwell Vale Hall, The Civic Centre, Aylesbury, Bucks
18 November 1979 – Poole Art Centre, Poole, Dorset
20 November 1979 – The Apollo Theatre, Ardwick Green, Manchester
21 November 1979 – The Apollo Theatre, Ardwick Green, Manchester
22 November 1979 – The Civic Hall, The Civic Centre, St Peters Square, Wolverhampton
23 November 1979 – The Gaumont, Southampton, Hants
24 November 1979 – The Gaumont, Southampton, Hants
25 November 1979 – Bingley Hall, Birmingham
26 November 1979 – Trentham Gardens, Stoke On Trent

27 November 1979 – The Royal Spa Hall, Bridlington, York
29 November 1979 – Deeside Leisure Centre, Liverpool
30 November 1979 – Lancaster University, Lancaster
2 December 1979 – The Rainbow Theatre, 232 Seven Sisters Road, London N4
3 December 1979 – The Rainbow Theatre, 232 Seven Sisters Road, London N4
4 December 1979 – The Rainbow Theatre, 232 Seven Sisters Road, London N4
6 December 1979 – The City Hall, Newcastle Upon Tyne
7 December 1979 – The City Hall, Newcastle Upon Tyne
8 December 1979 – The Apollo Theatre, Renfield Street, Glasgow
9 December 1979 – The Caird Hall, Dundee
10 December 1979 – The Odeon, Edinburgh
11 December 1979 – The Queens Exhibition Hall, Sovereign Streets, Leeds
12 December 1979 – King George's Hall, Blackburn, Lancs
13 December 1979 – Sophia Gardens, Cardiff [cancelled]
15 December 1979 – The Brighton Centre, Brighton Sussex
16 December 1979 – The Guildhall, Portsmouth, Hants
19 December 1979 – De Montfort Hall, Granville Road, Leicester
21 December 1979 – Bath Pavilion, Bath
11 February 1980 – The Corn Exchange, Wheeler Street, Cambridge, Cambs
12 February 1980 – University of Kent, Canterbury, Kent
13 February 1980 – The Winter Gardens, Malvern
15 February 1980 – Woking YMCA Centre, Goldsworth Road, Woking, Surrey
27 February 1980 – Emerald City New Jersey, USA
28 February 1980 – Stage West, West Harford, Connecticut, USA
29 February 1980 – The New York Palladium, 126 East 14th Street, New York, USA
1 March 1980 – Triangle Theatre, Rochester, New York, USA
3 March 1980 – JB Scotts, Albany, New York, USA
5 March 1980 – Motor City Roller Rink, Detroit, Michigan, USA
6 March 1980 – Park West, 322 West Armitage, Chicago, Illinois, USA
7 March 1980 – Old Chicago Amusement Park, 1-55 Stevenson and Route 53, Chicago, Illinois, USA
9 March 1980 – St Paul Civic Theatre, Minnesota, USA
13 March 1980 – The Shot Box, Seattle, USA
15 March 1980 – Fox Warfield, San Francisco, California, USA
16 March 1980 – Santa Monica Civic Centre, USA
21 March 1980 – The Palace, Houston, Texas, USA
22 March 1980 – Armadillo Works HQ, 525 Barton Springs, Austin, Texas, USA
28 March 1980 – The Capitol, 326 Monroe, St Passaic, New Jersey, USA
7 April 1980 – Rainbow Theatre, 232 Seven Sisters Road, London N4
8 April 1980 – Rainbow Theatre, 232 Seven Sisters Road, London N4
18 April 1980 – The Civic Centre, Guildford, Surrey
17 May 1980 – The Pavilion Eltard, 12th Avenue Victor Hugo, 94130 Nogent Su'marine, Paris, France
26 May 1980 – Pink Pop Festival, Geleen, The Netherlands
2 June 1980 – The Civic Hall, The Civic Centre, St Peters Square, Wolverhampton
3 June 1980 – King George's Hall, Blackburn, Lancs
4 June 1980 – Victoria Hall, Hanley, Stoke On Trent
21 June 1980 – Loch Lomond Festival, Loch Cameron Bear Park, Loch Lomond
3 July 1980 – Mainichi Hall, Osaka, Japan

4 July 1980 – Kaikan Hall, Kyoto, Japan
6 July 1980 – The Sun Plaza Hall, 4-1-1 Nakano, Nakano-Ku, Tokyo, Japan
7 July 1980 – Nippon Seinenkan, Tokyo, Japan
8 July 1980 – Nippon Seinenkan, Tokyo, Japan
11 July 1980 – ABC TV, 4151 Prospect Street, Hollywood, Los Angeles, California, USA
22 July 1980 – Guildford Civic Hall, Guildford, Surrey
2 August 1980 – Friars, Maxwell Vale Hall, The Civic Centre, Aylesbury, Bucks
3 August 1980 – Poole Arts Centre, Poole, Dorset
9 August 1980 – Turku Rock Festival, Finland
26 October 1980 – Top Rank, Sheffield, York
27 October 1980 – Newcastle City Hall, Newcastle Upon Tyne
28 October 1980 – Newcastle City Hall, Newcastle Upon Tyne
29 October 1980 – The Playhouse Theatre, 18-22 Greenside Place, Edinburgh
30 October 1980 – The Apollo Theatre, Renfield Street, Glasgow
31 October 1980 – The Apollo Theatre, Ardwick Green, Manchester
1 November 1980 – The Apollo Theatre, Ardwick Green, Manchester
2 November 1980 – Deeside Leisure Centre, Liverpool
3 November 1980 – The Queens Exhibition Hall, Sovereign Street, Leeds
5 November 1980 – Brighton Conference Centre, Brighton, Sussex
6 November 1980 – Brighton Conference Centre, Brighton, Sussex
7 November 1980 – Bracknell Sports Centre, Bracknell, Berks
8 November 1980 – Bracknell Sports Centre, Bracknell, Berks
9 November 1980 – Poole Arts Centre, Poole, Dorset
10 November 1980 – Sophia Gardens, Cardiff
11 November 1980 – Bingley Hall, Birmingham
12 November 1980 – De Montfort Hall, Granville Road, Leicester
13 November 1980 – De Montfort Hall, Granville Road, Leicester
15 November 1980 – Rainbow Theatre, 232 Seven Sisters Road, London N4
16 November 1980 – Rainbow Theatre, 232 Seven Sisters Road, London N4
18 November 1980 – The Odeon, Queen Charlotte Street, Hammersmith, London W6
19 November 1980 – The Odeon, Queen Charlotte Street, Hammersmith, London W6
22 November 1980 – Gothenburg, Sweden
25 November 1980 – Gota Lejon, Stockholm, Sweden
26 November 1980 – Gota Lejon, Stockholm, Sweden
27 November 1980 – Lund, Sweden
29 November 1980 – The Karregat, Eindhoven, The Netherlands
30 November 1980 – The Rockpalast, Gruga Halle, Dortmund, Germany
1 December 1980 – Utrecht, The Netherlands
2 December 1980 – Oosterpoort, Groningen, The Neverlands
3 December 1980 – Hofterlo, Antwerp, Belguim
6 December 1980 – Fort Regent, Jersey
8 December 1980 – St Austell Coliseum, Cornwall
9 December 1980 – Bristol [venue unknown]
10 December 1980 – Winter Gardens, Malvern
11 December 1980 – Guildford Civic Hall, Guildford, Surrey
12 December 1980 – The Music Machine, Camden Town, London NW1
14 December 1980 – St Austell Coliseum, Cornwall
14 February 1981 – The Cricketers, Westfield Road, Westfield, Woking, Surrey
16 February 1981 – Woking YMCA Centre, Goldsworth Road, Woking, Surrey

17 February 1981 – Sheerwater Youth Club, Woking, Surrey
21 February 1981 – Norwich University, Norwich, Norfolk
22 February 1981 – Nottingham University, Nottingham, Notts
23 February 1981 – The Leisure Centre, Crawley, Sussex
26 February 1981 – Pavilion Baltard, Paris
1 March 1981 – Olympen, Lund, Sweden
3 March 1981 – Oddfellows, Copenhagen, Denmark
6 March 1981 – Market Hall, Market Place, Hannover, Germany
8 March 1981 – The Metropole, Berlin, Germany
10 March 1981 – Ancienne Belguique, Brussels, Belguim
12 March 1981 – Tivoli Hall, Strasberg
13 March 1981 – Paradiso, Amsterdam, The Netherlands
15 March 1981 – Palais St Sauveur, Lille, France
16 March 1981 – Studio 44, Rouen
27 April 1981 – The Royal Court Theatre, Liverpool
13 May 1981 – Kinro Fukushi Kaikan, 1-13-14 Shintomi, Chou-Ku, Tokyo, Japan
14 May 1981 – Mido Kai Kan Hall, Osako, Japan
15 May 1981 – Sun Plaza Hall, 4-1-1 Nakano, Nakano-Ku, Tokyo, Japan
16 May 1981 – Sun Plaza Hall, 4-1-1 Nakano, Nakano-Ku, Tokyo, Japan
21 May 1981 – Le Club, Montreal, Canada
22 May 1981 – The Concert Hall, 888 Yonge Street At Davenport, Toronto, Ontario, Canada
23 May 1981 – The Concert Hall, 888 Yonge Street At Davenport, Toronto, Ontario, Canada
24 May 1981 – Ottawa Technical High School, Ottawa, Canada
26 May 1981 – The Ritz, New York, United State
10 June 1981 – Grona Lund, Stockholm, Sweden
12 June 1981 – Borlanger, Sweden
17 June 1981 – The Rainbow Theatre, 232 Seven Sisters Road, London N4
20 June 1981 – The Festival Pavilion, Skegness
22 June 1981 – Granby Hall, Leicester, Leics
23 June 1981 – The Guildhall, Portsmouth, Hants
25 June 1981 – St Austell Coliseum, St Austell, Cornwall
27 June 1981 – Bingley Hall, Stafford
30 June 1981 – Magnum Leisure Centre, Irvine
2 July 1981 – Royal Hall, Bridlington Spa, York
4 July 1981 – Market Hall, Carlisle
5 July 1981 – The Guildhall, Preston Lancs
7 July 1981 – Guildford Civic Hall, Guildford, Surrey
8 July 1981 – Guildford Civic Hall, Guildford, Surrey
23 October 1981 – The Rainbow Theatre, 232 Seven Sisters Road, London N4
24 October 1981 – CND Rally, Thames Embankment, London
12 December 1981 – Michael Sobell Sports Centre, Finsbury Park, London N4
13 December 1981 – Michael Sobell Sports Centre, Finsbury Park, London N4
14 December 1981 – The Hammersmith Palais, Hammersmith, London W6
15 December 1981 – The Hammersmith Palais, Hammersmith, London W6
19 December 1981 – BBC TV Theatre, Golders Green, London NW7
24 February 1982 – Central London Polytechnic, London WC1
12 March 1982 – The Guildhall, Portsmouth, Hants
13 March 1982 – The Conference Centre, Brighton, Sussex
14 March 1982 – The Conference Centre, Brighton, Sussex

15 March 1982 – The Fair Deal, Brixton, London SW2
16 March 1982 – Alexandra Pavilion, Alexandra Park Road, Wood Green, London N22
17 March 1982 – Royal Bath And West Showground, Shepton Mallet
18 March 1982 – Afan Lido, Port Talbot
20 March 1982 – Bingley Exhibition Hall, Birmingha
21 March 1982 – Bingley Exhibition Hall, Birmingham
22 March 1982 – De Montfort Hall, Granville Road, Leicester, Leics
23 March 1982 – De Montfort Hall, Granville Road, Leicester, Leics
25 March 1982 – The Apollo Theatre, Ardwick Green, Manchester
26 March 1982 – The Apollo Theatre, Ardwick Green, Manchester
27 March 1982 – Deeside Leisure Centre, Liverpool
28 March 1982 – Blackpool Opera House, Blackpool, Lancs
29 March 1982 – Top Rank, Sheffield
30 March 1982 – Top Rank, Sheffield
31 March 1982 – Top Rank, Sheffield
1 April 1982 – The Queens Exhibition Hall, Sovereign Street, Leeds, York
3 April 1982 – The City Hall, Newcastle Upon Tyne
4 April 1982 – The City Hall, Newcastle Upon Tyne
5 April 1982 – The Playhouse Theatre, 18-22 Greenside Place, Edinburgh
6 April 1982 – The Playhouse Theatre, 18-22 Greenside Place, Edinburgh
7 April 1982 – The Apollo Theatre, Renfield Street, Glasgow
8 April 1982 – The Apollo Theatre, Renfield Street, Glasgow
16 April 1982 – Johaneshovs Isstadion, Biljettbest, Stockholm, Sweden
18 April 1982 – Olympian, Lund, Sweden
20 April 1982 – Faulkener Theatre, Copenhagen, Denmark
21 April 1982 – Vesiby-Risskov Hall, Aar-Hous, Denmark
24 April 1982 – Paradiso, Amsterdam, The Netherlands
25 April 1982 – Paradiso, Amsterdam, The Netherlands
26 April 1982 – De Vereniging, Nijmegen, The Netherlands
27 April 1982 – Ancienne Hall, Due De Bruxelles, Brussels, Belguim
29 April 1982 – Pantin Hippodrome, Paris, France
30 April 1982 – Palais d'Hiver, Lyon, France
14 May 1982 – Richie Coliseum, Maryland, Washington, USA
15 May 1982 – The Palladium, 126 East 14th Street, New York, USA
16 May 1982 – Northstage, 96 School Street, Glen Cove, Long Island, New York, USA
18 May 1982 – The Palladium, 126 East 14th Street, New York, USA
19 May 1982 – The Trenton War Memorial, New Jersey, USA
20 May 1982 – The Orpheum Theatre, Hamilton Place, Boston, Massachusetts, USA
22 May 1982 – Verdune Auditorium, Montreal, Canada
24 May 1982 – The Coliseum, Canadian National Exhibition Centre Fairground,
Toronto, Canada
25 May 1982 – Michigan Theatre, Ann Arbor, Michigan, USA
26 May 1982 – The Riveria Theatre, Chicago, Illinois, USA
29 May 1982 – Perkins Palace, 129 North Raymond Avenue, Pasadena, Los Angeles,
California, USA
30 May 1982 – Perkins Palace, 129 North Raymond Avenue, Pasadena, Los Angeles,
California, USA
31 May 1982 – Perkins Palace, 129 North Raymond Avenue, Pasadena, Los Angeles,
California, USA

2 June 1982 – Fox Warfield Theatre, San Francisco, California, USA

5 June 1982 – Kerrisdale Arena, Vancouver, Canada

11 June 1982 – The Tokyo Kosei Nenkin Kaikan Hall, 5-3-1 Shinjuku, Shinjuku-Ku, Tokyo, Japan

14 June 1982 – The Sun Plaza Hall, 4-1-1 Nakano, Nakano-Ku, Tokyo, Japan

15 June 1982 – Mainichi Hall, Osako, Japan

16 June 1982 – Seinenkan Hall, Tokyo, Japan

17 June 1982 – Kinro Kaikan, Nagoya, Japan

26 June 1982 – QPR Stadium, Loftus Road, Shepherd's Bush, London

10 July 1982 – QPR Stadium, Loftus Road, Shepherd's Bush, London

20 September 1982 – Cliffs Pavilion, Westcliff on Sea, Essex

21 September 1982 – Showering Pavilion, Shepton Mallet

22 September 1982 – The Conference Centre, Brighton, Sussex

23 September 1982 – Granby Halls, Leicester, Leicestershire

24 September 1982 – Royal Court Theatre, Liverpool

25 September 1982 – Royal Court Theatre, Liverpool

27 September 1982 – The Edinburgh Ingliston Royal Exhibition Hall, Ingliston

28 September 1982 – Whitley Bay Ice Rink

29 September 1982 – Whitley Bay Ice Rink

30 September 1982 – The Queens Exhibition Hall, Sovereign Street, Leeds, York

1 October 1982 – New Bingley Hall, Weston Road, Stafford, Staffs

9 October 1982 – Gloucester Hall, Fort Regent, Jersey, Channel Islands

25 November 1982 – The Apollo Theatre, Renfield Street, Glasgow

27 November 1982 – Poole Arts Centre, Poole, Dorset

28 November 1982 – St Austell Coliseum, Cornwall

29 November 1982 – Afan Lido, Port Talbot

1 December 1982 – Wembley Arena, Wembley, Middx

2 December 1982 – Wembley Arena, Wembley, Middx

3 December 1982 – Wembley Arena, Wembley, Middx

4 December 1982 – Wembley Arena, Wembley, Middx

5 December 1982 – Wembley Arena, Wembley, Middx

6 December 1982 – Royal Spa Hall, Birmingham

7 December 1982 – The Apollo Theatre, Ardwick Green, Manchester

8 December 1982 – National Exhibition Centre, Birmingham

9 December 1982 – The Civic Centre, Guildford

11 December 1982 – The Conference Centre, Brighton, Sussex

SONG INDEX

The JAM SOUNDS FROM THE STREET